AF553354

Rural–Urban Dynamics

Rural–Urban Dynamics
Perspectives and Experiences

Edited by

S Rajagopalan

2010

Icfai Books
The Icfai University Press

RURAL-URBAN DYNAMICS: PERSPECTIVES AND EXPERIENCES

Editor: S Rajagopalan

First Edition: 2010
Printed in India

Published by

The Icfai University Press
52, Nagarjuna Hills, Punjagutta
Hyderabad, India – 500 082
Phone: (+91) (040) 23430–368, 369, 370, 372, 373, 374
Fax: (+91) (040) 23352521, 23435386
E-mail: info@icfaibooks.com, icfaibooks@icfai.org, ssd@icfai.org

ISBN: 9788131405963

Editorial Team: Sheena Mohanadasan and Ch Venkatesh

Contents

Section III

Bridging the Rural-Urban Gap

Section IV

Rural-Urban Scenario: Country Profiles

Overview

Viewing development through a rural-urban prism has engaged economists, policymakers, analysts, and sociologists for several decades now. Economic and social agenda of governments and the policies and priorities framed to accomplish them are to a great extent dictated by the development imperatives of the rural and urban sectors. The contrasting economic, social and cultural profiles of rural and urban areas pose challenges to policymakers in framing policies that ensure balanced development of both sectors.

The definition of what constitutes a rural and an urban area is universally based on demographics/dominant occupation, although the exact criteria may differ from region to region. For instance, a place with just over 5,000 people in India may qualify to be classified as an urban centre, while in Japan, any cluster with a population of less than 30,000 is considered rural.[1] A rural area is small geographically and is sparsely populated, with most of the inhabitants

[1] Sigurjón Mýrdal and Andrew Kristiansen (2004), "Distinguishing rural from urban," http://ust.khi.is/latira/what is rural.htm (Accessed October 11, 2006).

engaged in land-based occupations-farm and farm-based activities. An urban area, on the other hand, is bigger, and densely populated, with most of its inhabitants' livelihoods based on industries and services.

From a global perspective, the rural and urban areas are almost equal in the number of people that inhabit them: 3.2 billion people, or 50.8% of the world's population, live in rural areas.[2] However, that is where the equality ends; on practically every indicator of economic and social development, rural areas lag behind urban areas, especially in developing countries. Again, when the rural-urban population ratio is disaggregated countrywise, a striking observation is that in developing countries nearly 70% of the population is rural (China and India, for example). Another significant statistic is that rural population accounts for 70% of the world's poor.[3]

Rural-urban disparities, especially in developing countries, have for long been a major concern for policymakers. The disparities can be seen in all spheres of human life—economic and social. The income inequalities, lack of employment opportunities, lack of infrastructure and civic amenities, inadequate access to education, healthcare and other basic services are some of the major areas where rural areas lag behind urban ones. Globalization and the spread of the consumerist culture have further deepened these disparities, visible in the affluence and glitz of urban areas, which stand in stark contrast to the poverty, deprivation and squalor that characterizes the rural landscape in many parts of the world. The burgeoning slums in urban areas populated largely by migrants from rural areas are an outcome of these disparities. Seen in the context of countries like China and India, which together account for close to two-fifths of the world's population, and where 70% of the people still live in rural areas, the rural-urban divide assumes great significance.

---

2 Marcelino Avila, Lavinia Gasperini and David Atchoarena (2005), "Skills Development for Rural People: A Renewed Challenge" (Background Paper), http://www.norrag.org/wg/documents/%20IIPE%20background.doc (Accessed October 11, 2006).

3 ibid.

The rural-urban 'divide' is not the only perspective on the rural-urban equation; increasingly, experts and analysts point to the 'linkage' that exists between rural and urban areas that mutually strengthens the rural and urban sectors. Seen from the 'linkage' perspective, rural and urban areas form a continuum, rather than exist as discrete geographical territories with boundaries. Labour mobility from rural to urban areas, which balances the labour demand-supply situation in urban areas, is an example of rural-urban linkage. From the 'linkage' perspective, developmental policies are flawed to the extent they treat rural and urban areas as separate territories; ignoring the rural-urban linkage that tends to skew development.

A renewed focus on rural development, and strengthening and expansion of rural-urban linkage will serve to bridge the rural-urban gap, and bring about a balanced development.

This book explores the rural-urban dynamics from both the 'divide' and the 'linkage' perspectives, and looks at ways in which the rural-urban gap can be as well as being bridged in India. It also provides profiles of other developing countries—China, Bangladesh and Nigeria—with respect to the rural-urban scenario that exists in these countries, and also that of the United States, a developed country, which provides a striking contrast. Divided into four sections, the book contains a total of fifteen articles.

Section I: Rural-Urban Dynamics: The 'Divide' Perspective

The first article, **"Changing Role and Objectives of Rural Development in South Asia"**, a *UNESCAP* publication, talks about the varying degrees of attention and priority given by the South Asian countries to rural development, in the half century or so of their independent existence. It captures the major objectives pursued by the governments of these countries in their rural development policies and programmes, and points out that the motivations and objectives of public policies have varied over time and among countries owing to a complex combination of political, economic, and social factors as well as opportunities for development provided by foreign assistance and global economic trends. It makes a critical observation that the multiplicity of objectives, which rural development was expected to achieve in these countries, often deprived it of a central focus and contributed to its failure.

The relationship between the rural and the urban sectors in most developing countries is characterized by an economic dualism: the co-existence of a modern urban sector and a traditional rural sector. The second article in this section **"Rural and Urban Dynamics and Poverty: Evidence from China and India"** by *Sheggen Fan, Connie Chan-Kang* and *Anit Mukherjee,* explains that this dualism arose in countries like China and India, because the industrialization development strategy followed by both largely favoured the growth and development of the urban sector at the expense of the rural sector. It provides a historical perspective of the rural-urban dynamics in China and India, and examines the causes and consequences of the urban bias. The article points out that the urban bias in investment and development strategies needs correction in both countries through more investment in rural areas, particularly on infrastructure, and through strengthening of rural-urban linkage.

Besides plurality—in terms of languages, religions, customs, traditions—disparities also mark the landscape of India, and these are evident in the levels of economic and social development and the lifestyles in rural and urban areas. The third article in this section **"The Rural-Urban Divide in India"** by *S Rajagopalan* examines the various dimensions and the extent of rural-urban disparities in India by comparing the two sectors on key indicators of economic and social development. The dimensions of economic and social development that the article covers include demographics, poverty, education, healthcare, housing, access to safe drinking water, sanitation, electricity, road connectivity, banking services, penetration of ICTs, and the caste barrier. The article observes that, on almost all indicators of economic and social development, rural India lags behind urban India, although on some of them the gap is narrowing.

Section II: Rural-Urban Dynamics: The 'Linkages' Perspective

Focusing on the connections between urban and rural areas, rather than viewing them as separate worlds, can help to reframe our understanding of development in the two sectors. This is the central argument of the first article in this section **"Beyond Rural Urban: Keeping up with Changing Realities"** by *James Garrett*. The article emphasizes the point that a more integrated economy offers more choices and allows individuals and households to pursue their own best path out of poverty, depending on particular conditions, resources, and opportunities. Policies that support rural-urban integration and provide appropriate public investment to encourage the flow of goods and resources across sectors and locations are important steps in this direction.

"Rural Urban Linkages and Pro-poor Agricultural Growth: An Overview" by *Cecilia Tacoli* examines the various forms of rural-urban linkage, and how rural-urban linkage in the form of easy access to urban markets is a key to increasing incomes for poor rural farmers. Rural-urban linkage includes: flow of agricultural and other commodities from rural-based producers to urban markets; financial flow in the form of remittances from migrants to relatives and communities staying in villages, and investments and credit from urban-based institutions; livelihood engagement through multiple occupations ranging from farming to services to processing and manufacturing; and in the opposite direction, flow of manufactured and imported goods from urban centres to rural areas. The article points out that synergy between agricultural production and urban-based enterprises is often the key to development of more vibrant local economies and pro-poor regional growth.

Migration is perhaps the most dynamic form of rural-urban linkage. The third article in this section **"Rural-Urban Links in India: New Policy Challenges for Increasingly Mobile Populations"** by *Priya Deshingkar* emphasizes the need to recognize the importance of migration and commuting to the livelihoods of the poor, and to the economy, and examines the policy challenges that are arising in India due to increasing migration. On the one hand, the article says, the improvements in roads and information technology are making livelihood strategies multi-locational, that is, covering both rural and urban areas, and on the other, increasing migration raises the pressure on urban infrastructure, in which, public investment has been sluggish. The current set-up in urban areas proves inadequate in supporting migrant workers—it provides them little access to critical information on labour markets and rights, as well as to basic services like health, education, and shelter.

Section III: Bridging the Rural-Urban Gap

Appropriate policies and programmes to promote rural development are the key to bridge the rural-urban gap. The first article in this section "**How to Make Rural India Shine**" by *S Mahendra Dev,* examines some important indicators relating to rural India in the pre- and post-liberalization periods and finds that rural India is not 'shining.' The author makes suggestions in ten areas: employment, public investment, agriculture, water management, rural institutional reforms, rural non-farm sector, education and health, reduction in regional disparities, PURA model and basic services, and decentralization and governance, where he says policy attention is needed to make rural India shine. He points out that to make rural development more broad-based and balanced, investment, technology, and appropriate institutions are needed.

Little or no access to financial services of the formal institutions had stifled development in rural areas, where a majority of the poor resides, like in India. For instance, despite the presence of Regional Rural Banks and state-run programmes like the IRDP, people in rural India, until the early 1990s, relied largely on informal sources like moneylenders to access credit. Usurious interest rates charged by moneylenders and leakages in state-run programmes had made it difficult for rural people to access finance on easy terms. "**Microfinance: Providing Access to Financial Services in Rural India**" by *Vipin Sharma* discusses how, since 1992, microfinance has been changing the financial landscape of rural India with easy access to savings and credit services (and now insurance as well), through the entry of microfinance institutions that have adopted various delivery models and methods. Nearly 25 million poor in the country are being served by microfinance, which is gradually spreading across the country, and which promises to further deepen and expand access to financial services for rural India.

Technology has a key role to play in bridging the rural-urban gap, and ITC Ltd.'s 'e-choupal' concept presents a powerful demonstration of how technology can be harnessed to uplift the rural sector. ITC's e-choupal enables farmers to access information first-hand on crop prices in Indian and world markets, farm practices, and local weather forecasts. Based on the prevailing market prices, farmers can decide whether they want to sell their produce to ITC, or at the local mandi, or wait. Farmers are thus able to get higher prices and enhance their incomes, and at the same time are becoming more aware through access to the Net. Until the introduction of the e-choupal, the farmers were wholly dependent on commission agents—the middlemen—from whom they got low prices and often, manipulation in weighing of their produce. The e-choupal has become a hub for commercial activity at the village level, including a mall set up by ITC. **"E-Choupal: Transforming Rural India through Technology"** by *Nadarajan Gayatri Devi* discusses the various features of the e-choupal model and how it is empowering rural India.

Most of the 700 million rural Indians lack access to basic healthcare facilities; although 70% of Indians live in rural areas, more than 75% of Indian doctors are based in cities. **"Telemedicine in Rural India"** by *Sanjit Bagchi* talks about telemedicine, which promises to be an effective alternative to reach healthcare services to rural areas. The efficacy of telemedicine has already been demonstrated through the network established by the ISRO, which has connected 22 super-specialty hospitals with 78 rural and remote hospitals across the country through its geo-stationary satellites. Telemedicine may turn to be the cheapest as well as the fastest way to bridge the rural-urban health divide.

Section IV: Rural-Urban Scenario: Country Profiles

China accounts for about 20% of the world's population and for nearly 20% of the world's poor, and is the fastest growing economy in the world. Despite the urbanization that goes along with economic development, the rural population in China has grown in absolute terms, and a majority of the country's population (69%) lives in rural areas. Considerable disparities exist in rural and urban China with respect to incomes, access to education and healthcare, and housing. The first article in this section **"The Rural-Urban Divide and the Evolution of Political Economy in China"** by *John Knight, Li Shi* and *Lina Song,* examines the extent of the rural-urban divide in China—which is extreme; why and how it arose and persists till this day; whether it will be eroded; and views it from a political economy perspective. The article points out that the future of the rural-urban divide in China depends to a great extent on the forces driving economic policies in urban China, in particular, those relating to rural discontent, rural-urban migration, rising income inequality, and state-owned enterprise reform.

Bangladesh is one of the least urbanized countries in South Asia with densely populated rural areas composed of clustered villages that develop near roadways—72% of the total population resides in rural areas. Poverty is predominantly rural—93% of the very poor and 89% of the poor reside in rural areas. Migration has made rural and urban economies more integrated. The second article in this section, **"Rural and Urban Development Case Study – Bangladesh"**, by *Tim Ruffer* and *Nadia Masud* covers a number of aspects relating to rural and urban development in Bangladesh, which includes the agriculture sector, livelihood sources, migration and remittances, rural and urban policies of the government, and policy implications.

With a population of 125 million, Nigeria is Africa's most populous country, and has the highest urban population among sub-Saharan African countries (perhaps, one of the highest among developing countries). **"Rural and Urban Development Case Study – Nigeria"** by *Tim Ruffer,* like the previous case study on Bangladesh, covers a number of aspects relating to rural and urban development in Nigeria. Urban population has grown from 11% of the total population in 1952 to 46% in 2002. Poverty is higher in rural than in urban areas, and per capita incomes in urban areas are roughly a third higher than in rural areas. On the one hand, the continued growth of urban areas, coupled with improved transportation and higher literacy levels, has facilitated the incidence of commuting from peri-urban rural sites to towns and cities for employment; on the other, the rapid growth of urban populations has created challenges in Nigeria's largest cities, such as congestion and squalor, housing shortages, invasion of open spaces and green belts with low quality housing.

The last article in the book **"A Portrait of Rural America – Challenges and Opportunities"** by *LaStar Matthews* and *William H Woodwell, Jr.* gives a picture of rural sector in the US, a developed country, and provides comparisons with the urban sector in that country. Rural America, which covers 80% of US land, is home to about 59 million, or 21% of the population. This is in sharp contrast to the 70% and above proportion of population that reside in rural areas in developing countries. Another economic feature of rural America is equally striking: agriculture is no longer its predominant occupation; seven out of ten rural counties, today, are dominated by manufacturing, services, and other kinds of employment not related to farming.

Section I

Rural-Urban Dynamics: The 'Divide' Perspective

1

Changing Role and Objectives of Rural Development in South Asia

This article captures the major objectives pursued by the governments of South Asian countries in their rural development policies and programmes, and points to the growing significance of rural development in their development agendas.

The Post-Independence Scenario

In the half century or so of independent existence, South Asian states have given varying degrees of attention and priority to rural development. Moreover, the motivations and objectives of public policies have varied over time and among countries owing to a complex combination of political, economic and social factors as well as opportunities for development provided by foreign assistance and global economic trends.[1] Nevertheless, there have been some uniformities in the rural development policies of South Asian countries because of the similarities in their social and cultural milieu and a shared legacy of their colonial past which included institutions of governance and an agrarian structure suited to the needs of the colonial rulers.

The objectives of rural development followed and implemented by the various Governments have also been influenced by the overall plans for development and the performance of the economy in its global setting during this period. In particular, they have been conditioned by the international economic environment, especially for foreign assistance. Although rural development has been a priority area for external donors its importance has increased in the second half of the last 50 years as concerns about food security, the population explosion, environment and climatic changes, as well as poverty, equality and social justice have come to be increasingly perceived as being in the purview of global, rather than national policy agendas. Rural development stood at the cross-cutting path of these concerns. However, the multiplicity of the objectives which rural development was expected to achieve often deprived it of a central focus and often contributed to its failure.

The South Asian countries have, in recent years, tried to achieve some combination of the following major objectives, whose importance has differed both over time and among countries.

1. Raising Agricultural Productivity

This has been – and to a large extent continues to be – the primary objective of and the principal motivation for most rural development programmes, which were undertaken in the wake of rising population pressure on the land and the need for transferring resources for the pursuit of economic diversification. Before the advent of the green revolution in the 1960s most South Asian countries faced chronic food shortages, in some cases actual famine, and had to import substantial amounts of foodgrains, often financed from PL 480 imports from the United States of America and assistance from other countries.

It needs to be recognized that while raising agricultural productivity is an essential goal, it is a means for achieving larger development goals, such as increased welfare and the alleviation of poverty of the population. While increased agricultural productivity may ensure abundance of food availability for a given population, it may well not provide an adequate nutritional food intake for the majority of the population or, much more important, it may not provide sufficient access to those who need food, despite large surpluses of foodgrains. A striking example of this paradox is Brazil, which despite being one of the leading exporters (especially of soybeans and orange concentrate) is one of the most ill-fed nations in the world (Souza Silva, 1994).

The paradox is no less evident in India, where as a result of the Government's successful drive to raise food production and stocks about 70 million tonnes of wheat and rice lie in Government godowns while over 200 million children, women and men remain chronically undernourished. Pregnant women are the worst affected, since maternal and foetal undernutrition results in the birth of children with low weight (less than 2.5 kg). Such children are handicapped at birth in mental development (Swaminathan, 2002).

Also, as pointed out by Rao (2002) in the context of India, foodgrain security, though essential, cannot be equated with food security.[2] The share of consumer expenditure on cereals now accounts for a little less than 40 percent of total consumer expenditure on food in the country, the remaining 60 percent being incurred on items such as edible oils, sugar, milk, eggs, meat, fish, vegetables and fruits. Even for the poor these non-foodgrain items account for as much as half the total expenditure on food but in order to bring the intake of these items to adequate levels their consumption by the poor has to increase at least threefold. The demand for these items of food will therefore rise at a high rate due to population growth as well as the rise in per capita income. The goal of food security, therefore, goes far beyond attaining self-sufficiency in foodgrains and should aim at attaining physical as well as economic access to a balanced food basket, especially for the poor. However, achieving economic access to non-foodgrain items would require a much stronger effort to raise the purchasing power of the poor than ensuring the necessary supplies.

There is an urgent need for diversification of South Asian agriculture from its current focus on foodgrain and cash crop production to the production of non-cereal products, which will also serve to raise employment and increase the purchasing power of the poor, to a considerable extent. This is because the potential for employment generation in dairying, horticulture, etc., is much greater than in cereals. These activities also have the potential for greater human resource development which would in turn result in higher wage rates and provide the necessary purchasing power for both foodgrains and non-foodgrain consumption of the poor.

The objective of raising agricultural productivity in the context of rural development programmes is often postulated without any reference to the agrarian structure prevailing in a country. However, there seems to be a persistent bias in such programmes towards the larger farmers. As pointed out by Banerjee (2001), few historical phenomena share this remarkable tendency in the history of agrarian relations. "The state, it appears, has intervened always and everywhere in the markets for land, agricultural labour and other inputs into and outputs from agriculture to make life easier for larger farmers".[3]

Such a bias could be defended as a means of achieving food security if it could be demonstrated that large farmers were in fact more efficient than small farmers. On the contrary, however, there exists a large body of evidence to show that small farms in developing countries, including South Asia, tend to be more productive than larger farms.[4] The logic of the argument about the higher productivity of smaller farms is quite simple and is based on the higher costs of supervision of hired labour in larger farms and the relative scarcity of land in relation to the availability of family labour virtually at zero opportunity cost (Bhaduri 1997). The smaller farms are also able to grow additional crops and engage in subsidiary activities to supplement their incomes and for the survival of their family while the larger farms concentrate on only one major crop.[5]

2. Alleviating Poverty and Providing Employment Opportunities to Landless Labour

At the beginning of the twenty-first century there is general agreement, at the global as well as national level, that poverty is unacceptable as part of the human condition. The global family has come to recognize that the coexistence of pervasive poverty, with the affluence of a much smaller segment of the population, is ethically unacceptable, economically inefficient and politically unsustainable. Most developing countries put poverty alleviation as their primary development goal, at least in their official plans and pronouncements.[6]

The various global commitments to eradicate poverty have been endorsed, first at the World Summit for Social Development in Copenhagen in 1995 and then at the Millennium Summit in New York in June 2000, where the international community committed itself to halve extreme poverty by 2015. Such commitments to alleviate poverty are not new and have been reiterated in various forums for at least a quarter of a century, if not longer.

However, until recently, poverty alleviation was part of a broader agenda for development and viewed as a by-product of rapid growth. But now poverty has been prioritized as the primary objective of the global development agencies and many Governments. The international donor agencies, in particular, appear quite categorical in defining poverty reduction as the immediate priority of their various aid programmes.

The eradication of poverty, notwithstanding its prioritization in the global development agenda, however still remains a subsidiary concern of domestic development policy of most South Asian Governments whose focus is limited, at best, to alleviate poverty to a given target level.

For South Asia, which is home to about half of the 900 million poor people in Asia (with 450 million in India alone),[7] along with high rates of unemployment, this is undoubtedly an overarching objective for rural development programmes, especially since the bulk of poverty is in the rural areas. However, until recently rural development programmes did not pay much direct attention to the task of poverty alleviation. Most of the programmes, which were statist in character and were run by the Government adopted a top down approach.

3. Promoting a Suitable Environment for the Uplift of the Rural Community

Among the most fundamental changes in the evolution of rural development programmes is the continuing debate about the need for a change in their ethos and the way the protagonists of these programmes (who are often outsiders) relate to their beneficiaries. Most of the earlier programmes were either paternalistic in nature or were run by self-serving bureaucrats who were often closely allied to elite groups. There are still very few programmes of rural development which live

Table: Poverty in South Asia

	1990 Based on less than US $1 a day incidence (percentage)	US $1 a day Millions of poor	Latest year Based on less than US $1 a day incidence (percentage)	US $1 a day Millions of poor
Bangladesh	35.9 (1992)	–	29.1	37.9
India	52.5	438.4	44.2	442.9
Nepal	–	–	37.7	8.6
Pakistan	11.6	12.5	31	42.6
Sri Lanka	3.8	0.7	6.6	1.3

Source: ADB, Growth and Change in Asia and the Pacific (2001).

up to the motto of being of the poor, by the poor or for the poor. The induction of NGOs in poverty alleviation and rural development programmes has to some extent brought them closer to the ideal but the empowerment of the poor is still more rhetoric than reality in the South Asian context.[8]

In order to empower rural communities, the rural development programmes along with the Governments and institutions of civil society need to focus on a number of interrelated areas, particularly on human capital development.[9] Most South Asian countries are already committed to goals such as education or health for all, which should remain on every agenda. What is needed is not only the speeding up of the implementation of these goals, but also of moving beyond them in the direction of ensuring some affirmative action in favour of the poor. The priority should be to move towards substantially enhancing investment for the purpose of upgrading the quality and governance of rural schools and health care facilities to a level where the rural poor do not feel disadvantaged compared to the urban middle class.

Such a goal carries formidable implications as to costs and governance and may need some deployment of resources from non-priority projects. However, the resultant effect of such a process of quality enhancement efforts could enable the younger generation of poor households to compete on the basis of equality with the children of the elite for places in the universities and in employment. This would transform the competition between the children from poor and elite households into a more level playing field and would have "an empowering effect" on the poor to demand more rapid democratization of opportunities for human capacity development.

4. Providing and Helping Access to Basic Facilities and the Management of the Rural Commons

A common critique of most rural development programmes is that they fail to cater to the needs of the more vulnerable groups such as women, the landless, minorities and other deprived groups of South Asia. To reach and include them requires a deeper understanding of poverty and its underlying causes; an emphasis on building critical human, social and physical assets; and more effective delivery of basic services. For example, despite improvements, access to education and health care remain, along with other social indicators, below desired levels, especially in rural areas and among women and female children. Such poor delivery of basic services works to limit progress in human development.

Besides rural-urban differences in the availability of services, the country averages also disguise variations based on caste and geography. In Nepal, for example, "untouchables" have a life expectancy of 45 years, 15 years less than upper-caste Brahmins. In India, adult literacy rates among women of scheduled tribes, most of whom live in rural areas, was 29 percent compared to 39 percent for all Indian women. Country averages further mask the wide geographic diversity in these indicators within the country. In nutrition surveys by the National Nutrition Monitoring Bureau (NNMB) of rural areas in India (1994), the percentage of children underweight in nine large Indian states varies from 50 percent to almost 80 percent and severely underweight from 15 percent to 35 percent. Recognizing the persistence of rural vs. urban, gender, caste or ethnic and geographic biases may help in the design and targeting of development programmes.[10]

These imbalances can be reduced by interventions through rural development programmes that focus on increasing the access of the poor and vulnerable groups to essential services that are presently available only to the privileged and elite groups. In order to respond effectively to the needs of these vulnerable sections of the population, rural development programmes must have the following features:

(a) The adoption of decentralized, participatory and beneficiary-driven approaches designed to improve the delivery of such rural services as drinking water and rural sanitation, irrigation, extension, microcredit, education and health to the poorest sections of the population;

(b) Community management for the sustainable use of natural resources, such as joint forest management and watershed management programmes;

(c) Fiscal and administrative decentralization to local governments for enabling them to undertake the programmes identified above;

(d) Measures to improve governance and social inclusiveness of public sector institutions across income, gender and ethnic groups;

(e) Measures to reduce the vulnerability and risks faced by the rural poor and measures to help them recover from natural catastrophes such as floods, droughts and hurricanes (e.g., disaster and coastal management) and to improve the effectiveness of existing government safety nets (e.g., food and rural employment).

These measures will require the combined efforts of the Government (at the national, subnational and local levels) as well as foreign and private donors and non-governmental organizations, including the rural support programmes.

5. Bridging the Rural-Urban Gap in Incomes and Economic Opportunities to Enable Enhanced Economic and Social Mobility

Rural-urban disparities have been an endemic problem of most developing countries and a major source of the continuing increase in their urban population. Although the main reason for the rural-urban population drift is the push of rural unemployment and underemployment, a contributing factor is also the lure of greater access to the amenities of life which is in inverse proportion to the distance from urban metropolitan centres.

The disparity in the social indicators between rural and urban areas is widespread in South Asia. Literacy rates are less in rural than in urban areas and

Box 1: The Rural-Urban Divide

The rural-urban divide is not a discrete attribute but is a continuum, ranging from the urban suburb or periphery to the most isolated or distant rural communities. Rural development programmes need to be fine-tuned to take account of the specificity of the problems that are faced by communities lying between the two ends of the rural-urban spectrum. At least four major divisions of this spread with their own distinctive rural strategies can be distinguished.[11]

Peri-Urban Areas

The main issues arising in the urban periphery are not dissimilar to those in urban squatter settlements: creation of jobs in industrial and service sectors in neighbouring urban centres, provision of adequate transport facilities and housing. Many of these areas have been reduced to dormitories of adult residents who commute daily on bicycles or animal-driven vehicles to the urban centre. To the extent there still exists some scope for farming in these areas, the rural development programmes can help promote micro-scale, high-value-added farming, such as vegetables and dairying which would provide fresh produce, create jobs and avoid pollution. There also exists considerable scope for rural industrialization in these areas which could take advantage of backward linkages with agriculture and forward linkages with urban industry. For this there will be need for credit and new credit institutions which could provide venture capital for the establishment of small-scale industries and services to enterprising individuals or groups.

Accessible Rural Areas with Good Natural Resources

These areas are good candidates for agricultural development with the help of market incentives and institutional development. They have potential for higher absorption of both labour and capital and of producing market surpluses. With investment in human development and technology, these areas could become highly productive and their products could compete in world markets. These areas could provide employment to people of other less well-endowed areas, especially during seasonal peaks.

Accessible Rural Areas with Poor Natural Resources

The possibilities of productive employment are likely to be low in these areas and migration may be the only alternative for most people. However, possibilities of livestock farming could be considerable and may provide opportunities for employment in dairying and related activities, along with handicrafts for women. The main handicap is likely to be access to water and capital investment in tubewells and small irrigation projects are likely to yield beneficial results, as land itself is unlikely to be scarce. Since these areas are not remote it may not be difficult to access services from Government and non-Government organizations engaged in rural development activities. In particular, they could receive the services of teachers and health workers for training people and providing basic education.

Remote or Isolated Rural Areas

These are the most difficult areas to deal with as the costs of construction of infrastructure to reduce their remoteness are generally high. Nonetheless, measures to improve their productivity and incomes can be undertaken by subsidizing certain economic activities such as poultry farming and livestock. They could also be assisted in launching public works programmes to help build the needed infrastructure. Some remote areas have the advantage of being yet unspoilt by excessive human habitation and still preserve their pristine beauty. They could become attractive destinations for eco-tourism. Inhabitants of the area could be encouraged to preserve and protect wildlife and biodiversity and to guard against poaching by illegal hunters and fortune seekers.

among women than in men. In Nepal, the rural literacy rate (33 percent) in 1995/96 is more than 50 percent lower than in urban areas. In India, the adult literacy rate in rural areas (54 percent) in 1995/96 is significantly below that in urban areas (77 percent), with rural female literacy rates (31 percent) only about half of rural male literary rates. Even in Sri Lanka where literacy rates are higher than most other South Asian countries, it is estimated that only about 26 percent of all primary students master basic literacy skills and only 18 percent master basic numerical skills. Although infant and child mortality and malnutrition rates have improved considerably, the bias against rural areas means that other regions have made stronger progress in health. For example, in India the child mortality rate is 33 per thousand live births in rural areas compared to 17 per thousand in urban areas; while the malnutrition rate among children under three years old in rural areas is 50 percent compared to 38 percent for urban areas. A major objective of the rural development programmes should be to overcome the health services gap between urban and rural areas.

6. Enhancing the Role of Technology as a Means of Raising Productivity

Facing the increasing scarcity of arable land, South Asia must apply technological innovations to improve efficiency and sustain productivity growth. If the region's population nearly doubles, as projected from 1.4 billion in 2000 to 2.2 billion in 2045, the challenge of keeping agricultural growth rates at par with population growth will require putting available technology to better use and, through energetic research, developing new and more efficient growing methods. The average rate of agricultural growth per annum during the period 1990-98 was 1.5 percent in Sri Lanka, about 2 percent in Nepal and Bangladesh, 3.8 percent in India and 4.5 percent in Pakistan. This pace is particularly worrying as there are indications that the rate of growth of total factor productivity, despite considerable potential, is slowing down in many areas. In Pakistan, for example, it is estimated that large, existing productivity gaps in major crops indicate an opportunity to boost productivity by as much as 30-40 percent over the short to medium term. This projection is based on wider diffusion of available, improved crop production technologies, more efficient use of land, water, and other inputs and better post-harvest handling of produce. Other South Asian countries can score similar advances.

While the benefits of the green revolution are generally recognized to be scale-neutral and did benefit the poor in South Asia to a considerable extent, the gains from technological innovation remain unequally distributed between those with access to land, water and inputs, and those without. There is broad consensus that the main causes of rural poverty lie in low rates of agricultural growth and factor productivity and that the key to raising productivity in agriculture lies largely in measures to broaden access to land and complementary inputs, along with a more favourable policy environment towards agriculture (Fan and others, 1998). More equitable distribution of operational land holdings would create more equitable patterns of demand, which in turn would enhance growth in the rural non-farm sector and remove some of the biases in credit, marketing and research institutions that arise from the unequal distribution of assets and power (Singh, 1998). This is supported by recent evidence which suggests that countries with a more equal land distribution experience higher rates of economic growth.

The knowledge and information revolution is now being brought within the reach of the remotest areas by advances in telecommunications and information technology and needs to be harnessed not only for the rural elite but also for the rural poor. Formidable opportunities are being opened up in the area of distance learning and medicare, for urban standards of education, medical diagnosis and prescription to be delivered to the most remote villages. Here major investments to build the infrastructure to take the IT revolution to the villages, remains an important goal of public and global development policy. It also provides an opportunity for collaborative arrangements between the public and private sectors, as well as the NGOs. The example of *Grameenphone* in Bangladesh enabling poor, rural women to be brought into the communications revolution, as both providers as well as users of IT services, needs to be emulated elsewhere in South Asia.

Notes

1. For a recent extensive survey of the changing themes of rural development and their interaction with the parallel debates on development strategies (albeit mainly from the donors' perspective) see the special issue of ODI's *Development Policy Review*, December 2001, 19(4), especially the articles by Caroline Ashley and Simon Maxwell (*Rethinking Rural Development*) and by Frank Ellis and Stephen Biggs (*Evolving Themes in Rural Development 1950s-2000*).

2. C H Hanumantha Rao, Food Security, *The Hindu*, 23 March 2002.
3. Based on evidence contained in Binswanger, H, Deininger, K and Feder, G "Power, distortions, revolt and reform in agricultural land relations" in Behrman, J and T Srinivasan, eds., 1995 *Handbook of Development Economics, Volume III*, Amsterdam; New York and Oxford: Elsevier Science, North Holland.
4. For India, this has been found by a series of farm management studies going back to the 1950s. A summary of more recent evidence from a range of countries, both in Asia and Latin America, is given in Berry, R A and W R Cline, *Agrarian Structure and Productivity in Developing Countries*, Baltimore : Johns Hopkins University Press, 1979, showing much the same pattern. Similar studies are cited in Binswanger, Deininger and Squire (1995), op.cit. In Rosenzweig, M. R. and H. P. Binswanger (1993), "Wealth, weather risk and the composition and profitability of agricultural investments", *Economic Journal, vol. 103*, pp. 56-78, the authors using data from the semi-arid ICRISAT region of India, report that profit/wealth ratios are always at least twice as high for the farmers in the smallest category as they are for those in the largest.
5. For an interesting link of the inverse relationship between farm size and productivity and Chyanov's theory of the peasant economy, see Shanin, 1986.
6. The recent UNDP *Poverty Report 2000* on *Overcoming Human Poverty*, records that 69 percent of all developing countries have prepared explicit poverty plans or have incorporated poverty alleviation into their national plans. However, preparing plans on poverty alleviation is not always reflected in national policies or allocative priorities.
7. Based on a poverty line of $1 a day. Asian Development Bank, *Fighting Poverty in Asia and the Pacific*, Asian Development Bank, Manila, 2001.
8. For a discussion of empowerment in the Indian context – with wide applicability in other parts of South Asia – see, Andre Beteille, "Empowerment" in *Economic and Political Weekly*, Perspectives, 6-12 March and 13-19 March 1999.
9. The other important areas which are dealt with in the paper elsewhere are: access to land, increased participation and inclusion of women and lower caste communities and decentralization to local government, communities and organizations.
10. Based on information provided in World Bank, *South Asia: A Strategy and Action Plan for Rural Development*, Rural Development Sector Unit, South Asia Region, 2001.
11. For a more detailed discussion of the issues, see Wiggins, Steve and Sharon Proctor, "How special are rural areas? Implications of location for rural development", in *Development Policy Review*, December 2001, 19(4), pp. 427-436.

2

Rural and Urban Dynamics and Poverty: Evidence from China and India

Shenggen Fan, Connie Chan-Kang and Anit Mukherjee

This article examines the rural-urban dynamics in China and India, and the causes and consequences of the urban bias in the investment and development strategies adopted by both countries. It also analyzes the impact of economic growth on poverty reduction in both the rural and urban sectors in the two countries.

1. Introduction

Rural and urban areas are interdependent in many ways. A growing body of literature argues that rural and urban areas should not be treated as two distinct entities because the livelihood of many households includes both rural and urban components. Nonetheless, many developing countries have done exactly that. Development strategies in many countries have concentrated resources in the urban sector and consequently increased the development gap between rural and urban areas. Labor productivity and per capita income in rural areas have lagged behind that in urban areas, increasing the concentration of poverty among the rural population.

In particular, both China and India each followed a development path where policies treated rural and urban areas separately. Development strategies relied heavily on industrialization, which was viewed as a symbol of modernization and as a way to catch up with the higher-income Western countries. After the establishment of a new government in 1949, for example, China embarked on an urban-biased development scheme. India adopted a similar model after its independence in 1947. Economic rents and surpluses were transferred from rural to urban sectors through various explicit and implicit interventions, such as state pricing and procurement of agricultural products, fiscal transfers and investment, and restrictions on labor movement. These policy biases continued for decades.

In the late 1970s, however, China initiated agricultural reforms. India instituted macroeconomic reforms in the early 1990s. Whether intended or not by the policymakers, these changes began a process of correcting the urban bias in many respects. In China, agricultural prices were raised, the state procurement system was abolished, and many of the restrictions on movement of labor were lifted, improving rural-urban linkages. In India, the implementation of macroeconomic reforms led to an improvement of the terms of trade for agriculture. As a result of these corrections, agricultural growth accelerated, and rural poverty declined.

A better understanding of rural-urban linkages and of how urban-biased policies interfered with these linkages has important implications for the design of development strategies to promote growth and reduce poverty. Till now, however, little information has been available on the nature and the magnitude of these linkages and interdependence in China and India.

In this paper, we examine the history of the relationship between the rural and urban sectors in China and India, including the development of policies that influenced this relationship and their impact on poverty in China and India. Although the policy bias toward urban areas has diminished somewhat in both China and India, we will argue that continued action to redress urban bias is crucial to strengthening and exploiting the synergies between the rural and urban sectors in both countries.

This paper is organized as follows. We first present a conceptual framework to define and measure the extent of urban bias. We then review policies that have contributed to such bias and their changes over time in China and India. Next, we present an analysis that uses a panel data set to evaluate (1) the contribution of rural growth to the reduction of both rural and urban poverty, and (2) the impact of urban growth on rural and urban poverty reduction.

In the following section, based on evidence from the literature, we discuss how the government can use policy instruments, particularly investment policy, to correct urban bias, strengthen rural-urban linkages, and maximize the impact of policies on both growth and poverty reduction.

2. Definition, Causes, and Consequences of Urban Bias: A Conceptual Framework

The development literature has exhibited a growing interest in the linkages between rural and urban development. These linkages matter because rural and urban livelihoods are interconnected economically, financially, and socially. From a rural perspective, most farmers depend on urban markets to secure their livelihoods. Rural households also depend on urban centers or small towns for various services (e.g., hospitals, banks, and government offices) and for the provision of various private and public goods. Moreover, the rural sector benefits from remittances sent by urban-based family members (DfID 2003).

Likewise, urban areas are linked to the rural sector through several channels. For example, various urban businesses and enterprises depend on rural demand for their goods and services. They also rely on rural areas for the supply of raw materials. Urban consumers, on the other hand, benefit from cheap and sustained food supply from rural areas (Fan 2003; Fan, Fang, and Zhang 2003). Furthermore, many poor urban households partly depend on rural activities (e.g., farming) for their livelihoods (DfID 2003). The rural sector can also act as a buffer from the impact of macroeconomic shocks on the urban economy (World Bank 1999).[1] Links between the rural and urban sectors also include flows of information, such as markets and employment opportunities, as well as flows of people moving between rural and urban centers on a temporary or permanent basis.

Development policies that facilitate these rural-urban linkages can promote economic growth and poverty reduction. But how does this balancing and synergistic relationship work? Economic theory suggests that resources should move freely so that marginal returns are equalized between sectors and regions. An increase in agricultural productivity may precede the growth of urban settlements. But as new innovations take place in the urban sector, urban labor productivity and wages rise, making migration from the rural to urban sector attractive. In the meantime, urban development may also improve access to capital, inducing further mechanization or other innovations relevant to agricultural production. As a result, agricultural productivity grows, narrowing the productivity and income gaps between rural and urban areas. When innovations take place again in the urban sector, the gap in productivity and income widens between the two sectors. Rural labor begins to migrate to the urban sector, and capital moves to rural areas. A new equilibrium emerges.

This process of moving from disequilibrium to equilibrium due to technological innovations in both sectors is the major source of economic growth and development. But many developing countries disrupt this natural economic development process. Very often governments interfere in favor of the urban sector, distorting capital and labor markets to favor urban over rural areas, in an attempt to jumpstart development or leapfrog this process. As a result, overall efficiency is lost, as resources do not flow to their "free-market" locations where they would naturally earn the highest rate of return. As a consequence, the rural-urban gap increases, and the natural growth that would occur in rural areas, as well as in urban areas, is circumvented.

In fact, in developing countries, we typically observe the coexistence of a modern urban sector and a traditional rural sector. In these countries, the urban population is often better off than their rural counterparts. This rural-urban divide evolves when governments in developing countries give preference to the urban sector in their public policies. Such preferential practices may include, for example, price policies, public investment, and welfare transfers that favor the urban over the rural population. In part this urban bias may also occur because urban centers in developing countries may be better organized politically and thus have greater influence on policy makers than the rural population (Lipton 1977; Bates 1981).[2]

We see the effect of urban bias in the gap between urban and rural areas in terms of labor productivity, per capita income, and poverty rates. The greater the gaps among these indicators, the larger is the bias.[3] Naturally, per capita income and productivity differences have to be adjusted by labor quality and cost of living in the two sectors.

For India and China, urban bias has usually arisen from the combination of three different but related policies. The first and most common one relates to policies affecting the terms of trade (i.e., price policies). Very often agricultural outputs are underpriced, with levels that are much lower than those that would result from a free market situation or in the international market.[4]

Second, overvalued exchange rates in most developing countries exacerbate this bias, adversely affecting all traded goods, but frequently agricultural products in particular. If labor and capital are fully mobile, they may move towards the urban or industrial sectors if the returns there are more favorable. In the long run, however, even in the presence of distortion in the output markets, the marginal returns to different factors between rural and urban sectors will converge as long as there is no distortion in the factor (input) markets. Unfortunately, many countries like China have also heavily distorted factor markets by restricting the movement of labor and capital. The Household Registration System, or *hukou*, in China, for example, did not allow farmers to move to urban centers despite the presence of a huge labor surplus in the rural sector and the lower marginal return to labor there. After the reforms in 1978, farmers were allowed to migrate to urban areas, but many restrictions on their employment in urban centers remain.

Third, governments' tendencies to favor urban centers are reflected in their spending policies. Like other government policies, public spending endeavors to promote more equitable development and increase efficiency by correcting market failures.[5] In many cases, governments may have to trade off efficiency and equity goals. But it is also important to recognize that equity-efficiency trade-offs are not always present. Where market failures are more pervasive among the poor (i.e., the poor are poor because they are disproportionately affected by market failures), this leads to the presence of so-called "win-win" possibilities where government intervention leads to both a more efficient and a more equitable allocation of resources. For example, public investment in rural infrastructure has not only generated economic pay-offs by correcting market failures but has also led to poverty reduction.

The consequences of urban-biased policies are obvious. First, these policies lead to larger gaps between rural and urban areas in terms of many development indicators, such as education, health, nutrition, per capita income, and poverty. Second, rising inequality may lead to tensions that constrain the prospects for future growth through a variety of social, political, and economic mechanisms.

3. Rural-Urban Dynamics: A Historical Perspective in China and India

Using the framework developed in the previous section, we review below the major policies that have led to urban bias in China and India and discuss its consequences.

China

The urban bias that prevails in China finds its roots in the country's history. After the establishment of the communist regime in 1949, China adopted a development strategy that emphasized urban industries with capital-intensive technology through various implicit and explicit transfer programs.

The rationing system introduced in the 1950s enabled urban residents to have equal access to food and other necessities at much lower prices than would have occurred without state intervention. Almost all urban residents of working age had guaranteed jobs in the state – or collective-owned sectors. Because these jobs were permanent and labeled the "iron rice bowl," urban unemployment was virtually nonexistent. These jobs also provided urban residents with many benefits, such as free or subsidized housing and health care. On the other hand, rural residents were confined to their production units where they produced agricultural commodities under strict state planning. The government was able to monopolize agricultural production in the rural sector while controlling the distribution of food and other products in the urban sector. These commodities had to be sold at government prices that were lower than international prices. Huge rents were thus transferred to urban centers for the development of heavy industry. The surpluses arising from the agricultural sector not only contributed to capital accumulation in industries, but also supported urban-based subsidies.

The strict control of rural-to-urban migration through *hukou* reinforced the segmentation of China's rural and urban sector. *Hukou*, put in place in the 1950s, assigned a place of residency and employment for the entire population, and defined one's rights for social and economic activities within a specified locality.

Because of *hukou*, the share of urban population remained constant at 20 percent from 1952 to 1970s (Figure 1).

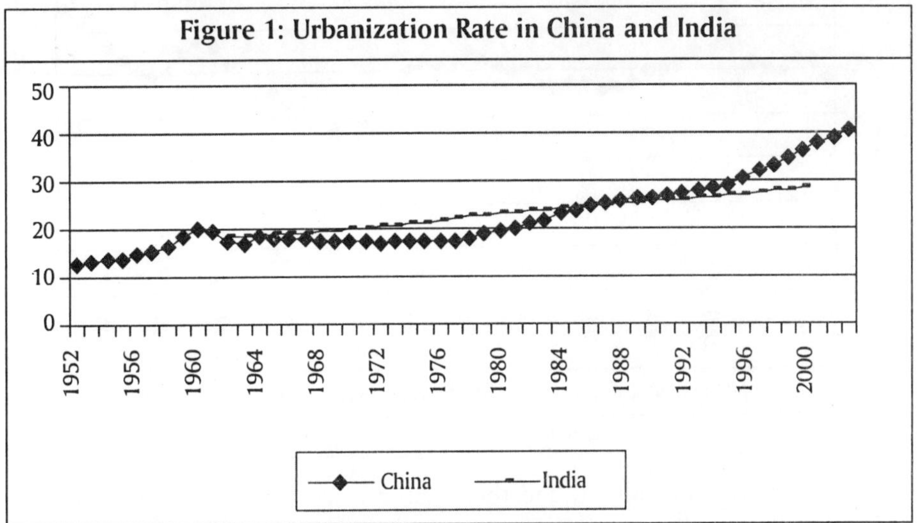

Figure 1: Urbanization Rate in China and India

The heavy-industrialization development strategy, combined with the *hukou* system, enabled the government to obtain agricultural products at lower prices, to maintain low urban consumption (through rations), to control the mobility of labor, and to increase industrial investments. All these elements contributed to the concentration of capital investment in the urban sector. Consequently, even accounting for cost-of-living differences, the income of urban workers was far greater than that of their rural counterparts (Figure 2). In 1978, for instance, per capita income in rural areas was only 34 percent than in urban areas.[6] Moreover, poverty in the rural sector was far more prevalent than in the urban sector. More than 75 percent of rural households were living below the poverty line in 1980 compared to 8 percent of their urban counterparts (Figure 3).

The economic reforms in 1978 promoted overall economic growth but included provisions focused on increasing farmers' income. In fact, the first phase of the economic reforms (1978 to 1985) targeted the rural sector. The most important institutional reform was the adoption of the Household Responsibility System (HRS). The HRS made the individual household, rather than the collective team, the main unit of agricultural production. The government also introduced price reforms that increased procurement prices for agricultural products. Moreover,

Figure 2: Urban-Rural Per Capita Income Gap in China

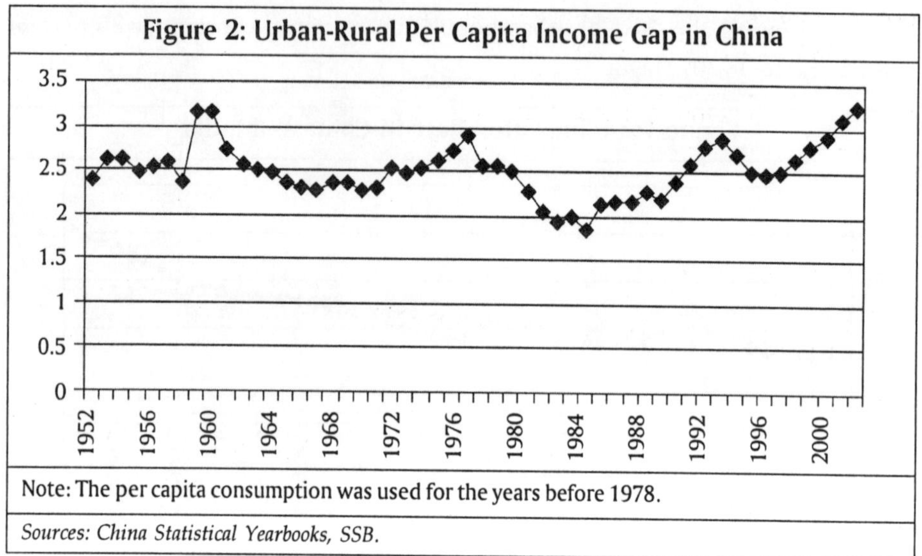

Note: The per capita consumption was used for the years before 1978.

Sources: China Statistical Yearbooks, SSB.

local markets were liberalized, and the number of commodities subject to state procurement was reduced. Consequently, agricultural production grew at more than 7 percent per annum from 1978 to 1984.

Figure 3: Rural and Urban Poverty Rate in China

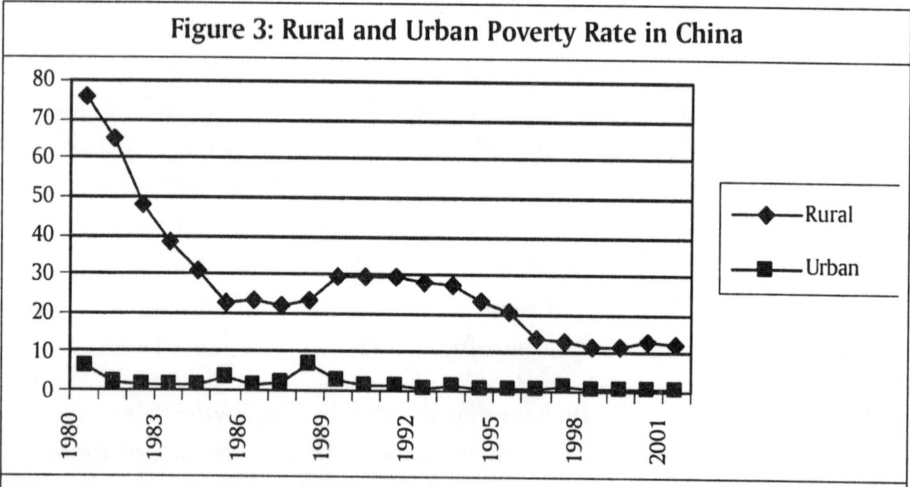

Note: The poverty line for rural area is 850 yuan measured in 2002 price, while the urban poverty line is 1,200 yuan measured in 2002 price.

Source: Chen and Ravallion (2004).

Another important development during the first phase of economic reforms was the emergence of rural industry clusters known as Township and Village Enterprises (TVEs). The development of TVEs strengthened the linkages between the rural and urban sectors due to the relaxation of restrictions on movement of labor out of agricultural production. For example, urban industries outsourced part of their production to the TVEs to benefit from the cheaper rural labor force, existing machineries, and more relaxed enforcement of environmental, health, and safety regulations in rural areas. Urban industries also used labor and raw materials from the rural areas, which led to an increase in agricultural labor productivity and farmers' income. These links promoted the development of many small rural towns that served as a bridge between rural areas and urban centers.

These reforms helped to counter the earlier urban bias. Rural per capita income tripled between 1978 and 1985. Consequently, the ratio of urban-to-rural per capita income fell below 2 during 1983-85, a historic low in China since 1949 (Figure 2).

The second phase of the reform program (1984-1991) broadened the reforms to include promotion of industrial enterprises in urban areas, creation of market institutions, and dismantling of the central planning system. Two particularly important policies were introduced: the dual-track pricing system for industrial goods and the enterprise contract responsibility system. Under dual-track pricing, prices were gradually deregulated and markets played an increasing role in setting prices. The enterprise contract responsibility system granted greater autonomy to particular enterprises to make their own production and employment decisions. But these policies caused high inflation in the economy, which in turn led to a deterioration of the terms of trade for agriculture. Soaring inflation led the government to allocate significant subsidies to urban workers and to increase subsidized credit for the urban sector during this period (Yang and Zhou 1996). Not surprisingly, rural-urban consumption and income differentials increased during the second phase of reforms and reached a historic high of 3.5 in 1993 and 1994 (Figure 2).

The third phase of the reform program (1993 to the present) established a socialist market economic system, under which the economy continues to remain primarily under public ownership but market forces are allowed to play a fundamental role in resource allocation and distribution decisions. To achieve this goal, several measures have been instituted to reform the financial and fiscal sectors, as well as to facilitate rural labor mobility. The government has also resumed agricultural price increases in order to further correct the former under-pricing of agricultural goods. Moreover, in order to achieve balanced growth on a regional basis, priority has been given to developing the central and western regions of China.

One of the most significant developments during this period is rapid urbanization (Figure 1). The share of urban population in the total population has risen from 28 percent in 1993 to more than 40 percent in 2003. This rapid urbanization has been accompanied by employment growth in the urban sector. The rate of job creation in the urban sector was five times the corresponding rate in the rural sector during the 1990s (Huang and Cai 1998). Consequently, the urban sector now accounts for an important share of non-farm employment.

Cities have become an attractive place to migrants. Millions have flocked to the urban areas of China in the past decade. An estimated 100 million rural workers and self-employed traders moved to the cities and coastal regions during the 1990s (Huang and Cai 1998). About 40 percent of rural residents[7] working in the non-farm sector are employed in the urban sector (Gale, Somwaru, and Diao 2002). The relaxation of the *hukou* registration system in the mid-1980s, combined with looser labor restrictions, have contributed to the growing number of rural migrants to the urban sector.

Most of the rural migrants send remittances back to the rural sector. In 1994, some 37 million rural migrants in 23 cities remitted 75 billion yuan to the rural sector (World Bank 1999). The remittances benefit the rural sector directly and indirectly. They have a direct impact on the income of the households that receive these remittances. An indirect impact occurs when the increase in household income stimulates local demand and therefore local production. Migration also benefits the rural sector by improving access to information and capital. Migrants that intend to return to their rural hometown or village often save to invest in a business. They also bring skills, contacts, and experience that they gain from the urban sector (Davin 1999).

Despite the policies aimed at modifying some of the regional and rural-urban imbalances, the ratio of urban to rural per capita income remains high, averaging 3.3 in 2003 (Figure 2). The causes of the rural-urban divide in China have changed over time. During the central planning period, the rural-urban gap was mainly a result of the government's pursuit of an urban industrialization development strategy. This conformed with economic thinking of the time. In the past two decades, however, political pressure from the relatively more powerful urban population has resulted in various transfer programs to promote income growth disproportionately in the urban sector (Yang and Fang 2000; Fang and Chan 2004). The central government maintains this urban bias to preserve regime stability and political legitimacy. Urban-based price subsidies still prevail; between 1985 and 1998, total price subsidies from the government increased from 26.2 billion yuan to 71.2 billion yuan. Thus, political factors, along with remnants of distortions in the labor and capital markets inherited from the centrally planned system, seem to have contributed to an urban bias in the economy that continues somewhat into the present time (Fang and Chan 2004).

India

India has followed a somewhat similar path. During the first three Five-Year Plan periods (1951-1966), the newly independent India emphasized self-reliance and gave priority to rapid industrialization. This development strategy required a substantial amount of investment in urban industries from the state at the expense of the agricultural sector (Teitelbaum 2004). The first Five-Year Plan (1951-56) allocated 31 percent of the budget to the agricultural sector (Chandra, M Mukherjee, and A Mukherjee 2000). Rural outlays, however, decreased thereafter to 20-25 percent as India formally adopted the socialist strategy of heavy industrialization during the Second Five Year Plan (1956-61). Under this strategy, agricultural policy was infused with a pro-urban bias. In order to provide cheap food and cheap basic inputs for industrial development, farm prices were kept artificially low and agricultural exports were curtailed through quantitative restrictions and an overvalued exchange rate. Moreover, basic food products were made available at subsidized prices in urban areas and food deficit regions. The government concerned itself with controlling the price of foodgrains because the relative price of foodgrains was thought to be an important determinant of savings and investment rates.[8]

An important element of India's food policy and food security system is the Public Distribution System (PDS), which started as a rationing system in the 1940s. The PDS aimed at "protecting low-income groups from increases in retail prices by purchasing grain from farmers (at the support price) and selling it to consumers at subsidized prices" (Persaud and Rosen 2003). But the urban sector profited most from the PDS. Suryanarayana (1995), for example, observed that the relatively more urbanized states of India, such as West Bengal, Maharashtra, and Tamil Nadu, benefited largely from the PDS allocation. Likewise, Gulati, Sharma, and Kahkonen (1996) indicated that the PDS was biased in favor of the urban sector and found that the quantities of foodgrains purchased through the PDS were higher in urban than in rural areas. Similarly, Suryanarayana (1985), Pinstrup-Andersen (1988), and Tyagi (1990) also found that the PDS favored mostly the urban sector.

After the mid-1960s, India's government began to prioritize the development of the agricultural sector. The government adopted an agricultural strategy aimed at improving productivity in the agricultural sector (Suryanarayana 1995). Under this strategy, various agricultural price support mechanisms and input subsidies were introduced, which helped the success of India's Green Revolution.[9] Emphasis was also given to the development of small-scale industries in rural areas. Various measures were adopted, including subsidized loans to promote the development of rural industries.

Beginning in 1991, India adopted a series of sweeping macroeconomic and structural reforms in nonagricultural sectors including industry, exchange rate, foreign trade, and investments. Although the reforms were implemented in the non-farm sector, they affected agriculture in at least two important ways. First, the reforms adopted between 1991 and 1993 resulted in rapid economic growth and therefore to a rise in per capita income. These improvements had a significant impact on food demand. Higher per capita incomes—which grew at 4.5 percent per annum in the early 1990s compared to 3.6 percent in the 1980s (World Bank 2004)—led to the diversification of food demand for non-foodgrain crops such as fruits and vegetables, as well as meat, poultry, and dairy products from a rising middle class. Second, the decrease in industrial protection significantly enhanced the incentive framework for the sector, as the domestic Terms of Trade

(TOT) between agricultural and industrial prices improved during the 1990s. The TOT rose from 0.9 to 1.2 between 1991 and 2000.

The improved TOT for agriculture resulted in an increase in the profitability of the primary sector relative to industry. As a result, private investments in agriculture rose substantially and are now double the amount invested by the public sector. These private investments were increasingly directed to horticulture, and poultry, fish, milk, and egg production, in response to booming consumer demand for these high-value agricultural products. These changes in demand led to a remarkable growth in the production of these high-value commodities during the 1990s relative to the previous decade.

Despite these improvements, government fiscal and investment policy is still oriented towards the urban areas. New investments under the Structural Adjustment Policies (SAPs) privileged mostly urban areas as well as more prosperous regions (Bhan 2001). Gujarat and Maharashtra, for example, received 37 percent of industrial investments between 1991 and 1994 and within these two states a large share of the investment was concentrated near the large city of Mumbai. Moreover, the focus of government policies, subsidies, and fiscal incentives has shifted away from agriculture towards industry under the SAPs. For example, government subsidies are directed mainly towards high-skilled industries such as the software sector. These industries also benefit from exemptions from custom duties and corporate income taxes (Bhan 2001).

Likewise, government subsidies in the health sector tend to favor urban areas while the provision of basic health services in rural areas is still lacking. Overall expenditures on social services have declined under the SAPs in relative terms. Even more disturbingly, subsidies have been redirected away from rural areas towards urban industrial centers. While the rural sector is home to about 65 percent of the Indian population, only 20 percent of the health subsidies are directed towards this sector, for example (Bhan 2001). Political intervention and economic forces, as well as government policies, have been identified as the sources of the skewed distribution of health care services in favor of the urban sector (Bhan 2001; Kumar 2004). A similar disparity exists between urban and rural areas in terms of literacy. Typically urban populations have better access to schools and also enjoy better quality education.

As a result of this urban bias in policies, an income gap also exists between rural and urban residents in India, even after adjusting for cost-of-living differences, although it is smaller than that in China (Figure 4). In 1951, the ratio of urban to rural per capita mean income was 1.4, and gradually increased to 1.6-1.7 during 1954-55. It then declined to a historic low of 1.3-1.4 during 1966-69 due to the adoption of new technologies and greater agricultural production during this initial stage of the Green Revolution. But the ratio has stayed at 1.5-1.6 since then (Figure 4).[10] The poverty rate in the rural areas is also higher than that in urban areas, although the difference is much smaller than in China (Figure 5). In 1999/2000, the incidence of poverty averaged 27 percent in the more populous rural areas, 3 percentage points higher than the poverty rate of 24 percent in the urban areas.

Figure 4: Urban-Rural Income Gap in India

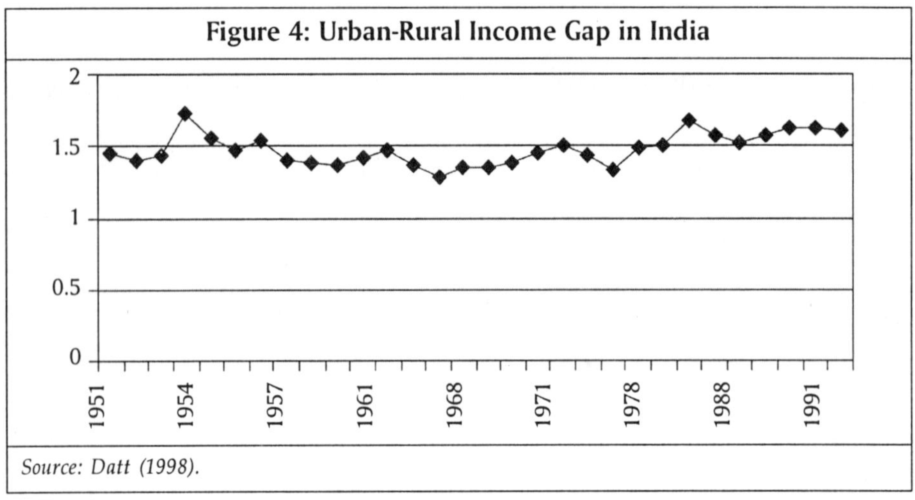

Source: Datt (1998).

4. Rural and Urban Growth and Poverty Reduction: An Empirical Analysis

The objective of this section is to analyze the contribution of sectoral growth on poverty reduction using state and provincial data from China and India. Our hypothesis is that growth in one sector (for example, rural) would reduce poverty both in that sector (rural) as well as in the other (urban). This section proposes to quantify these effects using panel data sets on poverty and sectoral growth for China and India.

Figure 5: Poverty Rates in India

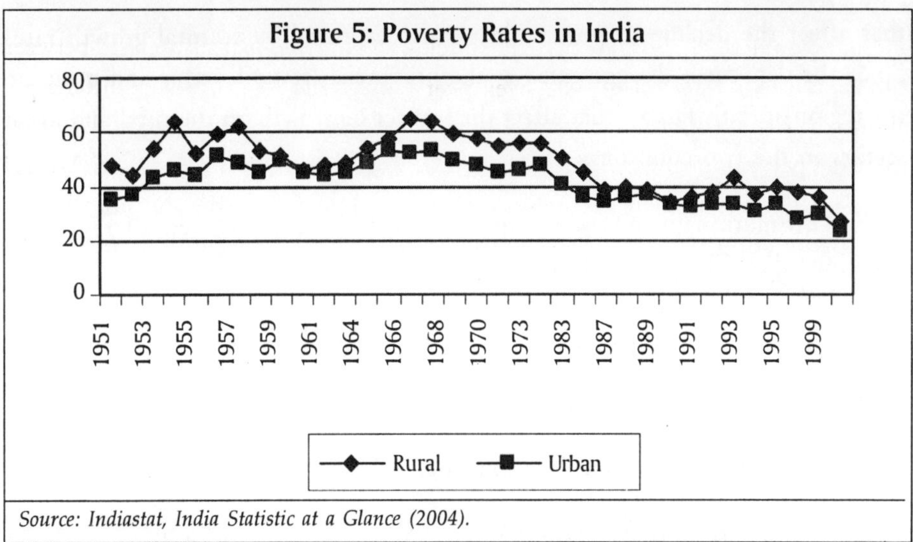

Source: Indiastat, India Statistic at a Glance (2004).

The variables in this analysis differ between the two countries as explained below. Data for India are fairly consistent and available over a long time period (1970-1997). On the other hand, for China, data are available only for a shorter time period; official poverty data at the provincial level are available from 1985 to 1996 for the rural sector, but only from 1992 to 1998 for the urban sector. Consequently, we examine the dynamic effects of rural and urban growth on poverty for India, but unfortunately, cannot do so for China. In this case, we can only draw conclusions on the total effects of growth on poverty reduction, and are not able to disaggregate the effects into long and short terms.

Model

For both countries, our basic model can be stated as:

$$RP_{it} = f\,(rg_{it}, ug_{it}, w),$$

$$UP_{it} = g\,(ug_{it}, rg_{it}, z),$$

where RP_{it} (UP_{it}) is the change in rural (urban) poverty in the ith province (state) in period t; rg_{it} (ug_{it}) denotes growth in the rural (urban) sector in the respective provinces (states) in period t; and w and z are socioeconomic factors that affect the decline in poverty levels not captured by sectoral growth rates. Since the data set is disaggregated at the provincial (state) level, *w* and *z* capture the region-specific factors that affect the impact of growth on the rural and urban sectors in the two countries.

For estimation purposes, we specify the following two sets of regression equations. For China, we estimate:

$$\Delta \ln (RP_{it}) = \alpha_0 + \alpha_1 \Delta \ln AgGDP_{it} + \alpha_2 \Delta \ln IndGDP_{it} + \mu_1 + \upsilon_{it}; \quad (1)$$

$$\Delta \ln (UP_{it}) = \beta_0 + \beta_1 \Delta \ln AgGDP_{it} + \beta_2 \Delta \ln IndGDP_{it} + \eta_1 + \xi_{it}. \quad (2)$$

For India, our estimation equations are:

$$\Delta \ln (RP_{it}) = \alpha'_0 + \alpha'_1 \Delta \ln Rincome_{it} + \alpha'_2 \Delta \ln Uincome_{it} + \mu'_1 + \upsilon'_{it}; \quad (3)$$

$$\Delta \ln (UP_{it}) = \beta'_0 + \beta'_1 \Delta \ln Rincome_{it} + \beta'_2 \Delta \ln Uincome_{it} + \eta'_1 + \xi'_{it}. \quad (4)$$

where $\mu_i(\mu')$ and $\eta_i(\eta')$ are province-specific factors, and $\upsilon_i(\upsilon')$ and $\xi_i(\xi')$ are the error terms. We estimate the two sets of equations with alternative specifications of the error terms, testing for heteroscedasticity and autocorrelation between the error terms and the explanatory variables.

Data

As stated above, the data for China and India are disaggregated at the provincial (state) level. Data on rural poverty in China are available between 1985 and 1996 and on urban poverty from 1992 to 1998 for 29 out of 31 provinces of the country. Although there was a minor reorganization of provinces in the late 1980s, the original classification is maintained throughout the period for our estimation purposes.

To capture the effect of rural growth, we use the log-difference of agricultural gross domestic product (GDP), which is available by province. We approximate urban growth by the log-difference of provincial industrial GDP, keeping in mind that there has been rapid growth of rural TVEs and other private enterprises over the last two decades in China. Some TVE clusters have grown into urban agglomerations, but are classified as rural. In our analysis, we would expect this close proximity of industrial clusters in rural China to exert significant impact on rural poverty.

For India, data at the state level are available for poverty, income, and State Domestic Product (SDP), separated by rural and urban areas. The data on some of these indicators are available from the 1950s. However, consistent data on poverty and income are available only from the early 1970s. Therefore, the time period of our analysis for India is from 1970 to 1997, covering 28 years.

Recent studies have pointed out certain irregularities in the SDP calculation in India.[11] Although SDP data are available at constant 1993-94 prices from the Central Statistical Organization (CSO), there are problems in extending the series backwards, especially before 1980. For instance, there are very long periods of unusually high agricultural growth reported for some states, as well as inconsistencies between input and output in agriculture and industry. In our estimations for India, therefore, we use rural and urban mean income as proxies for growth in the two sectors.

Results

For both rural and urban poverty in China and India, we estimate the effects of rural and urban growth on poverty using a number of models. The use of these models can give some indication of the robustness of the results. The fixed-effects model controls for region invariant effects, while Maximum Likelihood Estimation (MLE) corrects for standard errors. The Generalized Least Squares (GLS) estimation corrects for heteroscedasticity across panels (GLS1). To correct for serial correlation, GLS2 estimates the model assuming common autocorrelation of order one (ar1) across panels.

The estimated results for rural and urban poverty for China are shown in Table 1. With regard to rural poverty, rural and urban growth are statistically significant across all models, but with opposite signs (Table 1). That is, an increase in the rural growth rate (agricultural GDP) is associated with a decrease in rural poverty, while a rise in the urban growth rate is associated with an increase. Although this last result seems counterintuitive, we believe that barriers—such as inadequate infrastructure—still exist that prevent the spillover of urban growth

Table 1: Estimated Coefficients for Poverty in China

	Rural Poverty (1985–1996)				Urban Poverty (1992–1998)			
	Fixed Effects	MLE	GLS1	GLS2	Fixed Effects	MLE	GLS1	GLS2
	(1)	(2)	(3)	(4)	(1)	(2)	(3)	(4)
Rural growth	-5.261**	-5.261*	-4.421*	-4.974*	-0.310	-0.310	-0.320*	-0.311*
	(0.056)	(0.016)	(0.000)	(0.000)	(0.242)	(0.161)	(0.000)	(0.000)
Urban growth	5.182**	5.182*	2.541*	2.043*	-1.361	-1.361	-3.533**	-3.929*
	(0.058)	(0.017)	(0.004)	(0.015)	(0.666)	(0.606)	(0.069)	(0.019)
Constant	-0.326	-2.001*	0.813	0.918	0.073	0.131	0.302	0.333
	(0.247)	(0.047)	(0.484)	(0.301)	(0.845)	(0.672)	(0.367)	(0.183)
R-squared	0.132				0.028			
Log-likelihood		-116.7	132.9	-58.4		-64.3	-3.33	-28.4
Number of observations	348	348	348	348	203	203	203	203

Notes: GLS1: Heteroskedastic Panels; GLS2: GLS1 corrected for autocorrelation. * significant at 5 percent level, ** significant at 10 percent level.

effects to rural areas. Variation in rates of urban growth among regions may even counter efforts to reduce rural poverty. One factor might be that productive labor is being drawn away from agriculture to industry, especially from rural to urban areas in the Central and Western regions of the country. A number of studies are looking at the impact of rapid urban growth, especially in the coastal areas, to understand how this accentuates interregional inequalities. Large variation in the rates of growth of rural industries and skewed infrastructure investment between regions have been singled out as probable causes of this widening inter- and intra-regional inequality.[12]

In relation to urban poverty, only GLS models generate statistically significant results, but they are consistent: both rural *and* urban growth help to reduce uıban poverty. However, the effect of urban growth on urban poverty is much greater than that of rural growth.

In India, in contrast to China, the fixed-effects and MLE models show that only rural growth is associated with rural poverty, and only urban growth is associated with urban poverty (Table 2). The GLS models largely mirror this result, although they suggest that urban growth does have a slight impact on

Table 2: Estimated Coefficients for Poverty in India (1970–1997)

	Rural Poverty				Urban Poverty			
	Fixed Effects	MLE	GLS1	GLS2	Fixed Effects	MLE	GLS1	GLS2
	(1)	(2)	(3)	(4)	(1)	(2)	(3)	(4)
Rural growth	-0.917*	-0.927*	-1.058*	-1.049*	0.176	0.174	0.073	0.075
	(0.000)	(0.000)	(0.000)	(0.000)	(0.121)	(0.115)	(0.239)	(0.223)
Urban growth	0.006	0.011	-0.082**	-0.088**	-0.973*	-0.968*	-0.890*	-0.896*
	(0.935)	(0.878)	(0.102)	(0.081)	(0.000)	(0.000)	(0.000)	(0.000)
Constant	-0.011*	-0.011*	-0.004	-0.004	-0.012*	-0.012*	-0.012	-0.012
	(0.013)	(0.012)	(0.818)	(0.823)	(0.017)	(0.015)	(0.233)	(0.222)
R-squared	0.215				0.248			
Log-likelihood		415.5	498.8	499.1		358.7	519.5	520.2
Number of observations	420	420	420	420	420	420	420	420

Notes: GLS1: Heteroskedastic Panels; GLS2: GLS1 corrected for autocorrelation. * significant at 5 percent level, ** significant at 10 percent level.

rural poverty reduction. In any case, all models have the expect signs (i.e., an increase in growth is associated with a decrease in poverty). Except for the urban growth variable in the rural GLS models, the coefficients are approximately equal—around 1—so that, for example, one-percentage point change in rural growth rate will reduce rural poverty by similar magnitude. This makes sense when growth does not also alter income distribution.

Still, the lack of impact of rural growth on urban poverty reduction contrasts with other findings for both China and India (Fan 2003; Fan, Fang, and Zhang 2003) that show agricultural growth has a strong effect on reducing poverty in urban areas. Fan (2003) and Fan, Fang, and Zhang (2003) traced this effect through the reduction in food prices caused by increased agricultural production. But the current model and specification cannot capture this dynamic effect.

5. How to Promote Better Rural-Urban Linkages for Poverty Reduction

In both China and India, poverty is concentrated in the rural sector where the majority of the population resides. The results from our econometric analysis indicate that agricultural growth has a significant impact on rural poverty reduction, and can also, in the case of China, have an effect on reducing urban poverty. Therefore, policies that increase growth in agriculture and promote rural-urban linkages have the potential to reduce poverty.

China and India historically followed development strategies favoring the urban sector. However, in the past two decades, the terms of trade for agriculture have improved as part of the reform process, and have somewhat countered the previous urban bias. The explicit restriction on labor movement in China has also been abolished. However, various types of urban bias still prevail, particularly in terms of government investment priorities, which disproportionately favor urban areas in both countries. To some extent, this impedes the efficient allocation of factors, therefore contributing to the unequal development between the rural and urban sectors.

Increasing public investment in rural areas is therefore crucial in order to achieve greater poverty reduction. Adequate provision of infrastructure such as transportation and communication, for example, is essential for achieving better rural-urban linkages as this would facilitate mobility and therefore access to markets, employment, and services for the rural population. In addition, promoting non-farm employment, rural-to-urban migration, and the development of rural towns can also lead to much stronger rural/urban links and greater synergies between the two sectors.

Based on the results of this study and on previous research findings, we recommend the following policies to help correct urban bias, strengthen the links between rural and urban sectors, and promote growth and poverty reduction.

Increase Public Spending in Rural Areas

Past studies have consistently shown that public investment in the rural sector promotes rural growth in China and India. Growth in the rural sector can also benefit urban areas in many ways. For example, as discussed earlier, the development of China's rural industrial sector contributed to growth of urban industries and vice versa. Growth in the rural economy also generates fiscal and financial outflows from rural to urban areas (taxes from rural-based industries for example).

In a recent study, Fan and Chan-Kang (2005) estimated the returns of rural and urban road development on rural and urban growth as well as on rural and urban poverty reduction. The study finds that benefit/cost ratios for rural roads are about four times larger than for urban roads when the benefits are measured as a contribution to national GDP. Even in terms of urban GDP, these ratios are much greater for rural roads than for urban roads. In terms of poverty reduction, the study finds that for every yuan invested, rural roads raise far more rural and urban poor people above the poverty line than urban roads do.

One of the most direct impacts of agricultural growth on urban poverty is through reduced food prices. As the urban poor spend a very significant percentage of their income on food, a decline in food prices often benefits the urban poor proportionally more than the rural poor. For example, Fan, Fang, and Zhang (2003) and Fan (2003) illustrated that increased agricultural research investment (and therefore increased food production) has been one of the reasons behind the reduction in urban poverty in both China and India. Without agricultural research, food prices would probably be much higher today and as a result, urban poverty rates could be much higher.

The well-recognized linkages that exist between the farm and non-farm sectors in rural India also support the importance of public investment in the rural sector (e.g., Mellor 1976; Rangarajan 1982; Hazell and Haggblade 1990).[13] The types of linkages that exist between the farm and non-farm sectors include production, consumption, and investment linkages.[14] Rural economic growth consequently generates employment, income, and growth to the rest of the economy. Therefore, China and India need to continue to increase spending in rural areas in order to promote growth and reduce poverty in both urban and rural areas.

However, the share of government expenditures in the rural sector remains relatively low. In 2000, for example, nearly 65 percent of China's population resided in rural areas; however, rural investment accounted for only 20 percent of total government expenditures. Moreover, almost 50 percent of national GDP was produced by the rural sector (agriculture and rural township and village enterprises) in 2000. On the other hand, the government's rural spending as a percentage of rural GDP was only about 5 percent compared with 16.4 percent for the whole economy. India has a similar biased spending policy (Bhan 2001). These governments should therefore continue to prioritize public investments to the less developed regions of their countries; these would include the western part of China and the eastern region of India. The rural-urban linkages are particularly weak in those regions where rural non-farm employment, development of rural small towns, and rural-urban migration lag far behind more developed areas.

Reduce Restrictions on Rural-Urban Migration

One feature of rural-urban interdependence that has received considerable attention in the rural-urban linkage literature is rural-urban migration. Typically, as a country develops, urban economic growth takes place, which entices people to leave the countryside in search of new opportunities in urban areas. Following the economic booms of Japan, South Korea, and lately China and Thailand, rural-urban migration not only improved the well-being of the migrants, but also improved the land/labor ratio in the agricultural sector, enabling non-migrants to raise their labor productivity and income. For example, the increase in land/labor ratios in Japan and South Korea, and more recently in China, was the result of the net flow of rural labor to the urban and rural non-farm sectors.

The economic benefits resulting from rural-urban migration in China and India has been formally assessed in a number of studies. De Brauw, Rozelle, and Taylor (2001), for instance, investigated the impact of migration and migrant remittances on China's rural economy using econometric techniques on household survey data. They found that the remittances sent home partially or fully compensated for the loss of rural labor due to migration. These remittances have been particularly beneficial for households engaged in farm production, whose per capita income increased, on average, by 71 percent.

In India, Bhanumurthy and Mitra (2003) decomposed changes in poverty into a growth effect, an inequality effect, and a migration effect for two periods: 1983-1993/94 and 1993/94-1999/2000. The decomposition analysis showed that rural-to-urban migration contributed to poverty reduction in rural areas by 2.6 percent between 1983 and 1993-94. Poverty in the urban sector increased during the same period, but by a smaller rate than the reduction of poverty in rural areas. Therefore, the net poverty incidence for the country as a whole decreased over the period studied. Similar findings were reported for the 1993/94-1999/2000 period. Rural poverty declined by 1.64 percent as a result of rural to urban migration, while urban poverty increased by 1.43 percent.

Despite these overall positive effects generated by migration, formal and informal institutions and policy barriers still restrict the movement of the population. Lack of education and access to information and infrastructure are the most critical constraints. In China, many jobs in the urban areas still require urban residence. Farmers are, therefore, not eligible for many jobs. Even if farmers are employed, their rights are usually not protected. In addition, migrant farmers are not entitled to many social services, such as health care, education of children, retirement and unemployment benefits, to which urban residents are entitled. These restrictions and barriers should be removed to make large-scale migration possible, with additional investment targeted as needed to facilitate this movement and protect rural migrants.

Develop the Rural Non-farm Sector

The rural non-farm sector is important for the growth of the rural economy as well as for poverty reduction. It also provides opportunities for livelihood diversification for poor rural households. Hazell and Haggblade (1993) showed that the share of household nonagricultural income is inversely related to farm size, with landless and near-landless workers deriving between a third and two-thirds of their income from off-farm sources. In India, Dev (1986) indicated the bulk of the poor are landless or live on small farms with inadequate land for their own food needs. Consequently they depend heavily on earnings from supplying unskilled wage labor to other farms or to non-farm enterprises. Public investment in physical infrastructure (road, transportation, communication) as well as in education and health is crucial for the small farms to establish their own business and to access non-farm jobs in the rural non-farm sector.

Develop Small Rural Towns

The proximity and accessibility to small rural towns and urban centers by rural residents is crucial for the rural economy, especially for the development of the rural non-farm sector and for livelihood diversification (Bhalla 1997; Shukla 1992; Jayaraj 1994; Eapen 1995). These linkages are well discussed in Wandschneider

(2004), who studied the impact of small rural towns in local economic development in Madhya Pradesh and Orissa, two poor states of India. The author found that small rural towns and nearby villages are strongly linked through consumption, production, employment, and financial linkages, and various types of economic and social service provision. While villages benefit strongly from small towns through these linkages, the reverse is also true. Small towns and urban centers depend and benefit from labor, inputs, and markets of nearby villages.

The development of small rural towns is also associated with better infrastructure (in terms of quantity and quality), which in turn will facilitate access to markets and lower transportation costs. Moreover, by absorbing agricultural labor surplus, small rural town development in India and China helps to alleviate the pressure on bigger cities, while contributing to the growth of the national economy.

6. Conclusions

Like many developing countries, China and India followed development strategies biased in favor of the urban sector over the last several decades. These development schemes have led to overall efficiency losses due to misallocation of resources among rural and urban sectors. It also led to large income gaps between rural and urban areas. The urban bias was greater in China than in India. Indeed, official data show that both the income gap and the difference in poverty rates between rural and urban areas are much larger in China than in India.

Both countries have corrected the rural-urban divide to some extent as part of reform processes. But the bias still exists. Other studies also support the idea presented here that correcting this imbalance will not only contribute to higher rural growth, but also secure future urban growth (Fan and Chan-Kang 2005). More important, correcting the urban bias will lead to larger reductions in poverty as well as more balanced growth across sectors and regions.

Correcting a government's bias towards investment in urban areas is one of the most important policies to pursue. In particular, more investment in education, infrastructure, and agricultural research and development have proved to be both pro-growth and pro-poor. Facilitating the mobility of productive factors, such as labor, is another means to correct any bias. In particular, providing health, education, housing, and pension services for rural migrants in urban areas is essential to promoting human capital movement from rural to urban areas or to the industrial sector. Promoting the development of the rural non-farm economy and rural small towns is another effective way to correct rural/urban bias and to create significant synergies between the two sectors.

(Shenggen Fan is Director, Development Strategy and Governance Division, at IFPRI. He received his Ph.D in applied economics from the University of Minnesota. For the last ten years, his major work has been in the areas of technical change, institutional reforms, productivity measurement, and the effects of public investment on growth and poverty reduction in developing countries.

Connie Chan-Kang, University of Minnesota.

Anit Mukherjee, National Institute of Public Finance and Policy, India.)

Notes

1. The rural sector provides labor when the urban economy flourishes and absorbs labor back in times of economic contraction (Zhang *et al.* 1999).
2. Another source of the urban bias is the assumption by many policymakers that modernization results from industrialization not from improvement of the agricultural sector.
3. In this we argue that spending policy is an instrument that creates the gap, and not the measure of the gap. The measure of the gap is the income difference between rural and urban areas, adjusted for cost-of-living. Of course, the income differential is the result of many factors, which we do not discuss here, but these factors are nevertheless the causes of the gap, not the measure of it.
4. Recent studies have shown that the bias from this source has declined but is still present (Jensen, Robinson, and Tarp 2002).
5. The sources of market failures typically are: the absence of competitive markets, the existence of positive or negative externalities in consumption and production, the undersupply of public goods by the market, imperfect information on production and consumption opportunities, missing or imperfect markets, and coordination failures.
6. Since all prices were controlled by the government at the same level, the difference in cost of living between rural and urban was small prior to the reforms in 1978.

7. Despite the removal of some restrictions on labor movement, elements of *hukou* are still in place. Under Chinese law, each citizen is still required to register in one and only one place of regular residence.

8. It was thought that high food grain prices would discourage investment in the industrial sector as they would increase pressure to raise wages, which would in turn increase labor costs and consequently decrease profits (Suryanarayana 1995).

9. Important policies were introduced during this period, especially those involving procurement and minimum support prices. Under these policies, the government intervened when market prices were high, such as in difficult cropping years, in order to protect the consumers. Conversely, the minimum support prices protected the farmers when the market prices declined in good harvest years. The government also increased subsidies for fertilizers and other inputs.

10. Others report much higher rural/urban disparities. Using data from the *Human Development Report of India*, Datta (2004) indicated large discrepancies in consumption expenditures between the two sectors. In 2000, per capita consumption expenditure in rural areas amounted to 486 rupees compared with 855 rupees in urban areas. Likewise, per capita expenditure on rural basic services was 24 rupees in 1998, half the amount spent in urban areas in that same year. In terms of per capita expenditure on poverty alleviation programs, the per capita expenditure for rural poor was only one-eighth of what the urban poor received (28 rupees per capita) in 2001.

11. See, for example, Bhattacharya and Sakthivel (2004).

12. Fan, Zhang, and Zhang (2004); Zhang and Fan (2004).

13. Mellor's (1976) influential work established the important linkages that exist between the farm and non-farm sector in rural India. Mellor argued that rural income increases arising from agricultural productivity growth would be magnified by linkages with the non-farm sector. Since then, considerable emphasis has been put on the significance of the Indian rural non-farm sector. For example, Rangarajan's (1982) simulation results show that agriculture wields a significant influence on the growth of the industrial sector: 1.0 percent growth in agricultural output increases industrial production by about 0.5 percent and national income by 0.7 percent. Using an input-output model and data for 1979-1980, Hazell and Haggblade (1990) assessed the impact of agricultural growth on the national demand for non-farm products in India. They found that a 100 rupee increase in irrigated agricultural output will generate 105 additional outputs in manufacturing and 114 rupees of additional tertiary output, and so a total of 219 additional rupees for the non-farm sector.

14. The production linkages arise between these two sectors because increased agricultural output results in a growing demand for various goods such as inputs (i.e., fertilizers, equipments), usually supplied by non-farm enterprises. On the consumption side, rising per capita income in the rural sector induces demand for consumer goods, which is likely to be met by enterprises in the urban sector. A rise in income from the agricultural sector also translates into greater savings and investments, which in turn has an effect on the rest of the economy.

References

Arellano, M, and S Bond 1991. Some tests of specification for panel data: Monte Carlo evidence and an application to employment equations. *Review of Economic Studies* 58 (2): 277-297.

Bates, R 1981. *Markets and states in tropical Africa.* Berkeley, Calif., USA: University of California Press.

Bhalla, S 1997. The rise and fall of workforce diversification process in rural India. In *Growth, employment and poverty: Change and continuity in rural India* ed. G K Chadha and A N Sharma, 145-183. New Delhi: Vikas.

Bhan, G 2001. *India gender profile.* Report 62. Sussex, UK: Institute of Development Studies.

Bhanumurthy, N R, and A Mitra. 2003. *Declining poverty in India: A decomposition analysis.* Working Paper 70. New Delhi: Institute of Economic Growth.

Bhattacharya, B, and S Sakthivel. 2004. Regional growth and disparity in India. *Economic and Political Weekly* 39 (10): 1071-1077.

Blundell, R, and S Bond. 1998. Initial conditions and moment restrictions in dynamic panel data models. *Journal of Econometrics* 87: 115-143.

Chandra, B, M Mukherjee, and A Mukherjee. 2000. *India after independence, 1947-2000.* New Delhi: Penguin Books.

Chen, S, and M Ravallion. 2004. *China's (uneven) progress against poverty.* Policy Research Paper 3408. Washington, DC: World Bank.

Datt, G 1998. *Poverty in India and Indian states: An update.* Food Consumption and Nutrition Division Discussion Paper 47. Washington, DC: International Food Policy Research Institute.

Datta, P 2004. The great Indian divide. *Frontline* 21 (14), July 3-16. Accessible online *<http://www.india.eu.org/2035.html>*

Davin, D 1999. *Internal migrants in contemporary China.* New York: St. Martin's Press.

De Brauw, A D, S D Rozelle, and J E Taylor. 2001. *Migration and incomes in rural China: A new economics of migration perspective.* Singapore: Association of Pacific Rim Universities.

Dev, S M 1986. Growth in labour productivity in Indian agriculture: Regional dimensions. *Economic and Political Weekly* 21 (25-26): A65-A74.

DfID (Department for International Development). 2003. *Rural-urban transformations and the links between urban and rural development.* Environment & Urbanization Brief 7. London.

Eapen, M 1995. Rural non-agricultural employment in Kerala: Inter-district variations. *Economic and Political Weekly* 30 (12): 634-638.

Fan, S 2003. Agricultural research and urban poverty in India. *Quarterly Journal of International Agriculture* 42 (1): 63-78.

Fan, S, and C Chan-Kang. 2005. *Road development, economic growth, and poverty reduction in China.* Research Report. Washington, DC: International Food Policy Research Institute. Forthcoming.

Fan, S, C Fang, and X Zhang. 2003. Agricultural research and urban poverty: The case of China. *World Development* 31 (4): 733-741.

Fan, S, L Zhang, and X Zhang. 2004. Reforms, investment, and poverty in rural China. *Economic Development and Cultural Change* 52 (2): 395-421.

Fang, C and K W Chan. 2004. The political economy of urban protectionist employment policies in China. Photocopy.

Gale, F, A Somwaru, and X. Diao. 2002. Agricultural labor: Where are the jobs? In *China's food and agriculture: Issues for the 21st Century*, ed. F Gale, F Tuan, B Lohmar, H H Hsu, and B Gilmour, 44-46. ERS Agricultural Information Bulletin AIB775. Washington, DC: Economic Research Service, United States Department of Agriculture.

Gulati, A, P Sharma, and S Kahkonen. 1996. *The Food Corporation of India: Successes and failures in Indian foodgrain marketing.* IRIS-India Working Paper 18. College Park, Md, USA: Center for Institutional Reform and the Informal Sector, University of Maryland.

Hazell, P B, and S Haggblade. 1990. *Rural-urban growth linkages in India.* Working Paper Series No. 430. Washington, DC: World Bank.

Hazell, P B, and S Haggblade. 1993. Farm-non-farm growth linkages and the welfare of the poor. In *Including the poor,* ed. M Lipton and J van der Gaag. Washington, DC: World Bank.

Huang, Y, and F Cai. 1998. Myths and realities of China's rural industrial miracle. Photocopy.

Indiastat. 2004. Datanet India Private Limited. *<http://www.indiastat.com>* (accessed 2004).

Jayaraj, D 1994. Determinants of rural non-agricultural employment. In *Nonagricultural employment in India: Trends and prospects,* ed. P Visaria and R Basant. New Delhi: Sage.

Jensen, H T, S Robinson, and F Tarp. 2002. *General equilibrium measures of agricultural policy bias in fifteen developing countries*. Trade and Macroeconomics Division Discussion Paper 105. Washington, DC: International Food Policy Research Institute.

Kumar, N 2004. Changing geographic access to and locational efficiency of health services in two Indian districts between 1981 and 1996. *Social Science and Medicine* 58 (10): 2045-2067.

Lipton, M 1977. *Why poor people stay poor*. Cambridge, Mass., USA: Harvard University Press.

Mellor, J 1976. *The new economics of growth*. Ithaca, N Y, USA: Cornell University Press.

Persaud, S, and S Rosen. 2003. *India's consumer and producer price policies: Implications for food security*. Food Security Assessment/GFA-14. Washington, DC: United States Department of Agriculture, Economic Research Service.

Pinstrup-Andersen, P, ed. 1988. *Food subsidies in developing countries: Cost, benefits, and policy options*. Baltimore, Md, USA, and London: Johns Hopkins University Press for the International Food Policy Research Institute.

Rangarajan, C 1982. *Agricultural growth and industrial performance in India*. Research Report 33. Washington, DC: International Food Policy Research Institute.

Shukla, V 1992. Rural non-farm employment in India: Issues and policy. *Economic and Political Weekly* 27 (28): 1477-1488.

SSB, *China Statistical Yearbook*. Various years. Beijing: China Statistical Press.

Suryanarayana, M H 1985. *Public distribution in India*. New Delhi: Chugh.

Suryanarayana, M H 1995. PDS: Beyond implicit subsidy and urban bias—The Indian experience. *Food Policy* 20 (4): 259-278.

Teitelbaum, E J 2004. In the grips of a green giant: How the rural sector defeated organized labor in India. Paper presented at the Political Economy Research Colloquium at Cornell University, Ithaca, N Y.

Tyagi, D S 1990. *Managing India's food economy: Problems and alternatives*. New Delhi: Sage Publications.

Wandschneider, T 2004. Small rural towns and local economic development: Evidence from two poor states in India. Paper prepared for the International Conference on Local Development, Washington, DC, 16-18 June.

World Bank. 1999. *Rural China transition and development*. Report No.19361-CHA. Washington, DC.

World Bank. 2004. *World Development Indicators 2004*. Washington, DC.

Yang, D T, and C Fang. 2000. The political economy of China's rural-urban divide. Paper presented at the conference on Policy Reform in China at the Center for Research on Economic Development and Policy Reform, Stanford University, Stanford, Calif., USA, November 18-20, 1999.

Yang, D T, and H Zhou. 1996. Rural-urban disparity in sectoral labor allocation in China. Paper prepared for the annual meetings of the Association of Asian Studies in Honolulu, Hawaii, April 1996 and the Allied Social Science Association/Chinese Economist Society (ASSA/CES) joint session at New Orleans, 1997.

Zhang, L, A Hughart, S. Rozelle, and J. Huang. 1999. Coping with recession in rural China: Strategic labor supply decisions in periods of boom and bust. Center for Chinese Agricultural Policy, Beijing. Photocopy.

Zhang, X, and S Fan. 2004. Public investment and regional inequality in rural China. *Agricultural Economics* 30 (2): 89-100.

3

The Rural-Urban Divide in India

S Rajagopalan

This article examines the various dimensions and the extent of the rural-urban disparities in India by comparing the two sectors on key indicators of economic and social development.

Introduction

India is a land of diversities. The country's social and cultural fabric is textured with the mingling of several diverse cultures, customs, traditions, practices, languages, and belief systems brought about by migration and settlement of people from across the world over hundreds of years. Indeed, this bewildering plurality has led many commentators to remark that we have several 'Indias' within the one India that we know as a country.

Besides plurality, disparities also mark the landscape of India, and these are most evident in the levels of economic and social development and the lifestyles in rural and urban areas. The affluence and glitz of urban India stand in stark contrast to the abject poverty and squalor in rural India. The burgeoning slums in urban areas populated largely by migrants from rural areas are an outcome of these disparities. Rural-urban disparities, however, are not unique to India; they exist across the developing world.

With the advent of globalization, the rural-urban disparities are beginning to look even more glaring, with more and more of urban India adopting western practices, habits, and lifestyle choices, even as rural India remains far removed from these influences. Fuelling this 'westernization' of urban India are satellite television and the information and communication technologies, the two new-age phenomena to which rural India is only just opening up to.

In recent years, commentators have sought to capture the contrast between rural and urban India by using 'Bharat' (India in Hindi) for rural India, where the vast majority—nearly 75%—of the country's 1.1 billion people live, and 'India' for urban India.[1]

This article examines the various dimensions and the extent of the rural-urban disparities in India by comparing their relative status on key indicators of economic and social development.[2]

Definition of Rural and Urban Areas in India

Definition of rural and urban areas varies across the world; however, most countries use demographics and/or occupation as criteria to define rural and urban areas. Census of India 2001 defines an urban area (the conceptual unit for which is a 'town') as follows:[3]

1. All places declared by the state government under a statute as a municipality, corporation, cantonment board or notified town area committee, etc.
2. All other places which simultaneously satisfy or are expected to satisfy the following criteria:
   - A minimum population of 5,000;
   - At least 75 percent of the male working population engaged in non-agricultural economic pursuits; and
   - A density of population of at least 400 per square kilometre (1,000 per square mile).

Well-defined outgrowths (OGs) of statutory towns have also been included in the extended urban area.

Any area, which is not covered by the above definition of urban, is rural.

As per Census 2001, there were 6.38 lakh villages and 5,161 towns in India.

Comparison of Rural and Urban India

1) Demographics

According to the 2001 census, out of a total population of 1027 million (or 102.7 crores) in India, about 742 million, or 72.2%, live in rural areas and 285 million, or 27.8%, live in urban areas.[4] Rural India thus accounts for an overwhelming majority of the country's population. That is why the oft-heard statement, "India lives in its villages." However, in recent years, the population growth rate in rural India has come down to 1% per annum, while urban population is growing at 2% per annum[5]—a sign of increasing urbanization in the country.

Sex Ratio

The sex ratio (number of females per 1000 males) in the country as a whole was 933 in 2001[6]. Interestingly, the sex ratio in rural areas was higher at 946 than in urban areas, for which the figure was 901.[7] Even the child sex ratio (sex ratio in the age group of 0-6 years) was higher in rural India at 934 than in urban India, where it was 903.[8] This is one measure on which rural India shows a higher level of social development than urban India. The lower sex-ratio in urban India has been largely attributed to the prejudice against the girl child and the consequent high rate of female foeticide, which is enabled by the widespread availability of sex-determination technology (prejudice against the girl child exists even in rural India, but non-availability of sex-determination technology and doctors as in urban India, probably puts curbs on the practice of female foeticide there).

2) Poverty

26.1% of India's population is estimated to be living below the poverty line; in absolute terms, this number is 260 million. In the rural areas, the proportion of poor is 27%, while that in urban areas is 23.6%. However, close to 75% of all people living below the poverty line are in rural areas.[9] In absolute terms, 3.84 crore families live below the poverty line in rural areas, according to the Ministry of Rural Development.[10]

According to NSS (National Sample Survey) data, per capita expenditure in rural areas was Rs.499.90 in 2000-01, just about half of that in urban areas, where the figure was Rs.914.57.[11] The gap between the per capita expenditure in rural and urban areas had increased by over eight percentage points between 1987-88 and 2000-01.[12]

Agriculture is the predominant occupation of the rural population in India, but much of the agriculture is still rain-fed, exposing the farmers to the vagaries of nature. Lack of irrigation facilities, lack of information on best practices in farming, and lack of access to modern technology, credit facilities, and markets plague agriculture in India, making it increasingly difficult for farmers to sustain their livelihoods through it. While livelihood diversification does take place through adoption of alternative sources like animal husbandry and non-farm enterprises like handicrafts, the pursuit of such livelihood sources, again, is subject to severe constraints on both the demand and supply side, and very often, such livelihood sources like handicrafts are either erratic in their income stream, or yield low returns on investment. This is one of the major reasons why rural incomes and expenditures continue to remain far lower than those in urban areas, and why poverty persists on the scale and magnitude that we see there.

3) Education

Migration from rural to urban areas is driven by two major factors: education, and employment. The facilities for primary, secondary and higher education available in urban India are incomparably more to those in rural India. To make a fair comparison, however, one would need to focus mainly on literacy and primary education, which are considered necessary for every citizen of the country.

The Census defines literacy rate as the proportion of literates to total population in the age group '7 years and above'. The overall literacy rate in the country in 2001 was 65.2% in 2001. The literacy rate in rural areas was 59%, while that in urban areas was 80%—a gap of 21 percentage points. Only 46% of females in rural areas were literate, while the figure in urban areas was 73%; in the case of males, the disparity was lower, with the literacy rate being 71% in rural areas, and 86% in urban areas.[13] The overall rural-urban disparity in literacy rates is, however, reducing, as can be seen from the figures in 1981, which were 36% in rural areas, and 67% in urban areas (a gap of 31 percentage points).

According to NSS data (55th Round, January-June 1998), the adult literacy rate (the proportion of literate population in age group '15 years and above') was 57% in the country. In rural areas, the adult literacy rate was 50%, while in urban areas, it was 78%. Adult literacy rate among females in urban areas was nearly 68 percent, which was more than twice that of the ratio prevailing in rural areas. In case of males, the adult literacy rate in urban areas was 86%, while in rural areas it was 64%. What this data reveals is that even within the same gender, there is considerable disparity when disaggregated for rural and urban areas.

School Attendance

In the age-group of 6-14 years, 70% of girls were attending schools in rural areas in 1998-99, as compared to 86% in urban areas; in the case of boys, the corresponding figures were 81% and 89% respectively.[14] While these figures reveal the rural-urban disparities in school attendance, they do not tell the full story on the state of primary education in rural India.

The disparities in the quality of education in terms of content and coverage, and quantity in terms of number of schools, teacher-pupil ratio, and study materials, are significantly high between rural and urban areas. Teacher absenteeism is rampant in schools in rural areas. Recent studies have made disturbing observations—even after five years of schooling, a number of students in rural areas are not able to spell their names, or do basic arithmetic sums.

4) Healthcare

Access to healthcare has been recognized as one of the fundamental necessities, along with education, shelter, safe drinking water, and sanitation, for the well-being of individuals. On this score, the disparities between rural and urban India are particularly stark. Though, nearly 75% of the country's population lives in rural areas, more than 75% of the country's doctors are based in cities.[15] Often the only doctor practising in the villages is an RMP (Registered Medical Practitioner), who is at least a notch below the MBBS-qualified general practitioner that we find in urban areas. The ratio of hospital beds to population in rural areas is fifteen times lower than that for urban areas.[16]

The publicly-funded Public Health Centres (PHCs) form the backbone of healthcare in rural areas. However, the PHCs are woefully under-manned and under-equipped; a recent survey revealed that only 38% of all PHCs have all the essential manpower, and only 31% have all the essential supplies.[17] Besides, the PHCs are plagued by doctor absenteeism (much like the teacher absenteeism in rural primary schools). Despite the establishment of the PHCs in rural areas, per capita expenditure on public health is seven times lower in rural areas, as compared to that in urban areas.[18]

Health Indicators

The disparities in the health infrastructure and services in rural and urban India get reflected in the health indicators. For instance, life expectancy at birth in rural areas is 58 years, while that in urban areas is 64.9 years.[19] Infant Mortality Rate (number of deaths per 1,000 live births, before the infant attains the age of one) in rural India is 73.3; in contrast, the figure in urban areas is 47 (National Family Health Survey, Round 2, 1998-99).[20]

The emerging industry of medical tourism (or health tourism) highlights the wide disparities in the healthcare infrastructure and services in rural and urban India. The abysmal state of the public healthcare system notwithstanding, India is making rapid strides as a hot destination for medical tourism. The state-of-the-art private hospitals that provide first-world treatment at third-world prices to patients from across the globe, are all located in urban areas. With the government itself promoting medical tourism in a big way, many commentators have expressed concern over the possible further neglect of public healthcare.

5) Housing

According to NSS data[21], in 2002, only 36% of rural households lived in *pucca* houses (houses made of solid material), 43% lived in semi-*pucca* houses, and the remaining 21% in *katcha* houses (houses made of loose material). In comparison, 77% of urban households lived in pucca houses, 20% in semi-*pucca* houses, and only 3% in katcha houses. *Katcha* and semi-*pucca* structures are highly susceptible to damage in the event of a natural disaster, or can catch fire easily, which means the lives and property of rural people are a lot more vulnerable than those of people in urban areas. In villages on the coast, for instance, houses regularly go under when there is a cyclonic storm.

According to Census 2001, only 59.4% of rural households have a separate kitchen within the house, compared to 76% of urban households.[22]

6) Access to Safe Drinking Water

Access to safe drinking water is again a basic necessity for survival. While the situation is improving in both rural and urban areas, the rural-urban disparity is still considerable.

According to the Census of India, if a household has access to drinking water supplied from a tap or a hand pump/tube well situated within or outside the premises, it is considered as having access to safe drinking water. Based on this definition, as per the 2001 census, 62% of all rural households had access to safe drinking water in contrast to 83% of all urban households.[23] This contrast becomes sharper when only piped water ('tap' as supply) is taken into account: only 24.3% of rural households had access to piped water, as compared to 68.7% of urban households.[24]

According to Mr. Raghuvansh Prasad Singh, Minister of Rural Development (Government of India), about 5,000 villages in the country still have no source of safe drinking water, and some 50,000 villages have insufficient supply of water.[25] 216,000 habitations in the country have been affected by water quality problems.[26]

7) Access to Basic Sanitation

The scenario on basic sanitation in India is grim: as per Census 2001, just 36% of all households in the country had a toilet facility within the house.[27] This picture begins to look even grimmer when looked at from the rural-urban perspective. While 70.4% of urban households had a toilet facility within the house, a mere 22.8% of rural households could boast of the same.[28] Defecation in the open is widespread in the rural areas (this phenomenon is prevalent even in urban areas to some extent), where the fields serve as a convenient place.

Sanitation necessitates proper sewerage systems as a corollary to toilet facility. When the existence of sewerage systems and sewage treatment facilities in the country is taken into account, even in the cities hardly 30% of the total wastewater is treated before disposal, which means a large quantity of wastewater enters rivers, lakes, groundwater and coastal waters, causing considerable pollution.[29]

Lack of basic sanitation like insufficient access to safe drinking water is a major cause of diseases, and places enormous financial burden on the poor besides the physical suffering. It is important, however, to observe here that the scarce installation and use of toilets in households is more a problem of awareness than of resources.

8) Access to Electricity

In elections held in the country in the last few years—in both the general and the state assembly elections—a prominent slogan used by politicians to appeal to the electorate has been "*bijli, sadak, pani*" (literally, "electricity, road, water"). The slogan is not out of context—these three amenities are critical for everyday lives of people and for their social and economic development. That nearly sixty years after independence large sections of our people should still be deprived of such basic amenities is a telling comment on the implementation of policies and programmes in the country.

A high proportion of India's approximately 6.38 lakh villages still literally live "in darkness" as statistics bear out. According to the NFHS-II, the proportion of households having access to electricity in rural areas was just 48% in 1998-99, whereas 91% of urban households had access to electricity. The overall figure for the country was 60%. Lack of access to, or the perennially short supply of electricity severely paralyzes life in rural India.

Power supply has strong political overtones in India, especially in rural areas. State electricity boards, which account for the majority of power supply in the country, run on huge deficits accumulated through years of subsidized provision. Not surprisingly, power cuts on a daily basis and frequent power failures characterize power supply in large parts of the country. Although, some initiatives to remedy the situation have been undertaken in the past decade—like the Dabhol project in Maharashtra, which unfortunately has run into major problems—the overall picture still remains grim. Power is a key infrastructure, and reforms and initiatives in this sector are imperative for the social and economic development of the country.

9) Road Connectivity

Roads provide physical connectivity to people. A well-developed road network can shrink physical space by enabling people to move easily from one place to another. In the context of the rural and urban areas, roads assume great significance as roads within rural areas and between rural and urban areas can facilitate trade, commerce, labour mobility, and travel for education and healthcare. Easy commuting to a hub where most goods and services would be available would reduce or even eliminate to provide them in all villages.[30]

The road network in rural India is, however, far from satisfactory, as anyone who has travelled there will readily vouch for. 40% of the villages in India lack access to all-weather roads[31], and over 50% of villages with population with less than 1,000 are yet to be connected by roads.

10) Access to Banking Services

Penetration of banking services is very low in India, although the booming economy and the mushrooming bank branches would lead one to conclude otherwise. According to Census 2001, barely 36% of all households in India have access to banking services.[32] When seen from the rural-urban perspective, 30% of rural households are reported to have access to banking services, compared to 50% of urban households.[33] Although 68% of the 70,324 bank offices in 2005 were in rural and semi-urban areas, their share of deposits and credit was only 29.1% and 20.5% respectively.[34]

Despite the economic growth that the country has seen since the reforms in 1991, the services of the formal financial sector are still out of reach for a majority of the population. High transaction costs coupled with lack of requisite manpower is seen as the major hurdle for banks to reach remote, rural areas.

Lack of access to financial services from the formal financial institutions is what has given rise to the field of microfinance. A majority of India's poor live in rural areas, and microfinance with its focus on serving the poor, has created savings and credit products and services especially to suit the needs and capacity of the poor. Various microfinance models are in vogue, notably the Grameen Bank and the Self-Help Group (SHG) model.

11) Penetration of Information and Communication Technologies (ICTs)

The explosion of information and communication technologies (ICTs) in the last decade of the twentieth century brought about a revolution in the way people conducted their businesses, pursued education, accessed public services, sought entertainment, and managed their lives in general across the globe. Computers, the Internet, cellphones, and landline phones seem to have become all-pervasive. But, this phenomenon too, has been largely restricted to urban areas, in developing countries at least.

The ICTs explosion has given rise to another divide between people—the digital divide. 'The digital divide' refers to the gap between those who have access to or can use ICTs, and those that do not have access to or cannot use ICTs. Underpinning the digital divide, again, are all the other economic and social divides—rich and poor, literate and illiterate, rural and urban, to cite a few.

Consider the disparities in ICT diffusion in rural and urban India: in 2005, teledensity in rural areas was a meagre 2%, as compared to 31% in urban India, with the overall figure for the country being 11%.[35] PC (personal computer) penetration at an estimated 1.5%[36] and Internet penetration at 4.5%[37] in 2005 are abysmally low in the entire country, but even on this score, it is urban areas that are far ahead of the rural.

Low levels of literacy, low disposable incomes, high cost of the PC (although a low-cost model at Rs.10,000 is now available), and infrastructural bottlenecks like inadequate and unreliable power supply, are some of the reasons underlying the rural-urban digital divide.

Rural-Urban Disparities Across States

This article has taken an overall view with respect to the rural-urban disparities in India. But, as the National Human Development Report 2001 brought out by the Planning Commission observes, with regard to several economic and social development indicators, there are wide disparities between states in the extent of rural and urban development. Kerala and Punjab are states, for instance, where rural-urban disparities are among the least, while, states like Haryana and Madhya Pradesh still have significant rural-urban disparities.[38] In a state like Bihar, however, even though there are rural-urban disparities, the level of development in both sectors is considerably low; the level of development in urban areas is much lower vis-à-vis other states.[39]

The Caste Barrier

Any discussion on the Indian society would be incomplete without a reference to the caste system, which makes the Indian society a lot more complex than many others in the world. Established centuries ago, the caste system with its four broad caste categories—*Brahmin*, *Kshatriya*, *Vaishya*, and *Shudra*[40]—but with numerous sub-castes within each broad caste category, has created a social hierarchy in Indian society, which greatly influences access to social and economic opportunities and upward mobility across a spectrum of fields. While this phenomenon pervades both rural and urban areas, it is much more deeply entrenched in the rural. Political representation in the country is also to a large extent determined by the prevailing caste equation in different regions.

Education has served to be an effective leveller in bringing down the caste barrier to a great extent in urban India, but in rural India, where education facilities are woefully inadequate, the high caste-low caste divide persists and not only continues to deprive people of lower caste the opportunities to enhance their standard of living, but also perpetrates crimes of the most heinous nature on them. The caste barrier is a major reason why social and development indicators for a number of groups of people in rural areas have remained low for decades.

Conclusion

The comparison between rural and urban India vis-à-vis different parameters of economic and social development clearly reveals that rural India lags behind urban India on almost all parameters. Better access to social and physical infrastructure and livelihood opportunities in urban India creates better conditions there to survive and thrive, than in rural India. Even after nearly sixty years of independence, much of rural India is still deprived of two of the most basic necessities of life—safe drinking water and sanitation. The abysmal state of healthcare only compounds the situation, and not surprisingly, public health and hygiene are perennially at risk in large parts of the country.

While urban India races ahead on the path of development on the back of a booming economy and the forces of globalization, the economic and social backwardness of the rural hinterland (especially in states like Bihar, Uttar Pradesh, and Orissa) present a stark contrast. This is significant from the policy-making point of view, as over 70% of the country's population resides in rural areas. While the budgetary allocation for rural development is substantial, the progress on the ground is far from satisfactory. It does not help, as pointed out by a former prime minister, that only 15 paise in a rupee earmarked for development programmes actually reaches the beneficiary. Clearly, implementation and monitoring of development programmes are as crucial as framing appropriate policies. For India to join the league of developed nations, its vast rural population needs to have the same access to the opportunities and facilities that its urban population has.

(S Rajagopalan, Faculty Member, Icfai Business School, Ahmedabad.)

Notes

1. Mr. Sharad Joshi, founder of Shetakari Sanghatana, who was the first to use the descriptions 'Bharat' and 'India' in 1978, points out that he did not intend the descriptions to signify 'rural' and 'urban' India; he says, 'India' is that notional entity, largely Anglicised and relatively better-off, that had obtained the succession of colonial exploitation from the British; while 'Bharat' is largely rural, agricultural, poor and backward that was being subjected to colonial-like exploitation even after the end of the Raj." See "The Great India-Bharat Divide" by Sharad Joshi, *The Hindu Business Line* (February 23, 2003), *http://www.thehindubusinessline.com/2003/02/12/stories/2003021200050800.htm* (Accessed September 28, 2006).
2. Wherever not specifically indicated in this article, definitions and data have been sourced from the National Human Development Report 2001 brought out by the Planning Commission. *http://planningcommission.nic.in/reports/genrep/reportsf.htm*
3. *http://www.censusindia.net/results/eci14_page1.html* (Accessed September 22, 2006).
4. *http://www.censusindia.net/results/eNewsletter_1.html*, (Accessed September 14, 2006).
5. World Development Indicators, World Bank.
6. ibid.
7. *http://www.thehoot.org/ready.asp* (Accessed September 18, 2006).
8. *http://www.censusindia.net/results/eci15_page1.html* (Accessed September 22, 2006).
9. Calculated by the author.

10. Sudhansu R Das (2005), "Men, more than material, can bridge rural-urban divide," *http://www.thehindubusinessline.com/2005/09/30/stories/2005093000841100.htm* (Accessed September 24, 2005).
11. Prabhat Datta (2004), "The Great Indian Divide," *http://www.hinduonnet.com/fline/fl2114/stories/20040716002009000.htm* (Accessed September 27, 2006).
12. ibid.
13. Nirupam Bajpai and Sangita Goyal (2004), "Primary Education in India: Quality and Coverage Issues," pp.6 *http://www.earthinstitute.columbia.edu/cgsd/documents/bajpai_primaryeducation.pdf#search=%22school%20enrolment%20and%20drop%20out%20rates%20in%20rural%20and%20urban%20India%22* (Accessed September 27, 2006).
14. ibid (data originally from Dreze and Sen, 2002).
15. Sanjit Bagchi (2006), "Telemedicine in rural India" *http://medicine.plosjournals.org/perlserv?request=get-document&doi=10.1371/journal.pmed.0030082* (Accessed September 14, 2006).
16. Milind Deogaonkar (2004), "Socio-economic inequality and its effect on healthcare delivery in India: Inequality and healthcare," *http://www.sociology.org/content/vol8.1/deogaonkar.html* (Accessed September 14, 2006).
17. ibid.
18. Milind Deogaonkar (2004), "Socio-economic inequality and its effect on healthcare delivery in India: Inequality and healthcare," *http://www.sociology.org/content/vol8.1/deogaonkar.html* (Accessed September 14, 2006).
19. Prabhat Datta (2004), "The Great Indian Divide," *http://www.hinduonnet.com/fline/fl2114/stories/20040716002009000.htm* (Accessed September 27, 2006).
20. Table on Infant and Child Mortality Rates in India, *http://www.infochangeindia.org/indiastatsreport.jsp* (Accessed September 14, 2006).
21. *http://mospi.nic.in/nsso_pr_58round_housing_stock.htm* Accessed September 18, 2006.
22. eCensus India, issue no.17, 2003. http://www.censusindia.net/results/eci17.pdf (Accessed September 22, 2006).
23. Calculated by the author, based on data available at *http://www.censusindia.net/2001housing/S00-015.html* (Accessed September 12, 2006).
24. *http://www.censusindia.net/2001housing/S00-015.html* (Accessed September 12, 2006).
25. Raghuvansh Prasad Singh (2005), "When every rural home has its own bulb, tap and toilet," *http://www.indiaempowered.com/full_story.php?content_id=79320* (Accessed September 21, 2006).

26. ibid.
27. eCensus India, issue no. 17, 2003. *http://www.censusindia.net/results/eci17.pdf* (Accessed September 22, 2006).
28. ibid.
29. "India: Assessment 2002 – Water Supply and Sanitation" A Planning Commission Report, *http://planningcommission.nic.in/reports/genrep/wtrsani.pdf#search=%22India%3A%20Assessment%202002%20Water%20Supply%20and%20Sanitation%22* (Accessed September 27, 2006).
30. "Road Connectivity," NHDR 2001, pp.45. *http://planningcommission.nic.in/reports/genrep/reportsf.htm* (Accessed September 27, 2006).
31. "India Transport Sector" *http://web.worldbank.org/wbsite/external/countries/southasiaext/extsarregtoptransport/0,contentMDK:20703625~menuPK:868822~pagePK:34004173~piPK:34003707~theSitePK:579598,00.html* (Accessed September 21, 2006).
32. Saugata Bhattacharya, "Rural Banking: An Opportunity for Growth," *Professional Banker* (Icfai University Press), March 2006.
33. Barun Mitra (2006) "Grassroots Capitalism Thrives in India," Chapter 3 in "2006 Index of Economic Freedom," pp.45. *http://www.heritage.org/research/features/index/chapters/pdfs/Index2006_Chap3.pdf* (Accessed September 27, 2006).
34. Saugata Bhattacharya, "Rural Banking: An Opportunity for Growth," *Professional Banker* (Icfai University Press), March 2006.
35. Harsimran Singh, "Teledensity target to be revised for 2006, says DoT," *http://www.financialexpress.com/fe_full_story.php?content_id=113956* (Accessed September 25, 2006).
36. Kripa Raman, "Rebound in sight," *http://www.blonnet.com/ew/2005/10/24/stories/2005102400070100.htm* (Accessed September 26, 2006).
37. *http://www.internetworldstats.com/asia/in.htm* (original source: Computer Industry Almanac) (Accessed September 28, 2006).
38. NHDR 2001, pp. 12 - 23. *http://planningcommission.nic.in/reports/genrep/reportsf.htm* (Accessed September 27, 2006).
39. ibid.
40. The *Brahmin* in the Indian caste system is at the top of the social hierarchy, his primary function being acquiring and disseminating knowledge; the *Kshatriya's* function (being a warrior) is to provide defence and security; the *Vaishya* is the businessman, who engages in trade and industry; and the *Shudra*, who is at the bottom of the social hierarchy, provides manual labour.

SECTION II

RURAL-URBAN DYNAMICS: THE 'LINKAGES' PERSPECTIVE

4

Beyond Rural Urban: Keeping up with Changing Realities

James Garrett

The labels "urban" and "rural" fall far short of capturing the dynamism and diversity of reality. Conjuring up visions of crowded cities and isolated countryside, they suggest separate worlds and ways of living. They mask the many ways urban and rural overlap and intertwine, as well as the variety of livelihood strategies within urban or rural areas. This article emphasizes that focusing on the connections between urban and rural areas, rather than viewing them as separate worlds, can help to reframe our understanding of development in the two sectors.

Policies built on presumptions of separateness or on traditional notions of urban and rural livelihoods diminish the possibilities for economic growth and poverty reduction. More effective policies will take the diversity of livelihoods along the continuum into account and also appreciate the differences among urban and rural areas and the links between them.

Focusing on the connections between urban and rural areas can help to reframe our understanding of development in these areas. We can see that rural and urban lives and livelihood strategies span rural and urban geographies in integrated and interdependent ways. With better understanding of the current reality of urban and rural areas and the connections between them, policies will better reflect the ways people actually live. Policies will take into account the different livelihood strategies, links, and localities that exist across "urban" and "rural." And they will be able to promote synergies—such as market exchange—that benefit all, no matter where they live.

What is Happening?

Greater access to information technology, better roads, and improved education, among other factors, are helping to change and strengthen connections between urban and rural areas. Places do exist that correspond to the conventional vision and are "more rural" or "more urban," but increased flows of people, goods, services, information, income, and even waste and pollution contribute to a blurring of sectors and space. Thus, we should be careful that terminology doesn't unintentionally reinforce separateness or stereotypes and thus mislead analysis.

The food and agricultural system illustrates the complexities of urban-rural connections and the ways such complexities challenge attempts to divide policy actions into separate "rural" and "urban" spheres. Rural farmers,for instance, sell their products at both rural and city markets. Urban farmers raise and sell fruits, vegetables, and livestock. Urban shopkeepers look to rural residents as customers for food and non-food items and for agricultural inputs. Rural laborers migrate to nearby towns for work during the lean season. Rural dwellers complement farm income with proceeds from industries such as handicrafts or food processing. Agricultural production itself has benefited from more direct connections with urban-based agribusinesses and supermarkets that provide technical assistance, credit, and information on consumer demand.

Appreciating how the food and agricultural system integrates urban and rural areas and links agricultural production with industry and services gives a new perspective to other trends that seem to suggest agriculture is not so important—that agricultural production is declining as a percentage of many countries' economies and that the proportion of average rural household income from nonagricultural production activities is rising.

With a rural-urban "lens," we see that the food and agricultural system will in fact be important to the livelihoods of both urban and rural dwellers for some time to come. Take highly urbanized Argentina, Brazil, and Chile as examples. In these countries, agricultural production's contribution to the economy is relatively small (less than 10 percent of GDP), but agriculture and food-based manufacturing continue to make up around one-third of GDP (excluding difficult-to-assign components such as services and textile manufacturing).

Furthermore, this lens illustrates how the health of the agricultural sector is important to both rural and urban dwellers. Individuals can earn income directly from agricultural production or indirectly by participating in various jobs in the system that agricultural production supports in urban *and* rural areas, such as grocers, factory workers, and truck drivers. And, especially in more rural areas, the incomes of these workers increase demand for other goods and services provided by others not directly connected with agriculture.

Mismatch of Perception and Reality

These connections are not new, but they do seem to be increasingly important. Unfortunately, perceptions and policies do not seem to be keeping up. Many policymakers and researchers still hew to the rural-urban divide. They may not fully appreciate the importance of rural demand to urban businesses, the significance of income from nonagricultural production activities to rural households, or how, through remittances from seasonal or permanent migrants, rural households use links with cities to diversify their income sources. Economic models and national development strategies often reinforce spatial and sectoral divides, categorizing analysis or policies as urban and rural and assuming a corresponding division of industry and agriculture. In the past, such a division may have been a useful simplification; now it fails to reflect reality in important ways.

Institutional arrangements tend to do the same. Actions of public authorities can overlap and contradict. With some exceptions, such as Metro Manila in the Philippines, governance structures generally fail to appreciate the interdependence of cities with surrounding areas. Assessments by the United Nations Development

Programme in Nepal, for instance, show that conventional approaches to planning—dividing locales into rural and urban—impeded information flows and coordination between national, district, city, and village planners. Urban planners focused on urban infrastructure; rural planners focused on export markets and ignored ties to domestic ones.

What We Need to Understand

The mixtures of "urban" with "rural" activities are not anomalies but the reality of livelihoods in rural and urban areas today. Separating rural and urban or setting them against one another overlooks connections and potential development synergies. Training a rural-urban lens on policies makes clear that rural and urban development is not an either/or proposition.

For example, a rural anti-poverty strategy that focuses specifically on raising agricultural output can miss important issues of distribution and development, especially if it favors generating gains from large producers. How will small farmers and the landless fit with such a strategy? Will the strategy increase incomes and employment for them or worsen their prospects and actually encourage greater migration to cities? Without solid connections to local market towns and cities, how will agricultural producers, transporters, and traders even profit from increased output? And how will urban consumers reap the benefits of potentially lower food prices? A rural-urban lens suggests it is critical to focus on various components of the entire food and agricultural system, not on agricultural production alone.

As another example, a rural-urban lens raises cautions about national development strategies that strongly favor rural-urban migration or urban industrial growth as a solution to poverty. For example, even with rapid rates of rural-urban migration, a large proportion of the population remains in rural areas. What strategy will provide the engine of development for them? How will an urban-focused strategy take into account industrial production in small towns and rural villages? Or regard the essential role that intermediate-size cities play in connecting urban areas with rural goods and labor markets?

A rural-urban lens illuminates the present reality of livelihoods and connections that such policies should consider. For instance, rural-urban migration may indeed play an important role in reducing poverty. But population shifts can take generations. In tracking rural Filipino households over the past decade, one study found that a substantial majority of first-generation children stayed in rural areas, continuing to live with their parents or moving to another rural village. Many of those who did move to urban areas went to small and intermediate-size cities, not large metropolitan areas. Policies will need to address both urban and rural poverty for many more years and may need to pay more attention to rural villages and smaller towns and cities.

In addition, policies that promote the integration of rural and urban areas, and provide capacities and opportunities to individuals and households, can help people escape from poverty where they are, rather than simply helping them move. A study of two rural Vietnamese villages over the past decade, for instance, suggests that strong links with larger cities helped them successfully face significant economic and social change, transform their economies from traditional rice production, and continue progressing out of poverty. One village shifted to more varied crops, which they were able to sell in nearby urban centers. The other moved out of agriculture altogether to concentrate on handicrafts—again depending on urban links to reach domestic and international markets.

What We Need to Do

We may need *new language and new typologies* to comfortably distinguish differences in livelihood strategies and conditions within urban and rural areas as well as between them. Policymakers may no longer find it helpful to think of urban as "industry" and rural as "agriculture" but need to consider how to support economic and livelihood systems all along the urban-rural continuum.

Policymakers may need to *focus more on "systems" and less on "sectors."* They should pay more attention to economic activity and urban-rural integration within economic and political "catch-ments," including natural "regional economies." Thinking regionally will likely lead to greater support for the ways in which market towns and small and medium-size cities contribute to urban and rural well-being. It may also help policymakers consider development strategies in a more holistic way and move away from traditional divisions.

This highlights the importance of *understanding livelihoods and poverty contextually* so as to devise policies that cope with differences in problems, capacities, and opportunities. In addition to well-functioning markets, households need to have appropriate capacities and resources if they are to adapt successfully to economic and social change. Different participants within these systems—small farmers, the landless, migrants, or the urban poor, for example—may require different economic and social policies and investments.

Policies will need to *take dynamics into account.* Effective policies will adapt to shifting economic, political, and social conditions. Policies that support urban-rural integration and provide appropriate public investment to encourage the flow of goods and resources across sectors and locations are important steps in that direction. A more integrated economy offers more choices and allows individuals and households to pursue their own best path out of poverty, depending on particular conditions, resources, and opportunities. For instance, smallholders in Vietnam proved resilient and creative in the face of change, as long as they had the basics: access to markets, information, security of tenure, and the opportunity to generate alternative, non-farm incomes.

Given appropriately integrated planning, growth of urban and rural areas will not be antagonistic but complementary, enhancing and enlarging links and providing even greater opportunities for different groups in different locations. Migration and the rise of nonfarm activities will then become the results of positive transformations, rather than desperate coping strategies.

Of course, this assumes that *authorities have the means to encourage local and regional input into policies, programs, and plans.* To benefit from such input,they may need to adapt governance structures to coordinate government action both vertically and horizontally, as well as connect with other actors, including the private sector and civil society. Effective planning today may require examining the role of the smaller towns and intermediate-size cities in supporting regional economies and linking rural areas with even larger urban ones. These smaller towns and cities, in any case, are major destinations for migrants and still provide the most common urban experience for most rural folk.

Holding up a rural-urban lens to development is useful for illuminating new ways of thinking about development strategies and about urban and rural transformations, particularly as urbanization and migration continue, as rural livelihoods diversify, and as the agriculture and food system becomes more complex. Both rural and urban livelihoods can benefit from this perspective, but only if it leads to improved and closer interactions, not continued separations in mindsets, policies, and institutions.

(James Garrett is Research Fellow in Food Consumption and Nutrition Division at International Food Policy Research Institute.)

5

Rural-Urban Linkages and Pro-Poor Agricultural Growth: An Overview

Cecilia Tacoli

This article examines the various forms of rural-urban linkages, and how rural-urban linkages in the form of easy access to urban markets are key to increasing incomes for poor rural farmers.

Introduction

Rural-urban linkages include flows of agricultural and other commodities from rural-based producers to urban markets, both for local consumers and for forwarding to regional, national and international markets; and, in the opposite direction, flows of manufactured and imported goods from urban centres to rural settlements. They also include flows of people moving between rural and urban settlements, either commuting on a regular basis, for occasional visits to urban-based services and administrative centres, or migrating temporarily or permanently. Flows of information between rural and urban areas include information on market mechanisms – from price fluctuations to consumer preferences – and information on employment opportunities for potential migrants. Financial flows include, primarily, remittances from migrants to relatives and communities in sending

Source: Cecilia Tacoli, "Rural-Urban Linkages and Pro-Poor Agricultural Growth: An Overview," IIED. Prepared for OECD DAC POVNET, Agriculture and Pro-Poor Growth Task Team, Helsinki Workshop, 17-18 June 2004.

areas, and transfers such as pensions to migrants returning to their rural homes, and also investments and credit from urban-based institutions.

These spatial flows overlap with interlinkages between sectors both at the household level and at the level of local economies. They include backward and forward linkages between agriculture and manufacturing and services, such as production inputs and the processing of agricultural raw materials. Most urban centres, especially small and intermediate ones, rely on broad-based demand for basic goods and services from surrounding populations to develop their secondary and tertiary sectors. Overall, synergy between agricultural production and urban-based enterprises is often key to the development of more vibrant local economies and, on a wider level, to less unequal and more 'pro-poor' regional economic growth[1].

Some factors can be generalized as having a key role in the increase in the scale of rural-urban linkages. Decreasing incomes from farming, especially for small-scale producers who, because of lack of land, water or capital, are unable to intensify production and switch to higher value crops, mean that growing numbers of rural residents engage in non-farm activities that are often located in urban centres. For those who continue farming, direct access to markets is essential in the wake of the demise of parastatal marketing boards – and markets are also usually located in urban centres. Better access to markets can increase farming incomes and encourage shifts to higher value crops or livestock. Population growth and distribution patterns affect the availability of good agricultural land and can contribute to rural residents moving out of farming. With the expansion of urban centres, land uses change from agricultural to residential and industrial, and in the peri-urban interface these processes go hand in hand with transformations in the livelihoods of different groups – with the poorest often losing out.

Perhaps more significant than the absolute availability of natural resources in relation to population numbers and density are the mechanisms which regulate access to, and management of, such resources. These include land tenure systems and the role of local government in negotiating the priorities of different users and in providing a regulatory framework which safeguards the needs of the most vulnerable groups while, at the same time, making provision for the requirements of economic and population growth. Such mechanisms continue to call for attention, to make it possible for more vulnerable groups to successfully plot a course through this increasingly complex "landscape".

What is 'Rural' and What is 'Urban'? Some Problematic Definitions

The prevailing division between 'urban' and 'rural' policies is based on the assumption that the physical distinction between the two areas is self-explanatory and uncontroversial. However, there are three major problems with this view. The first is that demographic and economic criteria used to define what is 'urban' and what is 'rural' can vary widely between nations, making generalisations problematic (see Box 1).

Box 1: Variations in the Definition of Urban Centres

Asia remains a predominantly 'rural' continent, with two-thirds of its population living in rural areas in 1990. However, if both India and China were to change their definition of urban centres to one based on a relatively low population threshold of 2,000 or 2,500 inhabitants—as used by many Latin American and European nations – a large proportion of their population would change from 'rural' to 'urban'. Given the fact that India and China have a high share of Asia's population, this in turn would significantly change Asia's level of urbanization—and even change the world's level of urbanization by a few percentage points.[2]

A second problem is that of the definition of urban boundaries. In Southeast Asia's Extended Metropolitan Regions, agriculture, cottage industry, industrial estates, suburban developments and other types of land use coexist side by side in areas with a radius as large as 100 km, where the high mobility of the population includes circular migration and commuting.[3] In sub-Saharan Africa, agriculture still prevails in peri-urban areas, but there, as elsewhere, significant shifts in land ownership and employment patterns are taking place, often at the expense of both rural and urban poor people (see Box 2).

Box 2: Land Use Conversion in the Philippines

In Manila's extended metropolitan region, large swathes of rice land have been converted into industrial, residential and recreational uses. Alternatively, land may simply lie idle, with cattle grazing on grassed-over rice fields whose owners await either development permits or more propitious market conditions. Although the 1988 Land Reform Law protects from conversion lands eligible for redistribution from landlord to tenant farmer, it has in fact accelerated the process of land conversion. This is because landlords keen to avoid losing their land have converted it to non-agricultural uses, and in many cases tenant farmers have been evicted and the land left idle.[4]

The third problem in the definition of the boundaries between 'rural' and 'urban' areas is the fact that urban residents and enterprises depend on an area significantly larger than the built-up area for basic resources and ecological functions. In general, the larger and the wealthier the city, the more its industrial base and its wealthy consumers will draw on such resources and ecological functions from beyond its surrounding region.[5] The concept of a city's ecological footprint was developed to quantify the land area on which any city's inhabitants depend for food, water and other renewable resources such as fuelwood, and the absorption of carbon to compensate for the carbon dioxide emitted from fossil fuel use.[6] The concept makes clear the dependence of any city on the resources and ecological functions of an area considerably larger than itself (although urban areas with limited industrial bases and with most of their population having low incomes will have much smaller and generally more local ecological footprints than large and prosperous cities).

Flows of Goods, Access to Urban Markets and Local Economic Development

Exchanges of goods between urban and rural areas are an essential element of rural-urban linkages. The 'virtuous circle' model of rural-urban local economic development emphasises efficient economic linkages and physical infrastructure connecting farmers and other rural producers with both domestic and external markets. This involves three phases:

- Rural households earn higher incomes from production of agricultural goods for non-local markets, and increase their demand for consumer goods.
- This leads to the creation of non-farm jobs and employment diversification, especially in small towns close to agricultural production areas.
- Which in turn absorbs surplus rural labour, raises demand for agricultural produce and again boosts agricultural productivity and rural incomes[7].

However, spatial proximity to markets does not necessarily improve farmers' access to the inputs and services required to increase agricultural productivity. Access to land, capital and labour may be far more important in determining the extent to which farmers are able to benefit from urban markets. In Paraguay, despite their proximity to the capital city, smallholders' production is hardly stimulated by urban markets as their low incomes do not allow investment in cash crops or in production intensification to compensate for the lack of land.[8] Patterns of attendance at periodic markets also show that distance is a much less important issue than rural consumers' income and purchasing power in determining demand for manufactured goods, inputs and services.[9]

Nevertheless, access to urban markets is key to increasing incomes for rural and peri-urban farmers. Three aspects are crucial: physical infrastructure, including road networks and affordable transport; relations between producers, traders and consumers; and information on how markets operate, including price fluctuations and consumer preferences. Poor physical infrastructure can have far-reaching consequences on producers' prices, as inadequate roads usually entail prohibitive transport costs (see Box 3). Traders, often perceived as inherently exploitative, can in fact play an important role in providing credit and information to producers. In areas where production volumes are small and scattered between several small farms, local traders operating on a small scale are often the only link with markets. However, lack of storage and processing facilities and high transport costs increase the vulnerability of these trade networks.

Box 3: The Impact of Poor Physical Infrastructure on Farming

In Tanzania, collection, transport and sale of previously controlled cash crops has been liberalised since the mid-1980s. Cashew nuts from the southern region are primarily for export, and a small number of private companies control their purchase, collection and transport to the main shipping port of Mtwara. Road infrastructure in the area, however, is extremely poor, making transport costs prohibitive. Although private companies are only allowed to buy the nuts from farmer cooperatives in designated locations, in practice these are out of reach for small farmers, who can hardly afford transport costs. Smallholders tend to sell directly to agents, an arrangement which puts buyers in a strong bargaining position and weakens producers' ability to negotiate prices. It also makes it difficult for local government to effectively control the quantities traded and collect taxes from traders, despite this being a major source of revenue. In southeast Nigeria road and transport infrastructure is generally good, but some remote settlements can be cut off at certain times of the year, when soil erosion combined with heavy rains can wipe away feeder roads. Only large farmers have the means to hire tractors to transport produce to marketing nodes. Small farmers who cannot afford this expense often prefer to seek employment as waged labourers in large commercial farms, often belonging to urban-based landlords, or to abandon their own farms altogether and migrate to urban centres or to other rural settlements.[10]

Markets are also social institutions in which some actors are able to enforce mechanisms of control which favour access for specific groups and exclude others (see Box 4). Grain markets in South Asia tend to be dominated by large local merchants who control access to the means of distribution (transport, sites, capital, credit and information); even in the petty retailing subsector, caste and gender are major entry barriers.[11]

Box 4: Market Access and Control in Senegal's Charcoal Trade

In Senegal, forests are officially owned by the state and managed by the Forest Service, which allocates commercial rights to urban-based merchants through licences, permits and quotas. Village chiefs control direct forest access, ultimately deciding whether to allow merchants' woodcutters into the forests. Despite their control, villagers reap only a small portion of the profits from commercial forestry. More substantial benefits accrue to merchants and wholesalers who, through their social relations, control access to forestry markets, labour opportunities and urban distribution, and access to state agents and officials. Local control and management of natural resources is therefore weakened by the lack of economic benefits which would encourage maintenance.[12]

Understanding markets is essential for farmers. Direct access to information on consumer preferences has transformed, sometimes dramatically, the practices of farmers attending farmers' markets in Tamil Nadu, and helped them maximize their use of natural resources (see Box 5).

Box 5: Farmers' Markets in Tamil Nadu

This was initiated by the state government in 1999, and covered most of the towns and cities of Tamil Nadu, South India, where semi-drought conditions and labour shortages affect small-scale farmers. Dedicated marketplaces were constructed where vegetable farmers would sell their produce directly to urban consumers, with the explicit aim to exclude middlemen and traders. Direct contact with consumers has affected producers' practices in two main ways: through increased diversification of production to include a wider variety of vegetables, and through intensification, to maximise the use of water and land resources throughout the year.[13]

Rural-Urban Linkages and Livelihood Diversification

Transformations in the ways in which households and individuals make a living are perhaps the most striking aspect of rural–urban linkages and, in many cases, involve multiple occupations ranging from farming to services to processing and manufacturing. In most rural locations, there has been an increase among rural households in the time devoted to, and the income share derived from, non-farm activities, although diversification is not new. Nor is it a purely rural phenomenon, and the reliance of hundreds of millions of urban residents on agriculture, either for household consumption or as an income-generating opportunity, is well documented[14]. However, national employment data tend to underestimate the importance of diversification, as they usually record only people's primary activity. This neglects the fact that individuals are more likely to engage in multiple activities rather than rely on only one, and that there will often be variations over time, either seasonal (and therefore depending on changes in the labour demands of different activities) or related to individuals' life course (such as, especially for women, different demands on their time from childcare, caring for older people, etc). Recent survey data on employment patterns in southern Tanzania show that 67 percent of respondents living in villages and in the intermediate town of Lindi are engaged in more than one income-generating activity, including both farming and non-farm activities[15].

Information on rural households' income share derived from non-farm activities is usually based on relatively small and location-specific household or enterprise surveys. Rarely are there national data, and even where they are available, usually informal sector activities are omitted, including home-based work and petty trade which can be a significant part of non-farm income-generating activities for low-income groups. Available studies show that the proportion of rural households' incomes derived from non-farm sources, including migrant remittances, is between 30 and 50 percent in sub-Saharan Africa, reaching as much as 80-90 percent in some regions, such as southern Africa. In south Asia, the proportion is around 60 percent[16]. In Latin America, non-farm income constitutes roughly 40 percent of rural households' incomes[17].

A review of the main reasons behind the growth in rural non-farm employment in different nations and regions suggests that diversification is a response to a variety of factors. As in migration theory, these factors can be broadly divided into 'push' (or constraints) and 'pull' (or opportunities); however, this is more an analytical distinction, and empirical evidence shows that in most cases diversification is driven by a combination of both.

For example, in some regions of China and in the densely-populated Red River and Mekong deltas in Vietnam, increases in rural non-farm activities are primarily the consequence of large labour surpluses in the agricultural sector[18]. However, it should also be stressed that in both countries such labour surpluses emerged after the demise of the commune farm system in the 1979-84 period in China, and after 1986 in Vietnam. As households took over responsibility for farming, production levels increased and, in high-potential regions, this contributed to a decline in rural poverty and to increased demand for non-agricultural goods; at the same time, however, land scarcity gave rise to unprecedented migration to small and large urban centres[19].

In Brazil's central plains, since the early 1970s export-oriented agro-industry has taken hold with highly mechanised crops such as cotton, and has swept aside traditional staples' production by sharecroppers, small tenant farmers and rural squatters, forcing them to find employment in non-farm sectors[20]. In much of sub-Saharan Africa, the growth of non-farm occupation since the implementation of structural adjustment derives as much from the need for cash to cover user fees for basic services, as from the decline in farming incomes and, in some locations, the emergence of new types of employment in services for international tourism[21]. The latter are in most cases not the consequence of endogenous development but of the internationalisation of trade, production and services. Similarly, the development of many small and intermediate urban centres in northern Mexico, and the related growth in non-farm employment among their populations and that of the surrounding rural regions, is not locally induced but is based on foreign investment and production for international markets in *maquiladoras*[22].

Diversification Patterns, Inter-Household and Intra-Household Differences

Given the broad variations in the reasons behind diversification, and the ways in which local contexts affect both constraints and opportunities, it is useful to look at diversification patterns in relation to their potential contribution to poverty reduction and to greater equity.

A first distinction can be made between poor and vulnerable households and individuals, and better-off households and individuals. This cuts across both rural settlements and urban centres, as diversification and access to both rural and urban resources is important for residents of both areas. On the other hand, there are also significant differences in the ways in which different households straddle the rural-urban divide, and in how this contributes to their security and wealth.

Diversification can be described as an accumulation strategy for households with farming assets and with access to urban networks, and who often re-invest profits from urban-based activities in agricultural production and vice-versa, resulting in capital and asset accumulation. But for other groups, rural non-farm activities can be determined by lack or loss of land, labour or capital in what can be described as a 'survival strategy' that aims to reduce risk, overcome seasonal income fluctuations, and respond to external and internal shocks and stresses[23]. Land ownership can become increasingly unequal, as large farmers and wealthier urban households purchase land rights from small holders who cannot afford to buy inputs and have limited access to credit[24]. As a result, poorest households become less able to spread risk as they lose farming as part of their portfolio of activities. Indeed, reliance on non-farm income sources is much higher than average among rural residents with limited or no access to farming resources, such as, in many nations, women and the landless. But at the same time, households relying on farming only can be considered a high-risk category, especially in rainfed agriculture areas where they are susceptible to climatic vagaries[25].

As wealthier households' diversification of activities consolidates, multi-activity takes place at the household level, where individuals specialise in specific sectors of activities but resources are used to facilitate investments across sectors. By contrast, poor and vulnerable individuals lack the skills and education to specialise in any activity, and must engage in a multitude of low-paid income-generating occupations to make ends meet.

At the intra-household level, gender and generational relations are likely to have a significant impact on the ways in which different groups engage in diversification. In Tanzania, domestic trade liberalisation has opened up opportunities in local small-scale trade. These have been taken up especially by young women, who are otherwise expected to work as unpaid labour on their family's farm, which they would not expect to inherit; but young men are also moving out of farming, as petty trade replaces agriculture as their main activity. Their reasons for doing so are not only the decline in farming incomes, but also frustration at the almost absolute control still held by the older men over land and farming decisions (see Box 6).

Box 6: Age, Gender and Occupation in Northern Tanzania

In northern Tanzania, levels of multiactivity amongst younger generations are as high as 80 percent, against 50 percent for older respondents. Older women still shoulder much of the agricultural work as well as the domestic chores, but farming no longer provides employment opportunities or incentives to young people, who, in addition, no longer accept to provide unpaid family labour. As a result, almost 30 percent of households rely on waged labour for family farming and other household chores. This proportion reaches 46 percent in the plains settlement, Lotima, where houseworkers' main task is taking the cattle out to pasture, traditionally the sons' responsibility.

Young women are more likely than young men to engage in petty trading, either as a primary or as a secondary occupation. The main reason for this is that farming is usually in the form of unpaid family labour with little prospects, since daughters rarely inherit land from their parents who also control farming income and decision-making. By contrast, young women keep control of their earnings from trading, on which they also make independent decisions[26].

At the same time, widespread access to information, changing financial expectations and a view of farming as 'un-modern' also have a profound impact on employment patterns in many 'rural' areas. Hence, in densely populated southeastern Nigeria, which also has a comprehensive network of small and intermediate urban centres, young men in rural settlements are expected to find work, at least for a period of time, in nearby urban centres – should they decide not to do so, they risk being derided for being lazy[27].

Mobility and Migration

Mobility and migration are closely interrelated with livelihood diversification. Access to affordable transport expands the opportunities to find employment or to engage in income-generating activities through commuting. When mobility is constrained, as in the case of isolated settlements poorly served by road networks and transport facilities, migration is more likely to occur, although this may also be the case for well-served settlements in economically stagnating areas offering limited income opportunities.

Internal migration is often seen as essentially rural-to-urban and contributing to uncontrolled growth and related urban management problems in many large cities in the South. This has resulted in many policies to control or discourage migration. While migration restriction is infrequent, many countries have sought to make cities relatively inhospitable, for example bulldozing informal low-income settlements, or making it difficult for new migrants to secure property rights to land or access to public services. These measures generally have little impact aside from lowering welfare, especially for the poor. In fact, most of the growth in urban population is due to natural population increase. Since rural to urban migration is fastest where economic growth is highest – as migrants tend to move to places where they are likely to find employment opportunities – it is not in reality as problematic as it is made out to be. For example, secondary urban centres, especially in Latin America, have recently attracted new investment and industries which would have previously been directed to large cities. As a consequence, they have also increased their role as migration destinations.

Despite widely held beliefs that flows are always rural-to-urban, migration from the urban to the rural areas is increasing. This type of movement is often associated with economic decline and increasing poverty. In sub-Saharan Africa, significant numbers of retrenched urban workers are thought to return to rural 'home' areas, where the cost of living is lower.[28] Seasonal waged agricultural work in rural areas can also provide temporary employment for low-income urban groups.[29] Temporary and seasonal movement such as this is not reflected in census figures, and can make 'static' enumerations of rural and urban populations unreliable.

Complexity in migration direction and duration is matched by that in the composition of the flows, which reflect wider socio-economic dynamics. Although regional variations can be important, the number of migrant women has increased in many countries in the South. The age and gender of who moves and who stays can have a significant impact on source areas in terms of labour availability, remittances, household organisation and agricultural production systems. In some cases, decision-making power over the management of natural resources is invested with the actual migrants and not with those who 'stay behind'. This can limit the impact of policy and project interventions.

Multi-Spatial Households

Household membership is usually defined as 'sharing the same pot', under the same roof. However, the strong commitments and obligations between rural-based and urban-based individuals and units show that in many instances these are 'multi-spatial households', in which reciprocal support is given across space. For example, remittances from urban-based members can be an important income source for the rural-based members, who in turn may look after their migrant relatives' children and property. These linkages can be crucial in the livelihood strategies of the poor, but are not usually taken into consideration in policy-making (see Box 7).

Box 7: Multi-Spatial Households

In Old Naledi, a low-income settlement of Gaborone (Botswana), a third of all households own cattle and half retain land in their home village. This proportion does not decline with people's length of stay in the city. Rural assets have both monetary and social value, and serve as a safety net for low-income households with uncertain livelihood prospects in the city. However, although most of these households have no other assets, they are not eligible to relief or aid measures in case of loss as these are designed exclusively for rural dwellers.[30]

In Durban (South Africa), maintaining both an urban and a rural base also provides a safety net for low-income city dwellers in times of economic hardship or political violence. However, housing and rural development programmes do not acknowledge such multi-spatial, extended households: eligibility to subsidies and grants is based on the size of the co-resident household (either in town or in the countryside), and the funds can only be used in one of the two locations. Since urban housing subsidies are more widely available, this may encourage urban-based members of multi-spatial households to cut their rural links.[31]

Urban Centres and Rural Development

This is discussed in more detail in the other paper produced for this workshop, *'The Role of Small and Intermediate Urban Centres and Market Towns and the Value of Regional Approaches to Rural Poverty Reduction Policy'.* However, since it is a central issue in rural-urban linkages, this section provides some basic information and examples.

Since the 1970s, comprehensive rural-urban development frameworks have been formulated as an explicit attempt to promote rural development, and with the implicit aim of curbing migration to large cities. Integrated Rural

Development has contributed the view of rural development as holistic and multifaceted, and including non-agricultural as well as agricultural activities. However, it has rarely included explicit urban components, and whenever a spatial dimension is included it is usually limited to marketing functions.

Other attempts take urban centres as their starting point. In the 'urban functions in rural development' (UFRD) approach, the strategy for promoting rural development is to develop a network of small, medium-sized and larger centres each providing centrally located functions (such as services, facilities and infrastructure) hierarchically organised.[32] Rural development is expected to be stimulated by filling in the supposedly missing functions (for example banking services) through selective investment in rural towns (see Box 8). Translating this model into practice has been problematic for three main reasons:

- 'Urban functions' are assumed to benefit the entire surrounding region and all rural households irrespective of social and economic status: issues of access and control are not considered.
- The methods for selecting key towns for investment were not clear, and tended to focus only on the attributes of the towns themselves with no consideration of the rural potential.
- The model is based on generalisations which do not account for the rich variety in the roles of urban centres, which are determined by both the rural and regional context.

The underlying conceptual problem is the assumption that it is an absence of 'central places' that constrain development, rather than factors such as ecological capacity, land-owning structures, crop types and control on crop prices or access to markets, all of which in turn are shaped by rural-urban interactions within the specific regional context.

An alternative position on the role of small towns in rural development draws on empirical case studies from Africa, Asia and Latin America, it shows that universal generalisations and prescriptions, which form the basis of most spatial planning models, are not valid. Centralised policies, which do not take into account the peculiarities and specifics of small towns and their regions, may not be efficient.

Box 8: Application of the UFRD Approach in the Philippines

This USAID-funded programme was carried out in the Bicol Region in the late 1970s. A study conducted ten years later found that the selected towns were not performing the 'missing' functions and were themselves stagnating. Among the main reasons were that:

- The identified functions did not support rural development but rather the urban-based military and civil service personnel.
- Transport linkages to larger towns did not encourage the marketing and commercial functions of local towns, which were by-passed.
- Since agricultural productivity did not increase, rural household expenditures for non-agricultural goods and services did not rise and did not start the 'virtuous circle' of urban and rural expansion[33].

Real decentralisation of decision-making with investment and resource-raising at the local level may allow the articulation of local needs and priorities and stimulate both rural and urban development (Box 9). However, wider socio-economic issues such as inequitable land-owning structures and government crop purchasing policies and taxation are also likely to affect small towns and, by extension, migration to larger cities.

Box 9: Positive Links Between Rural and Urban Development

The Upper Valley of the Rio Negro and Nequen in Argentina shows how rapid growth in agricultural production can be accompanied by rapid growth in employment linked to agriculture and urban growth. The Upper Valley is linked by railway to Buenos Aires, giving local farmers access to both national and international markets. In the 1950s, the area acquired provincial status, which increased the power and resources available to the local government. The land-owning structure is relatively equitable, and most of the land is farmed by farmer-owners with sufficient capital to invest in intensive production, mainly fruit trees. The growing number of prosperous farmers has provided a considerable stimulus to local urban growth, with a chain of small centres developing along the railway. Urban based enterprises were stimulated by demand from agricultural producers both as forward linkages (cold storage plants, industries producing packaging material, plants for the processing into juices, jams, dried or tinned fruit) and as backward linkages (production of inputs such as fertilisers and pesticides, or tools and machinery).[34]

Conclusions: How Rural-Urban Interactions are Interlinked with Economic, Social and Cultural Transformations

Whilst, to some extent, flows and linkages exist between all rural and urban areas, their scale and strength are determined by the nature of economic, social and cultural transformations. These can be divided further into three broad categories: the global, the national and the local levels.

At the global level, the liberalization of trade and production has changed or reshaped rural–urban linkages in most regions. The increased availability of imported manufactured and processed goods affects consumption patterns in both rural and urban settlements; but since these are often cheaper than locally produced goods, local manufacturers and processors can be negatively affected. This is especially the case for small-scale enterprises using traditional or limited technology and often employing women, for example in traditional cloth weaving in southeast Nigeria and vegetable oil production in Tanzania[35].

In the agricultural sector, trade in export crops is largely controlled by international traders, who tend to by-pass local urban centres for processing and marketing, and who also retain much of the added value and do not necessarily invest it in the producing region or even nation. Moreover, stringent quality controls and quantity requirements, linked to demand in high-income nations and the preference of larger retailers there, often exclude small-scale farmers who do not have the financial capital to purchase the necessary inputs[36]. At the same time, the increase in the number of international tourist resorts and the establishment of export processing zones have created new, albeit limited, areas of employment that, in many cases, rely on migrant workers, especially women.

An often overlooked aspect of globalization is its impact on social and cultural values. Increased access to information on different and often distant places has an important role in younger generations' desire to migrate to experience the wider world, and to move out of farming in favour of more "modern" types of employment in services and – albeit less so – manufacturing. Changing employment opportunities can have a profound impact on traditional social structure. In South India, young men from landless low castes who find employment in urban centres openly defy the caste system as they are no longer dependent on their upper caste, land-owning employers for a living[37]. Whilst these transformations clearly encourage individual independence, and should be welcomed for breaking up social relations based on power imbalances, their economic and social consequences are far reaching and still not sufficiently understood.

What is clear is that the assumptions of rural households and communities as relatively stable units of production and consumption are no longer valid in many locations, and that this needs to be taken into account in the formulation and implementation of rural development initiatives.

At the national level, macroeconomic policies linked to reform and adjustment have an impact on rural–urban linkages. The sharp reduction in subsidies to agricultural inputs has affected the incomes of small-scale, under-capitalized farmers in most nations, whilst the retrenchment of workers in the formal sector has deepened financial insecurity in the urban centres. At the same time, the increase in the cost of food and the introduction of user fees for education and health services has forced many households to seek cash incomes through employment diversification – including non-farm occupations for rural residents, often located in urban centres – migration and urban agriculture.

The increased emphasis on producers' direct access to markets, following the dismantling of marketing boards which used to be the main outlet for small agricultural producers, has strengthened the links with urban centres, where local markets and links to wider regional and national marketing systems are located. This is not without problems, however, as limited information, inadequate infrastructure and storage and processing facilities can hamper increased returns for producers.

Whilst adjustment policies and economic reform have had a generally negative impact on low-income groups in both rural and urban areas, there are sometimes significant differences in the transformations that have taken place in the past 10–15 years, depending on each nation's position in the global economy, its resource base and technological know-how. Hence, some nations with higher levels of educational and technical skills and with national governments able and willing to invest in infrastructure facilities have been able to attract foreign direct investment – albeit usually in circumscribed areas.

At the local level, the nature and scope of rural–urban interactions is influenced by several factors, ranging from geographical and demographic characteristics (including the nature of agricultural land, population density and distribution patterns) to farming systems (based on land tenure and access to natural resources) to the availability of roads and transport networks linking local settlements to a number of urban centres where markets and services are located. Local governments, whose role in many nations has dramatically increased, at least in theory, with decentralization, can play an important role in supporting positive rural–urban linkages.

Local government and other local actors are best placed to identify local needs and priorities and provide an adequate response to them. Local decision-making can help avoid the neglect of forward and backward linkages between agriculture and services and manufacturing. It can also negotiate and regulate the use of natural resources by rural and urban residents and enterprises, which can otherwise become a major cause for conflict. However, although decentralization has great potential with regards to efficiency and democratic accountability, it is often accompanied by costs and constraints. Local government may be unable to provide the services needed, either because of the reduction in central government public investment or because it fails to generate sufficient revenue at the local level. And whilst local decision-making, supported by adequate resources, can support positive rural–urban linkages, wider issues such as land tenure systems, institutional structures of markets and broader national development strategies are likely to affect local initiative. Better integration of local development strategies in national planning is therefore crucial. Finally, especially in nations where decentralization is relatively recent, substantial efforts are necessary to ensure the legitimacy and the capacity of local institutions to carry out their new functions.

Figures 1 and 2 below describe the interrelations between regional rural areas, local urban centers and national and international urban centers, highlighting respectively positive and negative interactions with respect to regional development.

(Dr. Cecilia Tacoli is a senior researcher at the International Institute for Environment and Development. She is a specialist in rural and urban linkages, and migration and urbanisation patterns in the context of globalization.)

Figure 1: Positive Rural-Urban Interactions and Regional Development

International Context: Access to international markets for small and medium-sized producers, with stable commodities prices. Foreign investment supports local production, imports do not compete with locally produced goods.

National Context: Equitable distribution of and access to land; regionally balanced growth strategies including satisfactory provision of infrastructure, credit facilities for small and medium-sized producers, and basic services (education, health, water and sanitation); revenue support to local government; regulated institutional structure of markets.

Local Governance: Accountable, with adequate resources and capacity; identifies local needs and priorities and responds to them; supports forward and backward linkages between agriculture and services and industry located in local urban centres; regulates local natural resource management; integrated with national planning.

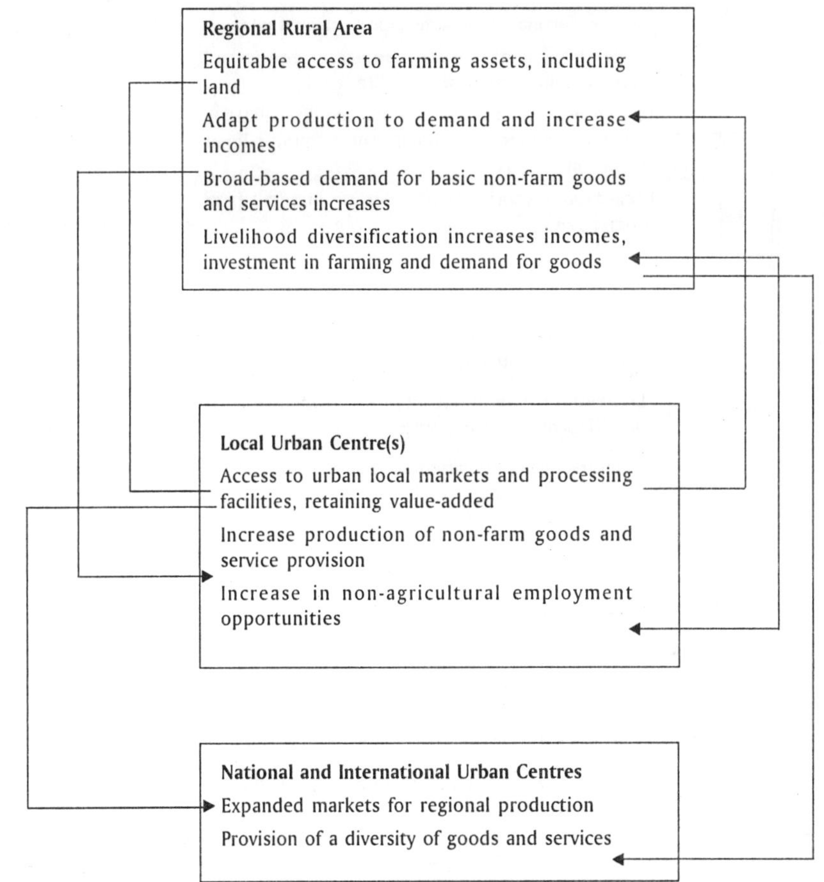

Figure 2: Negative Rural-Urban Interactions and Regional Development

International Context: Limited access to international markets for small and medium-sized producers, unstable commodities prices; foreign investment concentrates in large-scale export production, imports compete with locally produced goods.

National Context: Inequitable distribution of and access to land; regionally imbalanced growth strategies including limited provision of infrastructure, credit facilities for small and medium-sized producers, and basic services (education, health, water and sanitation); lack of support to local government; unregulated institutional structure of markets.

Local Governance: Unaccountable, with inadequate resources and capacity; not integrated with national planning.

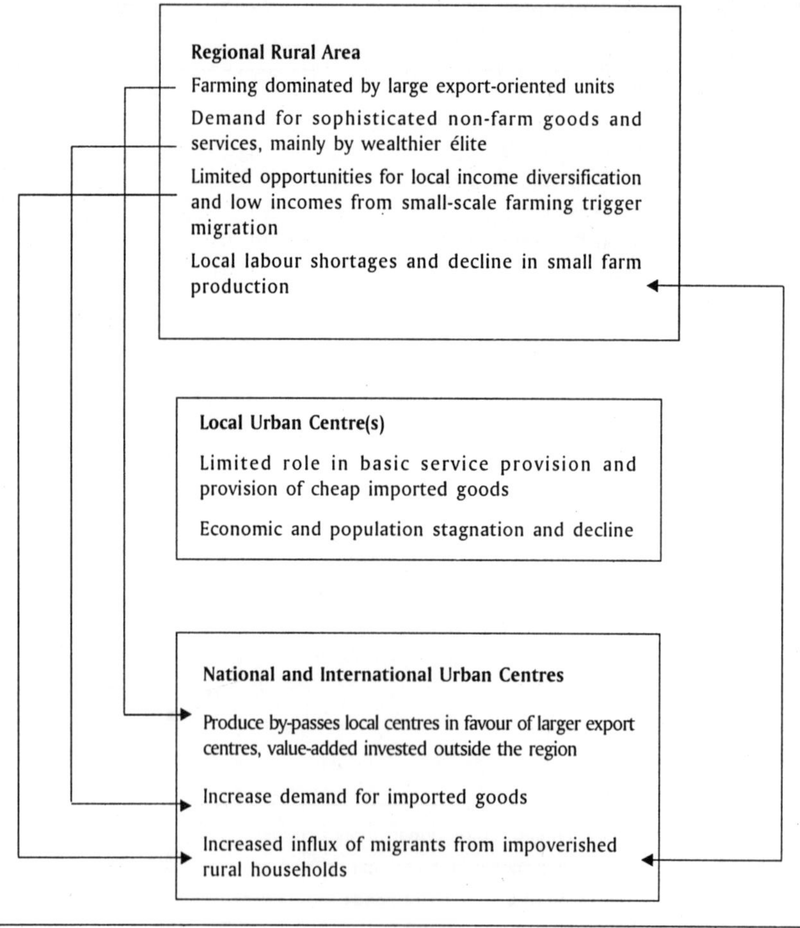

References

1. For a detailed discussion, see Tacoli, C and D Satterthwaite (2003) *The urban part of rural development* Rural-Urban Working Paper 9, IIED, London; also available at *http://www.iied.org/urban/pubs/rururb_wp.html*
2. United Nations Centre for Human Settlements (UNCHS) (1996) *An Urbanizing World: Global Report on Human Settlements 1996*, Oxford: Oxford University Press.
3. Firman, T (1996) Urban development in Bandung Metropolitan Region: a transformation to a Desa-Kota region, in *Third World Planning Review* 18:1, 1-22.
4. Kelly, P (1998) The politics of urban-rural relationships: land conversion in the Philippines, *Environment and Urbanization* 10:1, 35-54.
5. McGranahan, G, J Singsore and M Kjellén (1996) Sustainability, poverty and urban environmental transitions, in C Pugh (ed) *Sustainability, the Environment and Urbanization*, London: Earthscan,103-133.
6. Rees, W (1992) Ecological footprints and appropriate carrying capacity: what urban economics leaves out, in *Environment and Urbanization* 4:2, 121-130.
7. Evans, H E (1990) Rural-urban linkages and structural transformation, Report INU 71, Infrastructure and Urban Development Department, The World Bank, Washington DC; UNDP/UNCHS (Habitat) (1995) Rural-Urban Linkages: Policy Guidelines for Rural Development, Paper prepared for the Twenty-Third Meeting of the ACC Sub-Committee on Rural Development, UNESCO Headquarters, Paris, 31 May – 2 June 1995.
8. Zoomers, A E B and J Kleinpenning (1996) Livelihood and urban-rural relations in Central Paraguay, *Tijdschrift voor Economische en Sociale Geografie* 87:2, 161-74.
9. Morris, A (1997) Market behaviour and market systems in State of Mexico, in P van Lindert and O Verkoren (eds) *Small Towns and Beyond: Rural Transformation and Small Urban Centres in Latin America* Amsterdam: Thela Publishers, 123-132.
10. Tacoli, C (2002) *Changing rural-urban interactions in sub-Saharan Africa and their impact on livelihoods: a summary* Rural-urban working paper 7, IIED, London, also available at *http://www.iied.org/urban/pubs/rururb_wp.html*
11. Harriss-White, B (1995) Maps and landscapes of grain markets in South Asia, in J Harriss, J Hunter and C M Lewis (eds) *The New Institutional Economics and Third World Development* London: Routledge, 87-108.
12. Ribot, J C (1998) Theorizing access: forest profits along Senegal's charcoal commodity chains, in *Development and Change* Vol 29, 307-341.

13. Rengasamy, S *et al* (2002) *Farmers' Markets in Tamil Nadu: increasing options for rural producers, improving access for urban consumers* Rural-Urban Working Paper 8, IIED, London, also available at *http://www.iied.org/urban/pubs/rururb_wp.html*
14. Baker, J (1995) Survival and accumulation strategies at the rural-urban interface in northwest Tanzania, in *Environment and Urbanization* 7:1; Kamete, A (1998) Interlocking livelihoods: farm and small town in Zimbabwe, in *Environment and Urbanization* 10:1.
15. Lerise F, A Kibadu, E Mbutolwe and N Mushi (2001) *The case of Lindi and its region, southern Tanzania* Rural-Urban Working Paper 2, IIED, London.
16. Ellis, F (1998), op.cit
17. Reardon, T, J Berdegué and G Escobar (2001) Rural non farm employment and incomes in Latin America: overview and policy implications, in *World Development* 29:3.
18. Dang Nguyen Anh, Hoang Xuan Thanh and Cecilia Tacoli (2004) 'Stay on the farm, weave in the village, leave the home': livelihood diversification and rural-urban linkages in Vietnam's Red River Delta, and their policy implications, unpublished summary report, IIED, London.
19. Kirkby, R, I Bradbury and Gguangbao Shen (2000) *Small Town China – Governance, Economy, Environment and Lifestyle in Three Zhen*, Ashgate, Aldershot; Douglass, M *et al* (2002) *The Urban Transition in Vietnam*, UNCHS and University of Hawaii.
20. Chase, J (1997) Managing urban settlements in Brazil's agro-industrial frontier, in *TWPR* 19(2).
21. Bah M, S Cissé, B Diyamett, G Diallo, F Lerise, D Okali, E Okpara, J Olawoye and C Tacoli (2003) Changing rural-urban linkages in Mali, Nigeria and Tanzania, in *Environment and Urbanization* 15:1.
22. Beneker, T and O Verkoren (1998) Reception centre and point of departure: migration to and from Nuevo Casas Grandes, Chihahua, Mexico, in Titus, M and J Hinderink (eds) *Town and Hinterland in Developing Countries,* Thela Thesis, Amsterdam.
23. Baker (1995), op cit.
24. GRAD (2001) *Potentialités et conflits dans les zones péri urbaines: le cas de Bamako au Mali,* Rural-Urban Working Paper 5, IIED, London; and (2001) *Le cas de Mopti*, Rural-Urban Working Paper 6, IIED, London.
25. Baker (1995) op cit.
26. Lerise *et al,* (2001) op cit; Diyamett, B, M Diyamett, J James, R Mabala (2001) *The case of Himo and its region, northern Tanzania,* Rural-Urban working paper 1, IIED, London.
27. Okali, D, E Okpara and J Olawoye (2001) *The case of Aba and its region, southeastern Nigeria,* Rural-Urban Working Paper 4, IIED, London.

28. Potts, D (1995) Shall we go home? Increasing urban poverty in African cities and migration processes, in *The Geographic Journal* 161:3, 245-264.

29. Kamete, A Y (1998) Interlocking livelihoods: farm and small town in Zimbabwe, in *Environment and Urbanization* 10:1, 23-34.

30. Krüger, F (1998) Taking advantage of rural assets as a coping strategy for the urban poor, in *Environment and Urbanization* 10:1, 119-134.

31. Smit, W (1998) The rural linkages of urban households in Durban, in *Environment and Urbanization* 10:1, 77-88.

32. Rondinelli, D and K Ruddle (1978) *Urbanization and Rural Development: A Spatial Policy for Equitable Growth* New York: Praeger.

33. Koppel, B (1987) Does integrated rural development really work? Lessons from the Bicol river basin, in *World Development* 15, 205-220.

34. Manzanal, M and CVapnarsky (1986) The development of the Upper Valley of Rio Negro and its periphery within the Comahue Region, Argentina, in J E Hardoy and D Satterthwaite (eds) (op.cit).

35. Bah, M *et al* (2003), op cit.

36. See Pimbert, M at al (2001) Global Restructuring, Agri-Food Systems and Livelihoods, Gatekeeper Series No 100, IIED, London.

37. Anandhi, S, J Jeyaranjan and Rajan Krishnan (2002), "Work, caste and competing masculinities", *EPW Review of Women Studies*, 26 October. Available on *http://www.epw.org.in*

6

Rural-Urban Links in India: New Policy Challenges for Increasingly Mobile Populations

Priya Deshingkar

Migration is perhaps the most dynamic form of rural-urban linkages. This article emphasizes the need to recognize the importance of migration and commuting to the livelihoods of the poor, and to the economy, and examines the policy challenges that are arising in India due to increasing migration.

Introduction

Rural-Urban (RU) links in India take a variety of forms encompassing social, economic and political interdependencies. One manifestation of this is the migration of labourers from villages to small and medium towns and cities. Although migration has been an integral part of the development process for several decades there is still no consensus on its determinants, magnitude or impacts. Neoliberals perceive RU migration as an inevitable part of occupational diversification, urbanisation and accumulation by migrants, but structuralists tend to see it as exploitative and impoverishing. Policymakers worried about its effects on already overburdened urban areas generally seek to stem migration.

What is clear is that the influx of people into urbanising areas[1] is increasing with absolute numbers running into millions[2]. While macro-level data suggest a slowing of RU migration rates, the village studies cited in this paper show increasing temporary migration and commuting to urban centres. Livelihood strategies are becoming more multi-locational with improvements in roads and information technology. This has important implications for poverty reduction as work availability in remote rural areas is not keeping pace with population growth. Further, sluggish public investment in urban areas means rising pressure on urban infrastructure, which urgently requires policy responses. The evidence from village studies suggests that policy needs to become more flexible to provide services to people who are on the move. The current setup leaves poor migrants with little access to basic entitlements. New arrangements that can provide migrant workers with access to critical information on labour markets and rights as well as basic services in health education, shelter and food are needed.

1. Urbanisation and RU Migration Trends

Urban populations in India are concentrated in the six most developed states Maharashtra, Gujarat, Tamil Nadu, Karnataka, West Bengal and Punjab where rates of urbanisation remained the same or increased during the 1990s. On the other hand urbanisation rates slowed in the backward states of Bihar, Madhya Pradesh, Rajasthan and Uttar Pradesh (the "BIMARU" states). Overall, there has been a slowing in the growth rate of urban populations from the record level of 3.8% per annum in the 1970s, to 3.1% in the 1980s and further to 2.7% in the 1990s, and the slowing has been greater in the smaller towns[3].

Analyses of the 2001 National census and 1999-2000 NSS data show a slow down in permanent or long-term RU migration rates despite increasing inter-regional inequalities [Kundu 2003]. Kundu [pers comm] calculates that RU migration has declined by 1.5 percentage points, even allowing for a decline in the fertility rate, increases in urban boundaries and the emergence of new towns. This appears to be due to a combination of the low rate of sectoral diversification in rural areas, slow creation of job opportunities in urban locations [NSSO 2001] and policy measures that have discouraged migration into metropolises.

However, a number of recent village studies from all over the country show that there has been a sharp increase in population mobility including long term and temporary migration as well as commuting, particularly from drought-prone semi arid locations. While some of these studies are based on resurveys of villages [see for instance the work by Singh and Karan 2001, Karan 2003 in Bihar and Dayal and Karan 2003 in Jharkhand] others have used recall to arrive at this conclusion [Rao 2001 in Ananthapur, APRLP 2003 in Mahbubnagar, Khandelwal and Katiyar 2003 in South Rajasthan, and GVT (pers. comm. Meera Shahi) in Madhya Pradesh, Rogaly et al 2001 and Rafique and Rogaly 2003 in West Bengal]. The reasons for this are a combination of deteriorating employment opportunities at home, better prospects in urban areas and vastly improved communication and road networks.

A majority of immigrants and commuters are absorbed into the unorganised[4] sector. This is what 'over-urbanisation' theory [Hoselitz 1957] predicts: migrants supply far more labour than the organised sector can absorb. Labour absorption by the unorganised sector then leads to low productivity and limited prospects for exiting poverty. The experience of several decades in India has shown that most migrants never "graduate" to the formal sector[5], by contrast with the oft-cited conceptualisation of Harris and Todaro [1970].

Structuralists attribute this hiatus to the exploitative activities of middlemen and contractors[6]. For example, Breman [1974] argued from his study of migrant labourers in Gujarat that migration could never lead to accumulation and only ensured survival. Olsen and Ramanamurthy [2000] reached similar conclusions in their study of renowned *palamur* labourers who migrate out of Andhra Pradesh to work in urban construction. Likewise Singh [2002], based on a study of labourers working in the unorganised sector in Delhi, argues that hardly any had graduated to the formal sector and continued to work as underpaid, ill informed and exploited workers.

Nevertheless several observers suggest that migrants have been able to escape poverty even when they have remained in the unorganised sector. For instance, Gupta and Mitra [2002] also in a study of migrant labour in Delhi slums found that, with experience, migrants are likely to move from low income casual jobs to higher income, regular jobs. Rogaly and Coppard [2003] observe that wage workers in West Bengal now view migration as a way of accumulating a useful lump sum, rather than, as in the past, simply surviving. Deshingkar and Start [2003] document accumulative migration streams in both farm and non-farm work which have allowed several lower caste people in MP and AP to escape poverty.

The findings from the Livelihood Options project, a three year DFID-funded policy study[7] summarised next, show that migration and commuting are important livelihood strategies. The results are based on a synthesis of 12 months of primary data collected across 6 villages each in AP and MP. Based on participatory assessments and recall they show increased levels of mobility in all the locations studied. For a brief description of the villages see Annexure 1.

2. Findings from the Livelihood Options Project – Patterns of Population Mobility

People were more mobile for economic reasons in the more remote survey villages having low agricultural potential and a large proportion of very small holdings. Thus the MP villages, characterised by poor roads and communications, showed temporary migration rates that were several times higher than the AP villages (Table 1). On average nearly 47% of the households have at least one member migrating, with extremes in PT, the remote tribal village (75%) and MB the remote village in the moderately developed district with a feudal history (64%) of MP. The only comparable situation in AP was MD, the most remote and drought-prone village also with a feudal history, where 78% of the households had temporary migrants. Other AP villages were large and diversified, and had migration rates below a third of the population. MP villages on the other hand were much smaller, more agricultural and closer to the "classical" village. Non-farm options within villages were limited, and even in high productivity villages the opportunities for the lower caste poor were limited because operations were either mechanised or taken up by immigrants as in the case of PR village in the prosperous part of Ujjain district. There was therefore no other option but to move away for work, and temporary migration became the norm, partly to allow return for the agriculture season, and partly because small and medium towns lacked the infrastructure to provide a more permanent base.

Seasonal migration contributes significantly to household incomes. Earnings from migration were more important in MP locations with more than half of the total labouring income being derived from outside sources. In the AP villages income from wage work outside the village accounted for nearly a sixth of the annual household returns. Overall returns from in-village work are lower in all agriculturally backward and remote villages with more fragmented land holdings.

Table 1: Commuting, Temporary Migration and Long-Term Migration in the MP and AP Villages*

State	District	Village	Temporary Migration**		Commuting***		Long-Term Migration***	
			No. of HH	%	No. of HH	%	No. of HH	%
AP	Chittoor	OP	19	8.9	10	25.0	3	7.5
		VP	182	32.9	4	6.7	7	11.7
	Krishna	KO	139	9.7	13	16.3	13	16.3
		KA	71	15.3	3	5.0	9	15.0
	Medak	GU	64	4.1	10	12.5	3	3.8
		MD	331	77.5	2	5.0	9	22.5
		Total	**806**	**17.3**	**42**	**11.7**	**44**	**12.2**
MP	Ujjain	PR	82	58.6	6	15.8	2	5.3
		LJ	148	50	4	6.3	2	3.1
	Mandla	GG	81	43.3	4	10.0	4	10.0
		PT	132	75	5	12.5	2	5.0
	Tikamgarh	SM	78	21.1	6	7.7	9	11.5
		MB	82	63.6	4	9.5	2	4.8
		Total	**603**	**46.5**	**30**	**9.9**	**21**	**7.0**

* Includes both farm and non-farm work in rural and urban locations.

** Based on Census data covering 5944 households.

*** Seasonal Survey data covering 720 households.

Daily commuting, observed in 12% of households, was more widespread in AP than MP. Commuting offers the dual advantage of higher earning in non-farm work while keeping one foot in the farm economy and cutting some of the risks associated with longer term migration, and outgoings on food, shelter, healthcare and schooling. Commuting was predictably more important in the better connected villages: from OP, a semi-arid and largely rainfed village near the district headquarters, 25% of households had at least one member commuting. Next was KO, a rich coastal village with a highly diversified economy located in a prosperous belt of similarly diversified villages. Here commuting was to the numerous rice mills, shops, service industries and government establishments both around the village. Third in rank was GU, a prosperous village only 40 km from the capital city of Hyderabad.

In MP, 10% of the households on average had a commuting member. The proportion of households commuting from the better connected villages was slightly higher than the more remote villages. Commuting was to destinations as far away as 35 km which is a considerable distance on bad roads. Small urbanised conglomerates around highway junctions, known locally as "Kasbahs", were also important destinations to work in telephone booths, kiosks and open markets.

Long-term migration (more than one year) was more common in AP with 12% of the households on average reporting at least one member who was away more or less permanently. In the AP villages long-term migration was highest in the poorest and most remote village and also the two relatively wealthy coastal villages but the reasons were altogether different. In the case of the poorest village this was because livelihood options had become severely limited locally due to persistent drought and near total absence of non-farm activities close by, but also because of its relative proximity to Hyderabad which is just half a day's journey away. On the other hand in the coastal villages there had been significant outmigration of richer persons belong to the dominant castes to high income non-farm occupations in the capital city of Hyderabad and outside India. In MP only 7% of the households reported long-term migration, with the highest incidence in well-connected villages from where people settled in district headquarters and the medium and large towns of Jabalpur, Nagpur and Bhopal. Some had gone to Gujarat to work in cotton mills. While the importance of remittances[8] from long-term migration was undisputed as an important source of money for productive investment, in focus group discussions, it was difficult to quantify.

3. The Difficulties Faced by Migrants

Living conditions for migrants are tough and can remain that way for decades. Poor immigrants usually stay in slums or even less secure accommodation. The report of the Working Group on Watershed Development for the Tenth Plan preparation states that 50% of the population in Mumbai and 40% in Delhi lives in slums. Roughly 500,000 people migrate into Delhi every year mainly to work in the 95000 factories, or as workers in tea shops, vendors and drivers. Of these 400,000 go into the 1500 illegal colonies and 1000 slums in the city [Simha 2003], with very poor access to clean water, sanitation or electricity. Even those who earn reasonable amounts face constant threats of eviction, disease, sexual abuse, underpayment and police harassment.

Migrant workers have no access to subsidised grain at their destinations and spend a sizeable proportion of their wages on basic food supplies. Spending on rents is also substantial. Probably the most serious cost of migration is children's schooling. When entire families migrate, children stay behind to do household chores while the parents work. Data from the AP villages show that while 15% of migrating households had children out of school, against 10% for non-migrating households.

However migration brings significant benefits which are not immediately financial. Bhalla (pers comm.) observed that migrants in Nalgonda district, AP bring back an understanding of improved agricultural practices from coastal areas where they migrate. The evidence from Medak district, AP also suggests that migrants have brought back a range of small enterprise related skills that have enabled them to open tea shops, mechanics' shops and tailoring shops. In Chittoor district in AP, commuting workmen were able to learn sericulture skills and set up highly productive units of their own. In almost all the locations studied, migrants said that moving out of the village had allowed them to escape caste-based oppression.

Aside from travelling to find work, rural people are now increasingly mobile for a variety of other reasons (Box 1).

To sum up, the lives of Indians are no longer confined to either rural or urban spheres be it for economic or other reasons. People are increasingly mobile and there is a need for a more nuanced understanding of the complex dynamics of

Box 1: Other Rural-Urban Links
Health and Education: It is now commonplace for rural residents to travel to the nearest town to access specialised healthcare and higher education. As government continues to be fraught with bureaucratic procedures and inefficient services, more and more people are choosing private sector alternatives that are located in small and medium towns.
Contd...

Contd...
Political: In a situation where the legal and administrative system is prone to delays and irregularities, the fastest way of getting results is to approach a politically influential person for a reference. Trips to the block or *Mandal* headquarters to meet revenue officials or even the district headquarters to meet MLAs or MPs are undertaken routinely by those wishing to resolve disputes over loans, propoor schemes or land matters. *Social:* A sign of rising affluence is for families to cast the net wider when they are searching for a groom. Recent trends from Krishna district with the highest farm incomes show that a town or city based groom fetches a higher dowry in the marriage market than the son of a large farmer of similar income. This is a clear indicator of how villagers perceive future prospects in rural and urban livelihoods.

urban and rural change. Small and medium towns and even smaller urbanised conglomerations are important centres offering a range of services and economic opportunities and need to be strengthened.

4. Resource Allocation Patterns for Urban and Rural Development

Policies in India are currently geared to traditional perceptions of urban and rural and of rather static populations who live and work in the same area. Although not stated explicitly, many rural development programmes aim to control migration. The underlying rationale can be found in the literature on common property resource management, watershed management and agricultural development that is replete with statements of expected declines in migration flows due to successful employment creation and resource regeneration [see for instance IFPRI evaluation of NWDPRA by Kerr et al, and, studies of CPR rejuvenation in Rajasthan cited in Chopra 2000 and more recent evaluations of watershed programmes under the DRD pers comm. N K Singh].

The development of rainfed[9] and semi-arid locations has, rightly, been given high priority in planning, as witnessed in, for instance, the National Watershed Development Project for Rainfed Areas (NWDPRA) under the Department of Agriculture and Cooperation with an outlay of Rs.10.2 billion during the Ninth Five Year Plan. The total outlay of the Department for Rural Development is currently Rs.102.7 billion or 0.46% of the GDP[10] of which employment generation accounts for Rs.49 billion. The outlay of the Department of Land Resources which implements area based programmes such as the Drought Prone Areas Programme, the Desert Development Programme and the Integrated Watershed Development Programme is roughly Rs.10 billion[11].

Although on balance, total investment is greater in urban areas most of this is coming from private sources (pers comm. Shailendra Sharma) and is not focused on creating facilities for the poor. Public investment in urban development has not kept up with the growing need for more urban infrastructure and jobs. According to the National Commission on Urbanisation, the share of municipal expenditure of the overall government expenditure (sum of centre, state, and local) was only 8% in 1960-61 and fell to 4.5% in 1980-81. Over the same period, the urban population rose from 16% to almost 24% [Sharon et al 2002]. New economic reform policies have made it more difficult for municipal corporations to finance infrastructural investment [Kundu 2003]. Current public fund allocations for urban development are small, Rs.15.9 billion, roughly Rs.8.8 billion of which goes to Delhi alone. The only programme set up with a specific focus on the development of smaller towns is the Integrated Development of Small and Medium Towns scheme with an allocation of Rs.1 billion (0.004% of GDP) for 2003-4. It aims to develop infrastructure and create employment in small and medium towns with less than 500,000 people.

5. Rethinking Policies on Rural Development

There have to be questions over whether more could be done to facilitate the mobility of the population given the massive scale of investment needed to install even basic infrastructure in weakly-integrated rural areas and the growing search for jobs in urban areas. Experience has shown that the prospects of strong agriculture and NR-based growth in the more drought-prone areas can continue to be poor even with infrastructure in place.

Some lessons could be drawn from the recent experience of China. Stringent residency rules until recently meant that there were 70-120 million "floating" people who had no claims on state resources. A new household registration system is now under consideration to allow long-term city residents and business or property owners in cities to become legal residents. There are also proposals to facilitate migration. For example, experts at the Chinese Academy of Social Sciences recommended massive migration projects to move people out of the deforested upper Yangtze River[12]. Similarly the county government in Yongjing has decided that it will be more cost effective to move populations from inaccessible locations rather than struggle to provide them with the services that they lack [IDS 2003].

There are powerful arguments against enforced relocation and resettlement but serious consideration should be given to facilitating the existing movements of people into urban locations and occupations especially in small and medium towns. In any case governments and donors should query whether greater investments in low-potential areas are appropriate, given the growing mobility of people.

6. Migrant Support Programmes

Given the difficulties encountered by illiterate and under-informed migrants in accessing provisions that have been made for them by the State[13], there appears to be a need for support from elsewhere. A number of civil society organisations have taken up the cause of building the capacity of migrants to demand their rights from contractors and government officials.

A particularly striking example of a successful migrant support programme is the one initiated by the Grameen Vikas Trust in Madhya Pradesh under the DFID funded Western India Rainfed Farming Project. GVT has worked closely with the *panchayats* (local government) of source villages and has developed an informal system of identity cards for migrants. With these cards, migrants have something to show the authorities at railway stations and bus stands, common points in their journey when they are open to harassment. GVT has liaised with NGOs in the neighbouring state of Rajasthan to set up migrant resource centres that provide them with information on job availability, wage rates and rights. Other NGOs such as Sudrak in South Rajasthan are now thinking along similar lines and have formulated a proposal with the involvement of the UNDP.

By all accounts such migrant support programmes have achieved more success than official programmes in ensuring fair pay and better working conditions. The widespread system of subcontracting that operates in non-farm sector employment especially in construction projects fudges responsibility and accountability so that it becomes very difficult for government officials to implement protective legislation. Continued support from NGOs and donors is important.

7. New Challenges for Policy

There is currently no special government body or earmarked funding to deal with the issue of migration. Discussions with leading policy analysts in Delhi suggest that switching policy priorities should be the first course of action rather than setting up new bodies with separate funding. Different views emerged (Box 2) and what became apparent was that a key constraint in implementing changes of these kinds is the fiscal crisis being faced by municipal corporations.

Donor support could be an important way of assisting urban development in a way that helps the poor. The DFID-funded Andhra Pradesh Urban Services Project is certainly a step in the right direction but it does not cover small and medium towns. Current trends in population mobility suggest that investing more in smaller towns could have far-reaching impacts on increasing livelihood options and reducing poverty. In parallel, the existing laws that have been designed to protect poor workers need to be better enforced through the involvement of civil society organisations. Children's schooling is a major concern and greater efforts are needed to provide flexible education.

In conclusion there is a need to recognise the importance of migration and commuting to the livelihoods of the poor and the economy. A blanket policy is unlikely to help and more efforts should be made to understand regionally differentiated patterns. More resources are needed for the development of small and medium towns: these seem to be particularly important in providing rural people with remunerative employment and access to services. This would give the process of development and urbanisation a push without overburdening larger cities. But given the current fiscal climate there is a need for investment decisions to be informed by a refreshed understanding of rural-urban links and population mobility.

Box 2: Views from Leading Policy Analysts on Urban Development

Professor Amitabh Kundu, one of India's most prominent scholars on urbanization argues that government is sending out conflicting messages about migration into larger cities. On the one hand it is creating pockets of affluence which are bound to attract people but on the other hand the Master Plans are hostile to poor migrants. The result is that the poor are pushed to the peripheries and these are becoming increasingly violent and polluted. He thinks that lowered RU migration rates are not healthy and policy should support the process.

Dr. N C Saxena, ex Secretary of Rural Development and ex Member-Secretary of the Planning Commission, feels that government should try to create more growth in peri-urban areas and move industries and warehouses out of the heart of cities like Delhi. Current policies are actually providing incentives for people to move to the cities through lower registration fees and sales tax structures. There is a need to plan for 0% growth of the metropolises. He thinks the slums and colonies emerging there should be halted because it is more expensive to create jobs and provide infrastructure in urban areas[14].

Professor Sheila Bhalla of the Institute for Human Development, a leading researcher on the non-farm economy, believes that the government should follow a more proactive approach to migrants and work together with the private sector to ensure that immigrant labourers are provided with access to basic needs such as adequate housing and mobile schools for their children. She feels that leaving this responsibility to NGOs alone is dangerous because many that are not accountable to anybody.

(Priya Deshingkar has a multidisciplinary background, and was first trained as an agricultural scientist at the Indian Agricultural Research Institute in New Delhi, before completing a DPhil at the Institute of Development Studies, University of Sussex. She has over 20 years of research and consultancy experience in agriculture, rural development and poverty.)

Notes

1. This includes larger villages and peripheries of urban areas having high levels of non-farm activity and could be classified as urban on the basis of numbers of people engaged in nonfarm activities [in this connection see work of David Satterthwaite at the International Institute for Environment and Development who regards 60% of India as urban].
2. The Working Group on Watershed Development for the Tenth Five Year Plan estimates the number of rural landless who have migrated to urban areas at 100 million.
3. The growth rate of metros (population > 1 million) decreased from 3.25% to 2.88%, Class I towns (population up to 100,000) went down from 2.96% to 2.76%, Class II (50-90,000) from 2.75% to 2.38% and Class III (20-49999) from 2.59% to 2.27% [Kundu 2003] the rate of growth of smaller towns (Class IV, V and VI) declined sharply from 2.57% to 2.22% between 1981-91 to 1991-01.
4. Unorganised workers have been defined by the First National Commission on Labour (1966-69) as those who have not been able to organise themselves in pursuit of common objectives on account of constraints like casual nature of employment, ignorance and illiteracy.
5. According to the Second National Commission on Labour [2002] 369 m or 90.6% of the workers in India are in the unorganised sector.
6. Social networks are important and migrants will rarely move to locations without some personal contacts which are essential for reducing the many risks that they face. The more fortunate ones may find work under a contractor who, although paying them less than the legal minimum wage, will ensure that they find work and meet some of their expenses, thereby cutting transaction costs.
7. The Livelihood Options project, a three year DFID-funded policy study, that aims to identify how policies can be changed to support positive exits via diversification, and how negative impacts can be reduced. The research was led by the Overseas Development Institute (ODI).
8. Remittances were brought back in person or sent through a very close relative or friend. Losses and cheating were not reported.
9. According to the Ministry of Agriculture rainfed rural areas, cover roughly 63% of the total cultivable area.
10. The GDP was Rs.22494.93 billion in 2002-2003.

11. Apart from this are soil and water conservation programmes with a total outlay of Rs.290 million and the rural housing scheme IAY with an allocation of Rs.19 billion (0.08% of GDP). Another large programme aimed at rural areas is the Swaranjayanti Gram Swarozgar Yojna. (SGSY) which is a self employment programme with an allocation of Rs.8 billion (0.04% of GDP).
12. People's Republic of China – Migration in 1998 *http://www.scalabrini.asn.au/atlas/amatlas.htm*
13. For a list of laws that have been introduced to protect and ensure the rights of unorganised labourers see annex 1.
14. However Lanjouw [1999] maintains that the per capita cost of infrastructure provision is higher in rural than in urban areas.

References

APRLP 2003. Role Of Migration In People's Lives A Qualitative Study Of Four Villages In Mahaboobnagar and Anantapur districts. Andhra Pradesh Rural Livelihoods Project. Government of Andhra Pradesh.

Breman, J 1974. Patronage and exploitation; changing agrarian relations in south Gujarat, India. University of California Press, Berkeley.

Chopra K 2000 Environmental Issues In South Asia: Theory, Policy And Institutions For Governance. IEG Working Paper July 2000. Institute Of Economic Growth Delhi: 110007, India.

Dayal H and A K Karan 2003. Labour Migration From Jharkhand Institute For Human Development, New Delhi.

Deshingkar, P and D Start 2003. Seasonal Migration for Livelihoods in India: Coping, Accumulation and Exclusion Working Paper 220. Overseas Development Institute. London.

Fan S and P Hazell 2000. Returns To Public Investment: Evidence From India And China 2020 Focus 4 (Promoting Sustainable Development in Less-Favored Areas), Brief 5 of 9, November 2000 Washington, DC: International Food Policy Research Institute.

Fan, S, P Hazell and T Haque, 2000. Targeting public investments by agro-ecological zone to achieve growth and poverty alleviation goals in rural India. Food Policy 25: 411-428.

GOI 2001.Working Group on Watershed Development, Rainfed Farming and Natural Resources Management Planning Commission. Government of India.

GOI 2002. India National Commission on Labour II.

Gupta, I and A Mitra 2002. Rural Migrants and Labour Segmentation, Micro level evidence from Delhi Slums. Economic and Political Weekly. January 12 pp.163-168.

IDS 2003. Energy, Poverty, and Gender A Review of the Evidence and Case Studies in Rural China The Institute of Development Studies. The University of Sussex, UK 2003.

Harris, J R and M P Todaro 1970. Migration, Unemployment and Development: A Two-Sector Analysis. The American Economic Review. Vol LX No 1.

Hoselitz, B (1957): 'Urbanisation and Economic Growth in Asia', Economic Development and Cultural Change, Vol 6, No 1.

Karan, A Changing Patterns of Migration from Rural Bihar pp.102-139, in Iyer, G 2003 (ed) Migrant Labour and Human Rights in India, Kanishka Publishers, New Delhi.

Khandelwal, R and S Katiyar 2003. Aajeevika Bureau. An Initiative to Upgrade Labour and Migration Opportunities for the Rural Poor in South Rajasthan Sudrak, 283 Fatehpura, Udaipur Rajasthan.

Kerr, J, G Pangare and V Lokur Pangare Watershed Development Projects In India An Evaluation Research Report 127 International Food Policy Research Institute Washington, DC.

Kundu, A Changing Agrarian System and Rural Urban Linkages in India in the Context of Social Viability *http://www.fao.org/es/ESA/Roa/pdf/6_Social SocialViability_India.pdf*

Kundu, A 2003. Urbanisation and Urban Governance, Search for a perspective beyond neo-liberalism. EPW XXXVIII No 29, July 19 2003 pp 3079-3087.

Lanjouw, P 1999. The Rural Non-Farm Sector: A Note on Policy Options. Development Economics Research Group. The World Bank. Draft February 1, 1999.

Olsen, W and R V Ramanamurthy. 2000. Contract Labour and Bondage in Andhra Pradesh (India) Journal of Social and Political Thought. Volume One, No.2 June 2000 *http://www.yorku.ca/jspot*

Rafique A and B Rogaly Internal seasonal migration, livelihoods and vulnerability in India: A Case Study Paper Presented at Regional Conference on Migration Development and Propoor Policy Choices, 22-24 June 2003, Refugee and Migratory Movements Research Unit, Dhaka.

Rao, G B (2001) Household Coping/Survival Strategies in Drought-prone Regions: A Case Study of Anantapur District, Andhra Pradesh, India SPWD-Hyderabad Centre.

Rogaly, B J Biswas, D Coppard, A Rafique, K Rana and A Sengupta Seasonal Migration, Social Change and Migrants' Rights Lessons from West Bengal Economic and Political Weekly December 8, 2001 pp.4547-4559.

Rogaly, B and D Coppard 2003. 'They Used To Go to Eat, Now They Go to Earn': The Changing Meanings of Seasonal Migration from Puruliya District in West Bengal, Journal of Agrarian Change Volume 3 Issue 3 Page 395 - July.

Sharon S, M Barnhardt and Ramesh Ramanathan, 2002 "Urban Poverty Alleviation in India: A General Assessment and a Particular Perspective" (2002), with permission. Authors: Publishers: Ramanathan Foundation, 565, 3rd Block, RMV Extension, 2nd Stage Bangalore 560094. ISBN 81-901511-1-8 September 2003 Tackling urban poverty India Together *http://indiatogether.org./2003/sep/pov-upairev.htm*

Simha, R 2003 New Delhi: The World's Shanty Capital in the Making by One World South Asia, 26 August 2003.

Singh C S K 2002 Daily Labour Market In Delhi Structure And Behaviour, Economic and Political Weekly. March 2 Pp.884-889.

Singh, M and A K Karan 2001. Rural Labour Migration From Bihar. Institute For Human Development, New Delhi.

ANNEXURES

Annexure 1: Summary Information for Sample Districts and Villages in MP and AP

District (Region)	**Ujjain (Malwa)**	**Tikamgargh (Bundelkhand)**	**Mandla (Mahokoshal)**
Villages	PR (Well Connected) and LJ (Remote)	SM (Well Connected) and MB (Remote)	GG (Well Connected) and PT (Remote)
Village Characteristics	Agriculturally prosperous, semi-arid, tube-well irrigated, soyabean and wheat. • Mixed caste • Polarised land distribution	Average agricultural development. Semi-arid, well and tank irrigation, soyabean, pulses, and wheat. • Caste hierarchies from feudal legacy • Polarised land distribution	Hilly, forested, often infertile. Limited irrigation and limited spread of rice intensive agriculture. Rice & pulses • Large number of tribals • More equitable land holdings
District (Region)	**Krishna (Coastal Andhra)**	**Chittoor (Rayalseema)**	**Medak (Telangana)**
Villages	KO (Well Connected) and KA (Remote)	OP (Well Connected) and VP (Remote)	GU (Well Connected) and MD (Remote)
Village Characteristics	Agriculturally prosperous, canal irrigated, paddy, pulses, sugarcane • Mixed caste but upper caste dominated • Polarised land distribution	Semi-arid, tank and tube-well irrigated, well connected with large cities, groundnut, paddy, mulberry, tomato • Backward Castes have emerged as powerful in remote village recently • More equitable land holding	Semi-arid, socially backward, mainly tank irrigated or rainfed agriculture, sorghum, paddy, cotton, maize • Traditional caste hierarchy • Land distribution still along feudal lines in remote village

Annexure 2: Some of the Important Pieces of Legislation which Help Unorganised Workers

- Workmen's Compensation Act, 1923.
- Minimum Wages Act, 1948.
- Maternity Benefit Act, 1961.
- Bonded Labour System (Abolition) Act, 1976.
- Contract Labour (Regulation & Abolition) Act, 1970.
- Inter-State Migrant Workmen (RECS) Act, 1979.
- Building and Other Construction Workers (RECS) Act, 1996.
- Beedi and Cigar Workers (RE) Act, 1976.

Annexure 3: People Interviewed

Shailendra Sharma, Adviser, Labour, Employment and Manpower, Planning Commission, Government of India.

N K Singh, Director, Department of Land Resources, Ministry of Rural Development, Nirman Bhavan, New Delhi.

Amitabh Kundu, Professor, Centre for the Study of Regional Development, Jawaharlal Nehru University, New Delhi.

Anup Karan, Fellow, Institute for Human Development, New Delhi.

Sheila Bhalla, Visiting Professor, Institute for Human Development, New Delhi.

Alakh Sharma, Professor, Institute for Human Development, New Delhi.

N C Saxena, ex-Secretary Rural Development, ex-Member Secretary of Planning Commission, Government of India.

Meera Shahi, Gram Vikas Trust, State Coordinator, Western India Rainfed Farming Project, Government of India/DFID.

Section III

Bridging the Rural-Urban Gap

7

How to Make Rural India Shine

S Mahendra Dev

This article examines some important indicators relating to rural India in the pre- and post-liberalization periods and finds that rural India is not 'shining'. It makes suggestions for policy makers in key economic and social sectors, where it says attention is needed to make rural India shine.

I. Introduction

In the post economic reform period, there has been a debate about the impact of reform policies on important indicators such as economic growth and other macro variables, poverty, inequality, human development and employment. There have been improvements in some indicators such as the balance of payments, higher growth in services, higher accumulation of foreign exchange reserves, IT revolution, improvement in telecommunications, recent stock market boom, higher growth of exports, etc. It is, however, important to assess the impact of economic reforms on rural areas as more than 70 percent of India's population live in these areas. In this paper, first we examine some important indicators relating to rural India in the pre- and post-liberalization periods. This is important to understand the problems in rural India. Next, we give suggestions on how to make rural India shine.

Source: Economic and Political Weekly, October 2, 2004.

II. Rural India in Pre- and Post-Reform Periods

What is the impact of liberalization on economic and social development of rural India?

Macroeconomic Trends

Before analysing rural development, we assess trends in a few important macroeconomic areas in the pre- and post-reform periods. The post-reform period is again divided into the Eighth Plan and Ninth Plan periods. The conclusions from the assessment are the following.

(i) *Economic growth*: GDP growth in the 1980s was 5.6 percent per annum while it was 5.8 percent per annum in the 1990s (Table 1). In other words, GDP growth rates were more or less same in both the 1980s and 1990s. The two periods in the post-reform period show that the growth rate decelerated in the Ninth Plan. In 2002-03, GDP growth was only 4.3 percent; recently, Central Statistical Organisation (CSO) revised it to 4.0 percent. The euphoria about 'India Shining' was intensified with the growth of 8.1 percent in 2003-04. It may be noted that even with 8.1 percent growth in 2003-04, GDP growth in the period 1997-98 to 2003-04 is higher than that for the Ninth Plan.

(ii) *Agriculture growth:* Growth in agriculture GDP declined from 3.4 percent in the 1980s to 3 percent in the 1990s. In the post-liberalization period it declined from 4.7 percent in the Eighth Plan period to 1.8 percent in the Ninth Plan period. This is a matter of concern for rural areas. It was –3.2 percent in 2002-03. Due to the revival of the monsoon, agriculture growth in the second quarter of 2003-04 was 7.4 percent. It may be noted that the high growth in the year 2003-04 was due to better rainfall and a low base in 2002-03.

(iii) *Investment*: There was a 1 percentage point increase in total investment in the 1990s (23 percent) as compared to 1980s (22 percent). However, this increase was more due to the rise in private investment of the household sector. Public sector investment declined significantly from 10.0 percent in the 1980s to 7.8 percent in the 1990s. Within the

Table 1: Macroeconomic Trends in Pre- and Post-Reform Periods

Indicators	1980s	1990s	1992-93 to 1997-98 (Eighth Plan)	1997-98 to 2001-02 (Ninth Plan)	2002-03#	2003-04
GDP growth (percent per year)	5.6	5.8	6.7	5.5	4.3	8.1
Agriculture, forestry and fisheries	3.4	3.0	4.7	1.8	-3.2	7.4*
Industry	7.0	5.8	7.6	4.5	5.7	6.3*
Services	6.9	7.6	7.5	8.1	7.1	9.6*
Investment rate (percent of GDP)	22.0	23.0	23.3	22.5	22.1	–
Public	10.0	7.8	8.0	6.6	6.3	–
Household and private corporate	12.1	15.2	15.3	15.9	15.7	–
Private corporate sector only	–	7.1	7.3	6.1	–	
Inflation (wholesale price Index percent per year)	8.0	8.1	8.7	4.9	2.5	–
Government deficit (percent of GDP)	8.1	7.8	7.2	9.3	10.4	–
Current account balance (percent of GDP)	-2.1	-1.4	-1.2	-0.7	1.0	–
External reserves (months of goods and services imports, end of period)	3.3	5.6	5.9	7.0	14.5@	–

Notes: # Revised estimates for growth rates in 2002-03 given in RBI (2004); * Relates to second quarter; @ RBI estimate.

Sources: World Bank (2003) upto col 5; Reserve Bank of India (2004) for col 6 and 7; Investment rate, inflation, deficit, etc., for 2002-03 are estimates from World Bank (2003).

post-liberalization period, it declined from 8 percent in the Eighth Plan period to 6.6 percent in the Ninth Plan period. Similarly, investment in the private corporate sector declined from 7.3 percent in the Eighth Plan to 6.1 percent in the Ninth Plan. There was a marginal increase in the private sector investment from 15.2 percent in the Eighth Plan to 15.9 percent in the Ninth Plan. However, this was mainly due to an increasein household sector investment as the private sector corporate investment did not increase during the Ninth plan period.

On inflation and external reserves, India has done well in the 1990s. On the other hand, the government has not been successful in controlling the fiscal deficit.

Agriculture Sector

Agriculture is the most important sector in rural areas. We examine here some aspects of agriculture sector.

(a) *Growth:* There was a deceleration in the growth of production and yields of foodgrains and all crops in the1990s as compared to the 1980s. The growth rate in foodgrains production declined from 2.81 percent in the 1980s to 1.98 percent in the 1990s. Yield growth also declined drastically for foodgrains and all crops. This could have implications for farmers' incomes and employment. The main factors for the deceleration in agricultural growth include "(i) inadequate irrigation cover; (ii) improper adoption of technology; (iii) unbalanced use of inputs; (iv) decline in public investment; and (v) weakness in credit delivery system" [RBI 2003, p III-5].

(b) *Investment*: There has been a secular decline in public investment. As compared to the target of 3.4 million hectares per annum, the irrigation potential harnessed during the Ninth Plan was only 1.8 million hectares per annum. The investment in research and extension is still around 0.3 percent to 0.5 percent of GDP. The quick estimates show that in 2001-02 public investment was Rs.4,794 crore from Rs.3,919 crore in 2000-01. But it was still lower than that in the mid-1990s. It is true that private investment has increased in the 1990s. However, public and private investments cannot be treated as substitutes for each other as their compositions are different.

(c) *Credit*: The availability of credit for farmers is important for working capital and investment purposes in agriculture. (i) Despite having a wide network of rural branches and many schemes and programmes for the expansion of credit for agriculture and rural development, a large number of very poor people still continue to remain outside the fold of the formal banking system. The credit system should reach marginal and small farmers. In fact, the growth rate of agricultural credit for small and marginal farmers declined in the 1990s as compared with the 1980s [RBI 2002]. During the same period, there was no decline of growth in credit for large farmers. There is a deceleration in the commercial bank's disbursements of direct finance to marginal farmers; from 15 percent in the 1980s, to 11 percent in the 1990s. The growth rate of direct finance to marginal farmers decelerated to 13 percent from 18.1 percent during the same period [RBI 2003]. (ii) The credit-deposit (C-D) ratio increased from 55.1 percent in 1980 to 97.1 percent in 1990 (Table 2). But it declined significantly to 49.3 percent by 2000. The incremental CD-deposit ratios also declined from 106.1 percent in the 1980s to 36 percent in the 1990s. (iii) With rising income, there will be diversification of crops. Investment needs for the production of high income-elastic agricultural products, such as dairying and livestock, horticulture, agro-forests would rise much faster now. Due to these factors, rural credit has to expand at a rate faster than in the recent past.

Table 2: Credit-Deposit Ratios by Population Groups

Population Group	C-D-Ratios			Incremental C-D-Ratios	
	December 1980	March 1990	March 2000	December 1980 to 1990	March 1990 to March 2000
Rural	55.1	97.1	49.3	106.1	36.0
Semi-urban	47.9	48.3	40.0	48.5	37.6
Urban	56.5	52.9	42.1	51.9	39.0
Metro	81.1	58.0	73.2	51.6	76.8
Total	64.0	60.7	56.0	59.8	54.8

Note: Credit data based on utilisation.

Source: Shetty (2003).

(d) *Farmers' suicides*: In recent years, farmers' suicides seem to have increased in some states. This is particularly so in Andhra Pradesh and Karnataka and is one of the darker sides of Indian agriculture [Sainath 2004]. A study on liberalization and suicides of farmers in India shows that crop failure and indebtedness emerge as the main and causative factors while social and psychological factors also contribute to the problem [Rao 2003]. According to the study, "sharper decline in absolute productivity, price uncertainty due to trade liberalization and rise in costs due to domestic liberalization, decline in credit and non-farm work intensified the crisis".

Poverty

We examine here whether the decline in poverty was higher in the 1990s as compared to the 1980s. NSS provides consumer expenditure data for both annual surveys and quinquennial surveys. We concentrate on the estimates based on the latter as they are more reliable. It is known that the 1999-2000 NSS-based estimates on poverty are not comparable with earlier years because of changes in the reference period. The reference periods for 1999-2000 (55th Round) were changed from the uniform 30-day recall to both 7-day and 30-day questions for food and intoxicants and only 365-day questions for items of clothing, footwear, education, institutional medical expenses and durable goods. Official estimates have not adjusted for the changes in reference periods. On the other hand, individual researchers have made several adjustments to make the 1999-2000 data comparable with those of earlier rounds. The official estimates based on expert group method and approved by the Planning Commission and alternative estimates are presented in Table 3. The findings from Table 3 are:

(a) Official estimates show that rural poverty declined from 45.7 percent in 1983 to 37.3 percent in 1993-94. It declined by 8.4 percentage points over a 10 and a half year period implying 0.8 percentage points decline per annum. In the post-reform period, it declined from 37.3 percent to 27.1 percent. It declined 10.2 percentage points over a 6-year period, indicating 1.7 percentage points decline per annum. Similarly in urban areas, the average annual decline in pre- and post-reform periods were 0.80 and 1.47 percentage points respectively. Thus, if we go by official estimates, the rate of decline of poverty in rural and urban areas was higher in the 1990s as compared to 1980s.

(b) Deaton and Dreze (2002) provide alternative estimates of poverty. They make an attempt to 'adjust' the 55th round estimates to acquire comparability with the earlier rounds. They also use improved price indexes to update the poverty line over time. According to their estimates, the rate of reduction in rural poverty during 1993-94 and 1999-2000 was similar to that of the changes between 1987-88 and 1993-94. In both periods, rural poverty declined by 6 to 7 percentage points. Their estimates also show that urban poverty is only 12 percent, which is significantly different from the official estimates (Table 3).

(c) Sundaram and Tendulkar (2003a) used comparable mixed reference period (MRP) based measures in the 50th round in order to compare them with 55th round estimates. As mentioned above, till the 50th round, NSS had a uniform reference period (URP) of 30-day questions for food and non-food. In the 55th round, NSS used a mixed reference period of 30 days (leaving for the moment the 7-day question) for food and intoxicants and 365-day question for other items. Fortunately, unit level data for the 50th round contains mixed reference period estimates. Sundaram and Tendulkar used these comparable measures for the 50th round. Their estimates show that rural poverty declined from 49 percent in 1983 to 39.7 percent in 1993-94 (URP). Rural poverty declined by 9.3 percentage points during a ten and a half-year period, indicating a 0.9 percentage point decline per annum (Table 3). In the post-reform period, poverty declined from 34.2 percent in 1993-94 (MRP) to 28.9 percent in 1999-2000, showing a 5.3 percentage point decline (0.90 percentage points per annum) during the reform period. Their estimates for rural poverty thus show that the rate of poverty decline during the 1990s was similar to that of the 1980s. Sundaram and Tendulkar (2003a), however, divide the average annual decline with initial values of poverty ratios and show that the rate of decline in rural poverty was higher in both rural and urban poverty. But if we compare average changes the rate of decline was not higher in the post-reform period only for rural poverty. In fact, the rate of decline in urban poverty was lower in the 1990s as compared to 1980s.

(d) In an unpublished study, Sen and Himanshu (2003) made several adjustments in order to compare 1999-2000 data with earlier years. Basically, they make two adjustments: (a) using 50th round comparable mixed reference period (MRP) based measures; (b) adjusting for 7-day questions for food and intoxicants in the 55th round. It may be noted that Sundaram and Tendulkar (2003a) did not make adjustments for 7-day questions in the 55th round. Based on the two adjustments, Sen and Himanshu's study shows that rural poverty declined from 31.6 percent in 1993-94 to 28.8 percent in 1999-2000. In other words, it declined by only 3 percentage points with an average annual decline of 0.5 percentage points during 1993-94 to 1999-2000 (Table 3). Even if we take the average annual decline as a percentage of initial values, the rate of decline in poverty in the 1990s was not higher than in the 1980s. According to the Sen and Himanshu estimates, the decline in urban poverty was also similar (0.5 percentage points decline) during the period 1993-2000.

Table 3: Poverty Ratios – Official and Alternative Estimates, 1983 to 1999-2000

Sources	Rural						
	Poverty Ratios				Change in Percentage Points		
	1983	1993-94 URP (Uniform 30-day Reference Period)	1993-94 MRP (Mixed 30/365-day Reference Period)	1999-2000	1983-94	1993-2000 (URP)	1993-2000 (MRP for 1993-94)
Official	45.7	37.3	–	27.1	-8.4 (-0.80)	-10.2 (-1.70)	–
Deaton and Dreze (2002)	–	33.0		26.3	–	-6.7 (-1.12)	–
Sundaram and Tendulkar (2003a)	49.0	39.7	34.2	28.9	-9.3 (-0.89)	–	-5.3 (-0.88)
Sen and Himansu (2003)	–	–	31.6	28.8*	–	–	-2.8 (-0.47)
Sources	**Urban**						
	Poverty Ratios				Average Annual Change in Poverty		
	1983	1993-94 URP (Uniform Reference Period)	1993-94 MRP (Mixed Reference Period)	1999-2000	1983-94	1993-2000 (URP)	1993-2000 (MRP for 1993-94)
Official	40.8	32.4	–	23.6	8.4 (-0.80)	8.8 (-1.47)	–
Deaton and Dreze (2002)	–	17.8	–	12.0	–	5.8 (-0.97)	–
Sundaram and Tendulkar (2003a)	38.3	30.9	26.4	23.1	7.4 (-0.71)	–	3.3 (-0.55)
Sen and Himansu (2003)	–	–	28.0	25.1*	–	–	2.9 (-0.48)

Note: Figures in parentheses refer to annual average change.

* *Adjusted for 7 day question.*

(e) Table 4 provides the absolute number of poor for official and alternative estimates. Official estimates show that the number of rural poor declined by 50 million in the 1990s. Sundaram and Tendulkar's (2003a) study shows it declined only by 15 million during the same period. On the other hand, Sen and Himansu's (2003) study shows an increase of rural poor by 1.5 million. In the case of urban areas, both studies show an increase in urban poor in the 1990s. This is in contrast to official estimates, which showed a decline in urban poor by 11 million.

Table 4: Number of Poor – Official and Alternative Estimates, 1983 to 1999-2000

(In million)

	Rural						
Sources	Poverty Ratios				Change in Percentage Points		
	1983	1993-94 URP (Uniform 30-day Reference Period)	1993-94 MRP (Mixed 30/365-day Reference Period)	1999-2000	1983-94	1993-2000 (URP)	1993-2000 (MRP for 1993-94)
Official	252.0	244.0	–	193.2	-8.0	-50.8	–
Sundaram and Tendulkar (2003a)	268.1	261.4	225.3	210.5	-6.7	–	-14.8
Sen and Himansu (2003)	–	–	207.9	209.4*	–	–	1.5
	Urban						
Sources	No. of Poor				Change in No. of Poor		
	1983	1993-94 URP (Uniform Reference Period)	1993-94 MRP (Mixed Reference Period)	1999-2000	1983-94	1993-2000 (URP)	1993-2000 (MRP for 1993-94)
Official	70.9	76.3	–	67.1	5.4	-11.1	–
Sundaram and Tendulkar (2003a)	65.7	72.6	62.1	63.8	6.9	–	1.7
Sen and Himansu (2003)		–	65.7	69.4*		–	3.7

To conclude, official estimates show a 10 percentage points decline for rural poverty during 1993-94 to 1999-2000. Deaton and Dreze (2002) show a decline of 6.7 percentage points, while Sundaram and Tendulkar (2003a) show 5.3 percentage points decline during the same period. On the other hand, Sen and Himansu (2003) show a decline of only around 3 percentage points in the 1990s. Thus, the decline in rural poverty during 1993-2000 varies between 10 percentage points (unadjusted official estimates) and 3 percentage points of Sen and Himanshu (2003). Changes in the number of rural poor also varies from a 50 million decline (official estimates) to an increase of 1.5 million during 1993-2000. The study of Sen and Himanshu is more reliable than official estimates because the former makes adjustments for the non-comparability of 55th Round data.

Poverty profile: In rural areas, some groups gained in shares while others lost. As shown in Table 5, the proportion of agricultural labourers increased from 42.6 percent in 1993-94 to 48 percent in 1999-2000.[1] On the other hand, the share of the self-employed in agriculture declined in total rural poor. Similarly, scheduled tribes lost while other castes benefited.

Table 5: Percentage Distribution of Rural Poor in 1993-94 and 1999-2000

	1993-94	1999-2000
By occupation		
Self-employed in agriculture	32.33	28.25
Self-employed in non-agriculture	11.16	11.53
Agricultural labour	42.62	48.01
Other labour	7.84	7.12
Others	6.04	5.09
Total	100.0	100.0
By caste		
Scheduled castes	28.19	27.10
Scheduled tribes	15.46	17.41
Others	56.35	55.49
Total	100.0	100.00

Source: Sundaram and Tendulkar (2003a).

Regional disparities in poverty: Poverty is concentrated in some states. The share of six states (Bihar, UP, MP, West Bengal, Orissa and Assam), in all-India rural poor increased between 1993-94 and 1999-2000 (Table 6). In 1993-94, their share was 68.8 percent but increased to 74.4 percent in 1999-2000. In fact 54 percent of India's rural poor live in three states, viz, Bihar, Uttar Pradesh and Madhya Pradesh. As shown in Table 6, the total share of nine major states and others declined from 31.2 percent in 1993-94 to 25.6 percent in 1999-2000.

Regional Disparities: Investment and Capital Flows

Regional disparities have increased significantly in the post-reform period. This could be partly due to the disparities in investment and capital flows in the 1990s. We look at important indicators of capital flows in the end of 1990s

Table 6: Percentage Distribution of Rural Poor by States – 1993-94 and 1999-00

States	Share in All-India Rural Poor 1993-94	Share in All-India Rural Poor 1999-2000
Bihar	20.4	20.6
Uttar Pradesh	21.3	21.9
Madhya Pradesh	8.5	11.3
West Bengal	8.8	8.9
Orissa	6.2	7.2
Assam	3.4	4.5
Total of above six states	68.8	74.4
Andhra Pradesh	3.0	2.9
Gujarat	2.3	1.9
Haryana	1.4	0.6
Karnataka	3.4	3.2
Kerala	2.3	1.2
Maharashtra	7.5	6.5
Punjab	0.6	0.6
Rajasthan	3.4	2.9
Tamil Nadu	4.9	3.9
Other states and UT	2.4	1.9
Total of above nine states and other states and UT	31.2	25.6
All-India	100.0	100.0

Source: Estimated from data on the number of poor in Sen and Himanshu (2003).

across states. Ahluwalia (2000) examines the relationship between state plan expenditure as a percentage of GDP and growth rates in GSDP. The study finds that plan expenditure, as a percent of SDP declined in both the better performing states as well as poor performing states. Orissa had the highest state plan expenditure to SDP at 7.1 percent in the 1990s but showed low growth in GSDP. In contrast, West Bengal had the lowest plan ratio of 2.7 percent but recorded very high growth in the1990s. The lack of correlation between state plan ratio and growth rate of GSDP indicates that total investment, which includes private investment, is more important than state plan expenditure. In the post-liberalization period, private, institutional and external investments have tended to become more and more market determined. There is also a lot of interest in the pattern of investment distribution across states.

Table 7 provides information on per capita flows to different states. One can see significant interstate disparities in the five indicators in the table. Per capita public and private investment in Gujarat (Rs.33,875) was more than 10 times that of Bihar (Rs.2,852) and UP (Rs.3,304). If we take only per capita plan outlay, the disparities are lower than those for total investment. In the case of institutional investment also the disparities are lower than for total investment. Per capita total credit utilisation in Maharashtra was more than 20 times that of Bihar and nine

Table 7: Per Capita Capital Flows to States – 1999-2001

(in Rs.)

Major States	Per Capita NSDP 1999-2000	Per Capita Public and Private Investment	Per Capita Plan Outlay	Per Capita Institutional Investment	Per Capita Total Credit Utilisation	Per Capita Per Annum Externally Aided Projects (Average 1997-02)
Andhra Pradesh	14715	21447	1032	910	4668	221
Bihar	6328	2852	319	546	669	11
Chhattisgarh	NA	12209	631	32	1803	na
Goa	NA	56057	3423	1821	14489	25
Gujarat	18685	33875	1285	720	5827	138
Haryana	21551	9201	861	827	5098	106
Jharkhand	NA	9105	836	37	1759	na
Karnataka	16343	24775	1499	688	6420	125
Kerala	18262	12235	710	1173	5872	19
Madhya Pradesh	10907	7287	652	725	2528	62
Maharashtra	23398	17556	1120	660	14890	52
Orissa	9162	25525	627	1049	1706	118
Punjab	23040	12688	1244	1078	7707	68
Rajasthan	12533	6763	822	914	2419	35
Tamil Nadu	19141	26292	837	709	9194	83
Uttar Pradesh	9765	3304	293	619	1638	47
West Bengal	15569	7113	710	662	3674	89

Source: GoI (2003).

times that of UP. Shetty's (2003b) study shows that there has been a narrowing of regional disparities in the credit-deposit (C-D) ratios in the 1970s and 1980s. However, in the 1990s, the C-D ratios have fallen in all regions of the country – the decline being much more steep in backward states and regions. For example, in the eastern region, the C-D ratios had declined from 54 percent in 1981 to 50 percent in 1991 and to 37 percent in 2001. Similarly in the central region (MP and UP), C-D ratios declined from 50 percent in 1991, to 33 percent in 2001 [Shetty 2003b].

Table 8 provides a list of the top five leading states in the selected indicators. It shows that Karnataka and Goa figure in four, Orissa and Punjab in three and Gujarat, Tamil Nadu and Maharashtra in two out of five categories [GoI 2003]. Generally, there is a positive relationship between higher levels of infrastructure/ income and capital flows particularly the per capita total investment. There are some exceptions like Orissa. In the case of Orissa, relatively high levels of external aid and higher levels of private investment in the power sector could be reason for its figuring in three categories. Rajasthan, with lower infrastructure, figures in one category. On the other hand, Andhra Pradesh appears in one category due to very high per capita level of externally aided projects (EAPs).

Table 8: Leading States in Per Capita Flows

Per Capita Flows of	Top Five Among Major States
Plan outlays	Goa, Karnataka, Gujarat, Punjab, Maharashtra
Public and private investments	Goa, Gujarat, Tamil Nadu, Orissa, Karnataka
Institutional investment	Goa, Kerala, Punjab, Orissa, Rajasthan
Credit utilisation	Maharashtra, Goa, Tamil Nadu, Punjab, Karnataka
Additional central assistance for externally aided projects	Andhra Pradesh, Gujarat, Karnataka, Orissa, Haryana

Source: GoI (2003).

Employment and Real Wages

Faster growth through economic reforms is not always accompanied by a faster rate of poverty reduction. Poverty can be reduced if growth increases employment potential (quantity and quality). Similarly, the extent to which the working poor are able to integrate into the economic process also determines the impact of growth on poverty. For example, if there is a mis-match between the opportunities available due to economic reforms and the skills of the workers, the poor will not be able to take advantage of such opportunities and gain from the reforms.

Employment growth: The growth rate of rural employment was around 0.5 percent per annum between 1993-94 and 1999-2000, as compared to 1.7 percent per annum between 1983 and 1993-94. The daily status unemployment rate in rural areas has increased from 5.63 percent in 1993-94 to 7.21 percent in 1999-2000. Overall employment growth declined from 2.04 percent during 1983-94 to 0.98 percent during 1994-2000. Much of the decline in growth was in two sectors, viz, agriculture and community, social and personal services. These two sectors, which account for 70 percent of total employment have not shown any growth during the 1990s.

Real wages: Another indicator of purchasing power is agricultural wages. At the all India level, the growth of real agricultural wages declined from about 5 percent per annum in the 1980s to 2.5 percent per annum in the 1990s. Deaton and Dreze (2002) say that the healthy growth of real agricultural wages appears to be a sufficient condition for significant reduction in poverty in rural areas. In all the states where real wages have grown more than 2.5 percent (Gujarat, Karnataka, Kerala, Tamil Nadu), sharp reductions in rural poverty have been experienced. On the other hand, the entire eastern region (Assam, Orissa, West Bengal and Bihar), Andhra Pradesh and Madhya Pradesh, experienced low growth in agricultural wages and lower reduction in poverty. The NSS data, however, shows that there were no signs of decline in real wages for casual labourers in rural areas.

Using data from rural labour enquiries (RLEs) Chavan and Bedamatta (2003) reveal that real daily earnings of agricultural labourers recorded the highest growth in almost all states during 1983 to 1987-88. However, the growth rates of real daily wages of female and male agricultural labourers declined during 1987-88 to 1993-94 and during 1993-94 to 1999-2000 in majority of the states. This study also shows that daily labour earnings were higher than minimum wages for males in majority of the states. In the case of females, daily earnings were lower than minimum wages. There seems to be an increase in the male-female ratio of wages over time and it shows significant gender disparities in wages.

Public Distribution System

The public distribution system (PDS) is considered an important social safety net for the poor. Targeting was introduced in PDS in 1997. We computed the percentage of PDS purchases of rice and wheat to total consumption of rice and wheat based on unit level data from two NSS rounds (50th and 55th). The 55th round has a problem of comparability because of the change in the reference period. Since we are taking ratios, the problem may not be serious. The ratio for rural poor at all-India level increased from 6.8 percent in 1993-94 to 8.8 percent in 1999-2000 (Table 9). At the state level, a significant increase was noticed for Assam, Karnataka, Kerala, Orissa, Tamil Nadu and West Bengal. Regarding

Table 9: Percentage of PDS Purchases of Rice and Wheat to Total Consumption of Rice and Wheat in Rural Areas

States	Poor		Non-Poor		All	
	1993-94	1999-2000	1993-94	1999-2000	1993-94	1999-2000
Andhra Pradesh	33.12	29.62	20.05	18.66	21.48	19.48
Assam	5.32	8.79	2.37	4.16	3.57	5.79
Bihar	0.58	1.69	0.88	2.14	0.73	1.97
Gujarat	33.44	33.71	18.29	15.16	20.38	16.48
Haryana	0.60	0.74	0.87	0.37	0.80	0.40
Himachal Pradesh	34.00	35.99	32.66	26.47	33.00	27.11
J and K	19.85	5.79	2.87	23.17	5.19	22.79
Karnataka	29.23	41.52	13.92	21.48	16.46	23.38
Kerala	59.96	72.30	42.98	44.77	46.53	46.74
Madhya Pradesh	4.06	4.58	2.43	2.45	2.95	3.09
Maharashtra	20.09	22.58	14.83	15.66	15.95	16.87
Orissa	1.25	13.14	0.79	8.84	0.99	10.65
Punjab	0.67	0.00	0.40	0.02	0.43	0.02
Rajasthan	20.20	3.10	10.50	1.84	12.42	1.96
Tamil Nadu	23.85	44.20	17.82	30.56	19.40	32.68
Uttar Pradesh	1.73	2.25	3.03	1.73	2.54	1.87
West Bengal	1.96	9.50	1.75	1.83	1.83	3.85
Other states and UTs	26.45	34.11	21.15	17.36	22.02	18.74
Total	6.79	8.77	8.61	9.18	8.02	9.08

Source: Mahendra Dev and Ravi (2004).

dependence of the rural poor on PDS, Kerala has the highest percentage (72.3 percent) followed by Tamil Nadu (44.2 percent) and Karnataka (42 percent) in 1999-2000. There was a significant increase in the ratio in the case of Orissa. However, in three states (Bihar, UP and MP) where more than 50 percent of India's rural poor live, the ratio was less than 5 percent for the poor; it was less than 10 percent in Assam, J and K, Rajasthan and West Bengal. Thus, targeting has improved access to PDS in some states. However, poor states have not benefited significantly from targeted PDS.

Health and Education

Jawaharlal Nehru at the time of independence reminded the country that the task ahead: was of ending of poverty, ignorance, disease and the inequality of opportunity. That dream is largely unaccomplished, although this is not to deny the considerable progress in human development.

Rural literacy and education: India's overall literacy rate increased from around 17 percent 1951 to 65 percent in 2001. Literacy in rural areas increased from 36 percent in 1981 to 59 percent in 2001. During the same time, literacy in urban areas increased from 67 percent to 80 percent. The rural-urban gap has declined from 31 to 21 percentage points in the last two decades. Female literacy increased over time but still around 53 percent of rural females were illiterate in 2001. Also, 30 to 33 percent of rural girls in the age group 6-14 were not attending school in 1999-00. Similarly, among SCs and STs 40 to 45 percent of girls were not attending school.

There are significant interstate disparities in literacy and education. For example, rural female literacy in Kerala was 87 percent while in Bihar it was 30 percent in 2001. Similarly, the school attendance ratios for Kerala girls (6-13 years) were 97 percent but in Bihar they were 35 percent in 1995-96. There are also significant interstate variations regarding school facilities like access to schools teacher-pupil ratios, classrooms, etc.

Rural health: The life expectancy in rural areas between 1992 to 1996 was 59, while in urban areas it was 66. Although the gap between rural and urban areas, is narrowing it is still around seven years. Infant mortality declined in both rural and urban areas. In 1999-2001 infant mortality was 74 in rural areas while it was 43 in urban areas. In the post-liberalization period, the decline in infant mortality has been much slower in rural areas as compared to urban areas.

The health indicators for various social groups show that they are much lower for STs and SCs. For example, under five mortality was 127 for STs as compared to 83 for others. The percentage of undernutrition was also higher for STs and SCs. Health indicators for rural areas were much lower as compared to those of urban areas. In rural areas, nearly 70 percent of births are not attended to by professionals.

III. Suggestions for Making Rural India Shine

Our assessment has shown that 'rural India is not shining' in the post-liberalization period. It is true that there have been some improvements in infrastructure and levels of living. Poverty has declined but there is a debate on the rate of decline. Literacy also improved in the 1990s but there are many dark areas such as low employment growth, problems in health status, low agricultural growth, farmers' suicides, etc. There are more than 200 million rural poor in India. We provide here some suggestions to make rural India 'shine'.

In order to make rural development more broad based and balanced, major areas of concern have to be addressed. Rural investment, technology and appropriate rural institutions are needed for rural development. We suggest 10 areas where policy attention is needed.

(1) *Employment*: In the 1990s, employment was a major concern, particularly in rural areas. How do we create more employment opportunities and improve their quality? There are mainly two approaches. One is through sectoral programmes and the other is through direct employment programmes. There is some overlap in both the approaches. Employment can be increased if economic growth is labour-intensive. The development of agriculture and the rural non-farm sector mentioned below will improve employment and wages. Policies have to be framed for both unskilled and skilled workers and youth employment is an important focus area.

Direct employment programmes such as wage and self-employment schemes have to be effectively implemented. Labour-intensive employment programmes, if properly designed and implemented, hold high promise as instruments for addressing both short-term relief and long-term asset creation. Public works programmes have long been recognised as effective policy instruments of providing food security, particularly in rural areas. The Common Minimum Programme (CMP) of the new government also mentions the employment guarantee scheme.

(2) *Increase in public investment*: An important priority is to increase public investment in rural infrastructure. Infrastructure includes irrigation, electricity, agricultural research, roads and communications and new technology. We have seen above that public investment declined in the post-liberalization period. Increase in public investment will also encourage private investment.[2] Investment in rural infrastructure is more important for agricultural growth and rural development than trade liberalization *per se*.

(3) *Agriculture*: Although the share of agriculture in GDP has declined to 22 percent, the share of employment in agriculture is still 60 percent. Therefore, increase in agricultural growth is important for rural development. A two-pronged strategy is needed to improve the performance of agriculture. The first is to release the initiative and enterprise of farmers and the private sector in general by removing restrictions on agricultural trade, processing, etc. The second is to facilitate adequate supply responses to the incentives created by strengthening infrastructure, agricultural research and extension and delivery of credit while protecting the environment [Rao 2003]. The focus has to be more on dry land and marginal areas for higher returns. Agricultural subsidies have to reach small and marginal farmers.

(4) *Water management:* The management of water is going to be crucial for raising the standard of living in rural areas. Watershed development can be sustained in the long run only through social mobilisation and capacity building. Conservation of surface and groundwater can be improved when water and power are priced according to the volume of consumption. Community involvement is essential in setting the user charges as well as for assessing the individual consumption.

(5) *Rural institutional reforms*: Institutional reforms are important, particularly in the domain of public systems, for sustained technical progress and output growth in agriculture. "There is a limited scope for privatising irrigation, research and extension, and other infrastructure facilities. All of these will continue to be mainly the responsibility of public sector. Unless the public sector's efficiency in mobilising resources and managing these facilities is vastly improved, trade and price policy reform will not make a significant difference to the pace of agricultural growth" [Vaidyanathan 1996].

(6) *Rural non-farm sector:* Although India is one of the largest producers of raw material for the food-processing industry in the world, the industry itself is underdeveloped. Less than 2.5 percent of fruit and vegetable production is processed compared with 30 percent in Thailand, 70 percent in Brazil, 78 percent in the Philippines and 80 percent in Malaysia. By any standards, therefore, the unutilised potential of food-processing in India is enormous. Expansion of this sector is an ideal way of bringing industry to rural areas, expanding the value chain of agricultural production, providing assured markets for farmers enabling them to diversify into higher value horticultural crops and expanding employment by creating high quality non-agricultural work opportunities in rural areas [Mahendra Dev and Rao 2004].

(7) *Health and education:* We must focus on five aspects to improve health in rural areas: first, public expenditure on the health sector has to be increased. Public expenditure on health is now only around 1 percent of GDP. These percentages have been stagnant in the 1990s and there is a need to allocate more resources to this sector. However, along with this, the efficiency of public spending has to be improved. More resources should be spent on preventive care, as the poor benefit more from this. Primary healthcare services should be accountable to local governments and must ensure better services for money spent. The second issue is how to make the private sector accountable. The share of the private sector in total healthcare is high and has increased over time. One cannot ignore, therefore, the role of the private sector in the state. The government should promote institutions to regulate the private sector. Third, there is a need to promote community health

insurance schemes (e.g., SEWA's scheme) in order to provide health services at a low cost to the poor in rural areas. Fourth, a rights-based approach to the health sector, which can be improved with demands from the people, and social mobilisation is important. Fifth, health sector development has to be integrated with the overall process of development. For example, there is no synergy between the processes directed at improving drinking water facilities, sanitation and public hygiene, access to elementary education, nutrition and poverty alleviation and the processes that improve access to public health and medical services. An integrated approach is important to improve health sector performance.

Three aspects of improving basic education in rural areas are: First, more resources have to be allocated to education, particularly to primary education, from the budget. The international norm is 6 percent of GDP. India has been spending less than 4 percent of GDP. In rural areas infrastructure is poor and there is a need for greater spending. The 93rd amendment of the Constitution is in the right direction but funds are needed to realise universalisation of elementary education. Second, the quality of education in terms of curriculum, better infrastructure and teaching has to be improved. Third, retaining children in the schools is more difficult than enrolling them. While the demand factors are important in influencing the extent of literacy and dropout rates, access or supply or quality factors influence enrolment rates. Specific policies are required to address gender and social disparities.

(8) *'PURA' model and improving basic services:* The president of India A P J Abdul Kalam has been advocating implementation of the scheme PURA – Providing Urban Amenities in Rural Areas. PURA is a scheme to enhance physical, economic, knowledge, societal and electronic connectivity in rural areas. The union cabinet has recently approved the PURA scheme. This scheme should be taken up seriously throughout India. Generally, the performance of many basic services like drinking water, health, education, sanitation, electricity, transport are weak in rural areas. Effectiveness of these services have to be improved by a rights based and participatory approach. The demand to improve the performance of these basic services should come from the people.

(9) *Reduction in personal, regional and gender inequalities:* The experience of globalisation has shown that it increased interpersonal and regional disparities across many countries. The Chinese experience also shows an increase in inequalities. Stepping up public investment in physical and social infrastructure has immense potential for reducing regional disparities in the levels of development. The gap between the ultimate irrigation potential of major and medium irrigation projects, which can be undertaken only through public investment, and the potential actually created so far is quite high for drought-prone regions. Public expenditure on health and education needs to be stepped up substantially while focusing on the less developed areas.

(10) *Decentralisation and governance:* There is a need to devolve more finances, functions and powers to panchayats in order to make these institutions self-sustaining. Governments also have to integrate community-based organisations (CBOs) with panchayats. The actual performance so far in terms of genuine decentralisation/devolution to local bodies is far from satisfactory. Some people feel that decentralisation would lead to more corruption. It may be noted that decentralised corruption is better than centralised corruption. However, over time corruption can be reduced.

In recent years it has been shown that governance is the key factor for raising economic growth and human development. In this respect, several states are introducing many governance reforms given above to improve administration and delivery systems. These reforms, including e-governance, have yielded some results. But, the general impression is that inspite of reforms, improvements at the ground level are not visible. A change in the mindset of the bureaucracy, involving good NGOs in local development programmes, convergence of line departments with panchayats are some of the measures needed to improve governance in the country. Right to information, social mobilsation and involvement of panchayats would improve accountability of public expenditure. These measures can reduce the leakages in several government programmes.

IV. Conclusions

In the post-liberalization period, there have been improvements in foreign exchange reserves and physical infrastructure (like telecommunications and roads), a stock market boom, an IT revolution, and 8 percent growth in GDP in 2003-04. Due to these improvements, there was in early 2004 a feel good factor in the form of 'India Shining'. In this paper, we have examined the issue whether this was true for rural India. Our assessment shows that although there were improvements in some indicators, rural India is not 'shining'.

To conclude, rural investment (both public and private), technology, rural institutions and employment schemes are important for rural development. We have suggested 10 areas viz, employment, increase in public investment, agriculture sector, water management, rural institutional reforms, rural non-farm sector, health and education, reduction in regional, personal and gender disparities, PURA model and basic services, decentralisation and governance where policy attention is needed in order to make rural India 'shine'. India cannot 'shine' without the 'shining' of rural India.

(S Mahendra Dev is Director, Centre for Economic and Social Studies (CESS), Hyderabad. He has written extensively on agricultural development, poverty and public policy, food security, employment guarantee schemes, social security, farm and non-farm employment, and been a consultant to many international organizations like the UNDP, World Bank, International Food Policy Research Institute, and UNESCAP. He has also worked as a member in committees set up by the Government of India.)

Notes

[Revised keynote address delivered at the three-day 'National Seminar on Globalisation and Rural Transformation, organised by the Department of Economics, Kakatiya University, Warangal, February 20-22, 2004].

1 This increase was partly due to increase in their share in the rural population during the same period.

2 Nagaraj (2003) argues that lower public investment in the latter part of 1990s is responsible for decline in demand and stagnation in industrial growth.

References

Chavan, Pallavi and Bedamatta (2003): 'Trends in Real Wages in India', paper presented at conference on "Agriculture and Rural Society in Contemporary India", Bardhman, December 17-20.

Deaton, A and Jean Dreze (2002): "Poverty and Inequality in India: A Re-examination", *Economic and Political Weekly*, September 7.

GoI (2003): *Economic Survey, 2002-03*, Ministry of Finance, Government of India.

Mahendra Dev, S and C Ravi (2004): *Performance of PDS in India*, Centre for Economic and Social Studies, Hyderabad.

Mahendra Dev, S and N Chandrasekhar Rao (2004): *Food-Processing in Andhra Pradesh: Opportunities and Challenges*, Centre for Economic and Social Studies, Hyderabad.

Nagaraj, R (2003): "Industrial Policy and Performance Since 1980: Which Way Now?", *Economic and Political Weekly*, August 30.

Rao, C H H (2003): "Reform Agenda for Agriculture", *Economic and Political Weekly*, Vol 8, No 7.

Rao, Chandrasekhar, N (2003): "Liberalization and Suicides of Farmers in India", summary *Indian Journal of Agricultural Economics*, Vol 58, No 3.

RBI (2002): *Report on Currency and Finance 2000-01*, Reserve Bank of India, Mumbai.

– (2003): *Report on Currency and Finance 2001-02*, Reserve Bank of India, Mumbai.

– (2004): *Report on Currency and Finance 2002-03*, Reserve Bank of India, Mumbai.

Sainath, P (2004) "The Feel Good Factor", *Frontline*, Vol 21, No 5, March 12, Chennai.

Sen, A and Himanshu (2003): "Poverty and Inequality in India: Getting Closer to the Truth", Centre for Economic Studies and Planning, Jawaharlal Nehru University, New Delhi, mimeo.

Shetty, S L (2003a), "Credit Flows to Rural Poor", mimeo, *EPW* Research Foundation, Mumbai

– (2003b), "Growth of SDP and Structural Changes in State Economies: Interstate Comparisons", *Economic and Political Weekly*, December 6.

Sundaram, K and S D Tendulkar (2003a): "Poverty in India in the 1990s: Revised Estimates", *Economic and Political Weekly*, Vol 38, No 46, November 15.

– (2003b): "Poverty among Social and Economic Groups in India in 1990s", *Economic and Political Weekly*, Vol 38, No 50, December 13.

Vaidyanathan, A (1996): "Agricultural Development: Imperatives of Institutional Reforms", *Economic and Political Weekly*, Vol 31, Nos 35-37.

World Bank (2003): 'India: Sustaining Reform, Reducing Poverty', *A World Bank Development Policy Review*, Oxford University Press.

8

Microfinance: Providing Access to Financial Services in Rural India

Vipin Sharma

Little or no access to financial services of the formal institutions had stifled development in rural India, where a majority of the poor resides. This article discusses how, since 1992, microfinance is changing the financial landscape of rural India with easy access to savings and credit services.

April 1992: It was the first time that Hanuman Van Vikas Samiti's Raj Karan Yadav sat across the branch manager of the Sakroda branch of Mewar Aanchalik Gramin Bank in the Udaipur district of Rajasthan. A group of women had accompanied Raj Karan to negotiate for a loan for their SHG.[1] The brokering of this small loan of Rs.3,000 was a protracted process both for the reluctant banker as well as for the SHG members. It took a full day—copious paper work, many thumb impressions and detailed discussions. This was among the first SHG loans given by a bank in India and a part of a pilot project initiated by NABARD to link 500 SHGs in the country.

August 6, 2005: Malik the CEO of Biswa, an MFI from Sambhalpur, sits comfortably in a hotel lobby in Bhubaneswar discussing a Rs.30 cr bank loan with visitors from ICICI Bank, Mumbai. The meeting lasts about an hour, and once Malik submits a few more documents, the deal will be finalized.

Source: Chartered Financial Analyst, November 2005. Originally published as "Microfinance in India: Coming of Age."

The Origin

After NABARD was carved out of the Reserve Bank of India in 1982, the apex financial institution for the development of agriculture and rural areas was constantly challenged to strengthen the rural credit delivery system so as to enable the rural poor to access small loans from formal financial institutions. With perhaps one of the most impressive institutional infrastructures, this should not have been a difficult task, particularly given the fact that most of the banks were government-owned.[2] To supplement credit provision in the rural areas, Regional Rural Banks (RRBs) were established across the country in 1975, in addition to the already existing institutional infrastructure of the cooperative and land development banks. Coupled with stringent statutory priority-sector lending obligations, the flow of finance to the rural poor under this regime should not have been an issue. However, the only loans going to the poor seemed to be under the subsidy-linked IRDP[3] of the Government of India.

Although the program had a long run, its impact with wrong identification of 'beneficiaries', leakages, misuse of subsidies, and low recoveries, was at best marginal. The program never found favor with the bankers, who lent under extreme pressure from the state governments. Few other avenues for the poor existed, which resulted in their reliance upon the ubiquitous local *mahajan* for their credit requirements. Despite the infrastructure, large poverty-alleviation programs and statutory obligations, almost 65% of the poor were still borrowing from informal resources.

Linkage Banking and Other Microfinance Models

The year 1992 marks the formal beginning of microfinance in India. Although its growth was cautious and erratic in the initial years, in the last half-decade, the microfinance sector has grown at a fairly significant pace. From a pilot project, it became a full-fledged program; and today, the linkage-banking model is known, particularly in the NGO sector, as the 'SHG movement'.

Linkage-banking is the predominant national model. Many actors are involved in making the program operational. The primary stakeholders are the poor women who come together as an SHG. These SHGs are broadly promoted by NGOs, who, for the purpose of the program, are called Self-Help Promoting Institutions (SHPIs). For promoting SHGs, the SHPIs are usually provided with small grants from NABARD; the government also provides grants in case the purpose of promotion of SHGs is for their participation in the 'Swarnajayanti Gramin Swarojgar Yojana'; or under large multilateral funded programs like 'Swashakti' or DPIP or 'Swayamsiddha' or by bilateral donors. The size of grants for SHG promotion differs from agency to agency ranging between Rs.60,000 under the recently concluded 'Swashakti' Project to Rs.3,900 that NABARD provides. In recent years, a few banks like Canara Bank and ICICI Bank, too have started providing SHG promoting grants to NGOs. Bank branches link the SHGs with loans. As per the current guidelines from NABARD, the loans are linked to the savings made by an SHG and can go up to four times the level of these savings. Under the linkage-banking model, typically the SHGs get loans at a rate of interest of 8-9% and, in turn, lend it to their members between 18-24%. Their lending rate is fixed as per the by-laws agreed to by the SHG members.

Banking Infrastructure in India

Banks	Total Branches	Of which:		
		Rural	Semi-Urban	Urban
Com. Banks (27)	46,068	19,266	10,900	15,902
Foreign Banks (40)	237	0	2	235
Other scheduled and non-scheduled banks (35)	5,420	1,143	1,776	2,501
RRBs (196)	14,483	12,062	2,045	376
Total	66,208	32,471	14,723	19,014

Till recently, the program was primarily supported by the public sector banks, but in the last couple of years, there has been a lot of interest among private-sector as well as multinational banks. In the last half-decade, a large number of NGOs too has shed their traditional social intermediation role and has begun to undertake financial intermediation. Among these, there are a few like BASIX, SPANDANA, SHARE, CASHPOR, ASA which have established themselves as commercial MFIs (NBFIs)/Grameen replicators. There are about 100 such MFIs in the country now. While SEWA is an urban cooperative bank model, the BASIX group also has a Local Area Bank. Another model that has emerged in the country is the aggregation of SHGs into federations. This has particularly become popular in Andhra Pradesh, made possible by the introduction of the Mutually Aided Cooperative Act 1995.

There are no clear guidelines, as yet, on lending by banks to community-based federations. The schematic below represents the structural arrangements for the delivery of microfinance services in India.

The Current Status

Despite a slow-growth rate in the initial period, as of 2005, India today has the highest number of poor being served by the microfinance sector (25 million), having overtaken its neighboring Bangladesh, one of the first countries to have adapted microfinance route as an effective poverty-alleviation strategy. A snapshot view of the SHG-bank linkage program is given below:

Bulk of the SHG linkage targets have been achieved through the public-sector banks, and even today, 73% of all microfinance loans are provided by these government-owned banks. However, in the past few years, the private-sector and the multinational banks, despite the lack of rural bank branches and understanding of rural areas or the rural clients, and with their very upmarket, urbane culture, have shown a keen interest in microfinance. To overcome constraints of infrastructure, these banks have evolved innovative mechanisms and models to expand their microfinance portfolio. ICICI Bank, among the newcomers, has been the most aggressive. The ICICI Bank through its 'partnership model' has already achieved an outstanding of Rs.720 cr and among all commercial banks, has the second largest microfinance portfolio after SBI. It plans to achieve a portfolio of about Rs.2,000 cr by the end of this year. Other private-sector banks like HDFC Bank (Rs.175 cr), UTI Bank (Rs.100 cr), IDBI Bank, etc., too are looking at microfinance as a serious business opportunity. Among the multinational banks, ABN AMRO Bank (Rs.85 cr), Standard Chartered Bank (Rs.15 cr), and HSBC (Rs.12 cr), among others, have also developed their own strategies and models for lending to the sector.

The scale which the sector has been able to attain, and the pace at which it has grown consistently over the last few years, is now attracting a host of foreign investment funds, venture capital funds, and even private-equity investors. During the last couple of years, Grameen Capital, USA, Lok Capital, UNITUS and Bellweather Fund have set up their operations in India. Institutions like the IFC and CDC are also getting interested in this sector and looking at investment opportunities. Given the size of India's population below poverty line, even international microfinance retail institutions like FINCA are preparing to set up operations in India.

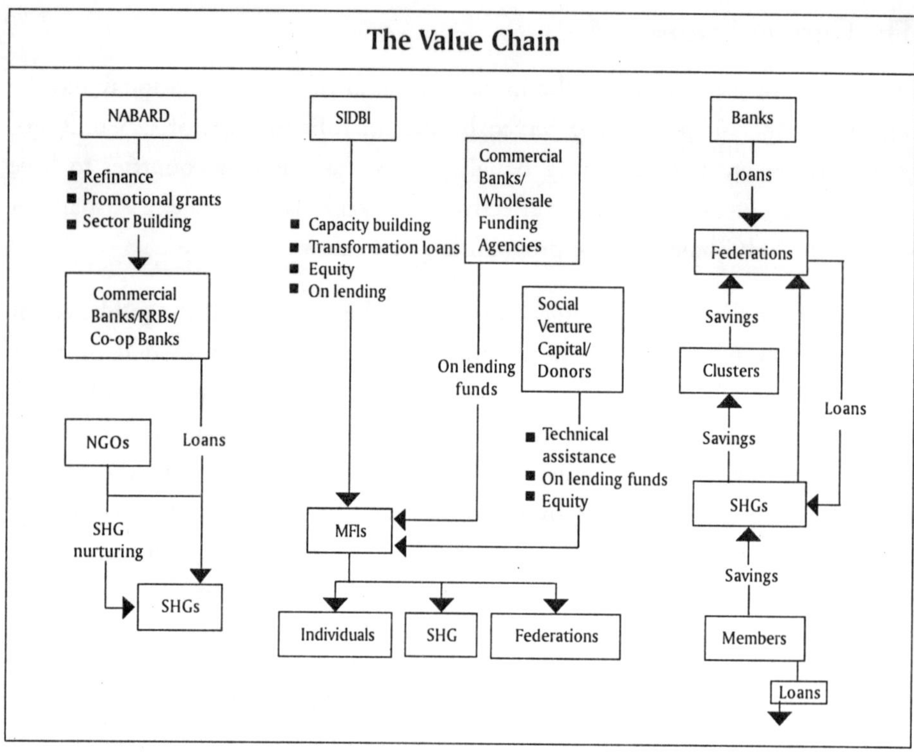

The MFIs together account for about Rs.500 cr of outstanding portfolio with a cumulative disbursement of over Rs.1,600 cr. Some large MFIs like SHARE have an outstanding portfolio of Rs.370 cr. While a few MFIs are registered as NBFIs, most of them are either societies or Section 25 companies. While SIDBI (through its SIDBI Foundation for Micro Credit) is the apex institution supporting the growth of MFIs in the country, a few large bilateral-funded programs like CASHE (Credit and Savings for Household Enterprises) being implemented by CARE India, too support the incubation of community-based microfinance institutions. Almost 90% of all microfinance clients are in the rural areas, with most of the urban poor being left out of this program.

Policy Shifts

In the last one year, the sector has seen a lot of action. Moving beyond setting targets for NABARD to link SHGs to Banks, the Union Finance Minister, in his last budget speech, made some major announcements for the sector. For the first time, certain legitimacy was given to the growing contribution of the MFIs. To start with, he expanded the scope of the Microfinance Development Fund to include equity, and doubled the fund size to Rs.200 cr. The fund will be managed by an independent board comprising of representatives from both financial as well as NGO sector. He also announced the opening up of the External Commercial Borrowing (ECB) route for the MFIs to allow cheaper foreign funds for the sector. In addition, he also allowed banks to channel their services through banking correspondents. And, finally, responding to the demands of the sector, he announced the introduction of a legislation for the sector. While this is seen as a major achievement for the sector, there still remain demands, particularly of the MFIs for deposit collection, lowering the entry barriers for registration of NBFCs, and a legislation that allows a defined institutional space to the microfinance institutions.

Future Challenges

While the sector has grown significantly in the last half-decade, several challenges still remain. Microfinance still reaches only about 10 to 12% of the poor in the country. Sixty-seven percent of the population in the country have no bank accounts

Microfinance Landscape	
No. of SHGs Linked to banks	1.67 million
Cumulative loans disbursed by banks	Rs.6,878 cr
Total Loans disbursed by commercial banks during the last year (2004-05)	Rs.2,800 cr
No. of participating banks	560
• Commercial Banks	48
• RRBs	196
• Cooperative Banks	316
No.of bank branches lending to SHGs	35,294
No. of NGOs and other agencies associated	Approx. 1,000
Average member level loan-size	Rs.3,024
Average loan-size for SHGs	Rs.46,000

and 80% have never taken a loan from a formal source. About 40% continue to borrow from informal sources. The demand and supply gap is still huge. As per estimates, it varies between Rs.50,000 to 1,50,000 cr and only 20% are currently met through the program. Regional skew is another area of concern. Almost three-fourths of all microfinance clients are located in the four southern states. Andhra Pradesh, with over 5,00,000 SHGs, accounts for almost a third of all clients in the country. Large parts of the northern and north-eastern states are still underserved by the sector. NABARD has identified 13 states for special focus in the coming years. Financial deepening also requires urgent attention. With an average loan size of about Rs.3,000, the loans can, at best, serve consumption smoothening. For asset acquisition, new models and greater conviction is required from the banks. The sector needs to grow beyond meeting survival credit/subsistence credit needs of the poor and provide for sustainable livelihoods. Linking credit with enterprises/livelihoods finance is a new focus area. Through the program, there are few opportunities for long-term loans, and there are very few investments in product development. Within microfinance, it is largely microcredit services that the poor are being offered. Large population of the poor is not covered by any microinsurance product. Although both NABARD and SIDBI have assigned allocations for capacity building, these are released in driblets and are far short of the requirements for upscaling the program.

Impact

There are very few studies that empirically support the claim that microfinance is helping the poor in asset acquisition and moving out of poverty. However, the big contribution of the sector has been the organization of the poor, particularly women, to access critical financial services. Since 90% of the SHG members are women, the program has had an impact not just in economic terms, but also in terms of the improvement in social indicators, resulting in double bottom lines. Empirical evidence shows that the mobility of women associated with the microfinance programs has increased, resulting in greater awareness and confidence amongst them. An impact assessment of CARE's microfinance program 'CASHE' demonstrates that microfinance program results in better health and nutrition, greater role of women in household decision-making, and their empowerment to contribute to the community decision-making process. With women having access to financial resources, they also influence critical decisions like sending the girl child to school. The households have also been able to report higher levels of assets, though the change from the baseline is only marginal. Overall, microfinance clearly is a path towards empowering the most marginalized among the poor to take charge of their lifecycle-related requirements. Through microfinance, they are better positioned to access not only financial services, but also resources, markets, and their entitlements. While microfinance is looked upon as a financially viable approach to address economic vulnerability, more importantly, it has demonstrated the potential of building the social capital of the poorest communities.

(Vipin Sharma is Program Director, Microfinance in CARE India for the last six years. He comes with a diverse and extensive experience of about twenty-four years in the areas of policy formulation, coordination, networking with national/international partner agencies, and building strategic linkages at various levels in the government and the development sector. He is a member of the UNIDO supported think-tank on cluster development; member of the Governing Board of Sa-Dhan, the national network of MFIs in India; and is a part of the Regional Leadership team of CARE in Asia.)

Notes

1. SHGs are the primary affinity groups of 15-20 rural poor women who come together on weekly/fortnightly/ monthly-basis to save and borrow loans from banks and to rotate these among their members for petty and emergent purposes.
2. In 1969, 19 banks were nationalized, with 6 more in 1974.
3. Integrated Rural Development Program was initiated by the Government of India in 1972 as a large national poverty alleviation program in which the poor were provided with income-generating assets through a mix of subsidy from the government and loans from banks.

9

E-Choupal: Transforming Rural India through Technology

Nadarajan Gayatri Devi

Technology has a key role to play in the bridging the rural-urban gap, and ITC's 'e-Choupal' model presents a powerful demonstration of how technology can be harnessed to uplift the rural sector. This article discusses the various features of the e-Choupal model, and how it is empowering rural India.

"A quiet digital revolution is reshaping the lives of farmers in remote Indian villages. In these villages, farmers grow soyabeans, wheat and coffee in small plots of land, as they have for thousands of years. A typical village has no reliable electricity and has antiquated telephone lines. The farmers are largely illiterate and have never seen a computer. But farmers in these villages are conducting e-business through an initiative called e-Choupal, created by ITC, one of India's largest consumer product and agribusiness companies."

– Mohanbir Sawhney, McCormick Tribune Professor of Technology, Kellogg School of Management, USA.[1]

Source: The Icfai Knowledge Centre. Originally published as "ITC: Rural Transformation through Technology."

"ITC wants to create a high-quality low-cost fulfillment channel for rural India. The e-Choupal was the first step in the last mile towards complete backward integration. But it's also the first mile on a new information highway around which multiple suppliers and buyers can converge. It is transformational in its implications and can make a huge contribution towards rural well-being."

– Y C Deveshwar, Chairman, ITC.[2]

Introduction

Towards the end of 2004, the cigarette and tobacco giant ITC set up its first rural shopping mall Choupal Sagar in Rafiqganj, a small village about four kilometres from Sehore town in Madhya Pradesh, India. The mall stood on an eight-acre plot with a shopping area of 7,000 square feet. Along with soaps, detergents and toothpaste, Choupal Sagar sold almost everything from television sets, pressure cookers, room heaters, watches, sewing machines, and grinders to motorbikes and even tractors. There were other unique services like a fuel pump for which ITC tied-up with Bharat Petroleum Corporation Limited (BPCL), a cafeteria, a primary healthcare facility serviced by a private healthcare service provider and banking facilities. The ITC management preferred to call the initiative the 'second layer' of its agri-business model, e-Choupal. Started in 2000, e-Choupal had won several business awards. E-Choupal was perhaps the single largest information technology (IT) – initiative by a corporate entity in rural India.[3]

Background Note

The 'Imperial Tobacco Company of India Limited' was incorporated on August 24, 1910 in Kolkata, India by British American Tobacco (BAT). The name of the company was changed to ITC (Indian Tobacco Company) Limited in 1974 and later 'ITC Limited' (the dots were removed) on September 18, 2001.

The company devoted the first six decades of its existence towards the growth and consolidation of the Cigarettes and Leaf Tobacco businesses. The Packaging and Printing Business Division was set up in 1925 as a backward integration for the Cigarettes business. In 1975, ITC ventured into the Hotels business with the acquisition of a hotel in Chennai which was rechristened 'ITC-Welcomgroup Hotel Chola'. ITC chose the hotels business for its potential to earn high levels of foreign exchange. Since then ITC's hotels business had grown to occupy a position of leadership, with 66 owned and managed properties spread across India. The company also had a marketing and reservation arrangement with the Sheraton Corporation, the reputed international hotel chain.

In 1979, ITC entered the Paperboards business by promoting ITC Bhadrachalam Paperboards Limited. Bhadrachalam Paperboards was merged with the company effective March 13, 2002 and became a division of the company. In 1990, ITC acquired Tribeni Tissues Limited, a specialty paper manufacturing company and a major supplier of tissue paper to the cigarette industry. The merged entity was named the Tribeni Tissues Division (TTD). TTD was merged with the Bhadrachalam Paperboards Division to form the Paperboards and Specialty Papers Division in November 2002.

In 1990, ITC set up the International Business Division (IBD) for export of agricultural commodities. By 2005, the division contributed over 60% of the ITC group's total foreign exchange earnings. ITC-IBD dealt in agricultural commodities like:

- Feed Ingredients – Soyameal, rapeseed meal;
- Food grains – Rice, wheat and wheat products, pulses;
- Coffee;
- Black pepper;
- Edible nuts;
- Marine products – Shrimps and prawns;
- Processed fruits – Mango, papaya and guava products.

In 2000, ITC's Packaging and Printing business launched a line of greeting cards under the brand name 'Expressions'. In 2002, the product range was enlarged with the introduction of gift wrappers and autograph books. In the same year, ITC also launched 'Expressions Matrubhasha', a vernacular range of greeting cards in eight languages and 'Expressions Paperkraft', a range of stationery products. In 2003, the company rolled out 'Classmates' notebooks in the school stationery segment.

Meanwhile, ITC established a nationwide retailing presence in 2000, through its Wills Lifestyle chain of exclusive specialty stores. Beginning with its initial offering of 'Wills Sport' relaxed wear in July 2000, it expanded its basket of offerings to the premium consumer with 'Wills Classic' formal wear and 'Wills Clublife' evening wear. With a distinctive presence across segments at the premium end, ITC also made a foray into the popular segment with its men's wear brand 'John Players' in 2002.

In August 2001, ITC entered the packaged foods business with the launch of the 'Kitchens of India' brand. In 2002, ITC launched 'Candyman' in the confectionery and 'Aashirvaad atta' (wheat flour) in the staples food segments. In 2003, 'Sunfeast' biscuits were launched. Later, the 'Aashirvaad' brand was extended to ready-to-eat foods, ready-to-cook pastes and salt.

In 2002, ITC began marketing popular safety matches brands like iKno, Mangal Deep, VaxLit, Delite and Aim. In 2003, ITC forayed into the marketing of incense sticks. Its brands included Spriha and Mangal Deep across a range of fragrances like rose, jasmine, sandalwood etc.

Genesis of e-Choupal

One day in 1999, ITC Chairman Y C Deveshwar (Deveshwar) was closeted with some of his key managers in the company's headquarters, Virginia House in Kolkata to discuss the slow growth of the company's International Business Division (IBD). In the financial year 1998–99, IBD, one of India's largest exporters of agricultural produce, (including soya, wheat, sesame, pepper, shrimp, and coffee) had generated Rs.450 crores in agricultural commodities sales, compared to the Rs.7701 crores of sales generated by ITC's other divisions.

India's archaic laws regarding agriculture and a legacy of fragmented land holdings made this business a difficult one to manage. It was replete with inefficiencies, middlemen, and logistical problems. Deveshwar suggested to one of ITC's young managers and the CEO of IBD, S Sivakumar that a new business model was the need of the hour.

While sourcing soya in the central Indian state of Madhya Pradesh, the IBD team experienced first hand the various difficulties involved. Conventionally, a farmer sold his produce to a small trader called the 'kaccha adat' who in turn sold it to a larger trader called the 'pakka adat'. From there, the produce found its way to the local mandi[4] where it was auctioned. The Agricultural Products Marketing Act[5] had created mandis to enable an equitable distribution of the gains from agriculture among producers and traders. The mandi played a key role, and acted as a delivery point where farmers brought produce for sale to traders.

In the soya growing areas of Madhya Pradesh, a mandi on average served around 700 square kilometers. With traditional grains, large portions were used by the farmers or bartered for different crops. Since soya was not native to the Indian palate, its major market was the crushing plant. This made the mandi a critical part of the soya chain. At the mandi, a government appointed bidder valued the produce and set the initial bid after which government licensed buyers called Commission Agents (CAs) bid upwards until the crop was sold. ITC contracted with a specific CA in each mandi to bid on behalf of the company.

There were many disadvantages with the mandi system. The CA would pay the farmer a low price and sell the produce to ITC at the market price. The farmers who had no proper storage facilities to store the soyabeans had no option but to accept the CA's price offer. After a CA won an auction, the farmer took the produce to the concerned CA's shop at the mandi to be weighed on a manually operated balance scale, which was often manipulated. Once the produce was weighed, the CAs paid the farmers. Sometimes, in case of small mandis, the farmers were even paid after an unofficial credit period. Once the transaction was complete, the CA brought the produce to ITC's processing facility where the company paid for the produce. For ITC, the procurement costs went as high as Rs.700 per tonne of soya.[6]

The idea of e-Choupal – a hybrid word ITC created combining the e of e-business with choupal, the Hindi word for a village gathering place – flowed logically from the need to re-engineer the supply chain for ITC's benefit as well as the farmers, who invariably were at the receiving end.[7] ITC realized it could not do away with intermediaries because each of them performed a valuable function. While one aggregated the produce, another took care of logistics etc. ITC realized that the solution to the problem lay in empowering farmers with information.[8]

In June 2000, ITC decided to implement its new Internet enabled model at Misrod, a village in Madhya Pradesh, with a population of 3000. An Internet kiosk enabled the village population to access the World Wide Web and visit the IBD portal soyachoupal.com (available in Hindi and Marathi). Each e-Choupal was equipped with a PC with Internet connectivity, printer and UPS (Uninterrupted Power Supply). In case the power supply was erratic, a solar panel was provided. Where Internet connectivity was not up to the mark, a VSAT[9] connection was provided along with another solar panel.

Before the e-Choupals, trading outside the mandi was not possible. The government had restricted agricultural transactions to mandis to prevent exploitation of the farmers. Open auctions were considered the best way of protecting the interests of farmers. ITC had to sell the potential benefits of the e-Choupal to the government. The transparency of the soya choupal website which enabled the government to cross check ITC's prices at any time helped in convincing the government to amend the Agricultural Produce Marketing Act to legalize agricultural transactions outside the mandi.

The Sanchalak

ITC placed the computer at the house of a lead farmer called the 'sanchalak'. The sanchalak who was trained to use the computer, helped farmers readily access the portal and learn online the best farm practices; the prevailing prices and price trends for the crop in the Indian and world markets, the intricacies of risk management; and the local weather forecast. Local agricultural universities, state meteorological departments, banks, and technical analysts were the sources of this information and knowledge. A team from ITC ensured that the content was relevant and updated. Access to this information was absolutely free of cost to any interested farmer.[10]

The sanchalak was also trained by ITC to assess the quality of the crop and provided moisture meters and other tools to measure quality. The portal soyachoupal.com gave information about the prices for best quality beans. When farmers brought in samples, the sanchalak was in a position to price the crop based on its degree of variance with the best quality sample. Farmers then took their produce to the ITC collection centres. The sanchalak who was responsible for driving the farmers to the collection centres was paid a commission of 0.5% for each tonne of soyabean originating from his choupal[11].

The Samyojak

ITC also had the task of dealing with the Commission Agents (CAs) who had been very powerful till then as they controlled information on prices. The e-Choupal model understandably had upset them. ITC envisaged a new role for the CAs. ITC mandated that CAs, who represented the company in the respective mandis, become coordinators called samyojaks for the e-Choupals set up in their areas. These samyojaks used their ties in the villages to nominate sanchalaks. They looked after the warehouses attached to the company's processing facilities where the soyabean purchased from the farmers was stored. They took care of cash disbursements to the farmers. They were also responsible for aggregating the produce bought from far off villages and bringing the same to the company.

Before e-Choupal, the farmers were a harassed lot, dependent on others in the value chain for price information, receiving poor treatment at the mandi (sometimes waiting for days before their produce could be sold) and realizing only 70 to 75% of the end prices. e-Choupals changed the way farmers conducted business. Farmers could trust the e-Choupal because they could see for themselves the prices being offered on the computer screen. The portal carried the mandi prices across the state fed in daily by the samyojaks. Along with the information on prices available at the ITC hub, the farmer was able to take a better decision. He could compare the costs associated with transporting his crop to the mandi and the price he would get for his beans. The benefit of the published prices offered by ITC versus the uncertainty at the mandi, made a lot of farmers shift from the mandi to the ITC hubs. An additional attraction was that ITC offered to reimburse the cost of transporting the soyabeans to the company's hub.

At ITC's processing centres, the layout was designed such that waiting times were reduced to two hours. Material handling systems ensured that tractors, trucks or trolleys could directly unload the produce without spilling a single grain. A modern weighbridge ensured precise weighing and the farmer got his payment in less than ten minutes. Besides, tests were done on the produce to assess quality standards across the choupals. Based on the test results, the concerned sanchalak was counseled, who in turn advised his community to improve the yield and quality standards.

For ITC, apart from the cost savings, there was another benefit of buying directly from farmers. Because farmers were less likely to mix impurities than middlemen, the company could source produce of a far better quality. Consequently, ITC commanded a higher price in the international market.

Wanting to scale up the project, ITC did a cost benefit analysis. On an average it cost around Rs.40,000 to set up a basic e-Choupal. In villages where telephone connectivity was very poor, ITC had to invest in VSATs, which hiked the cost to around Rs.1,00,000.[12] ITC believed that it could recoup its investments in 18 months, i.e., three sowing seasons. With such a cost benefit ratio, ITC decided to extend e-Choupal to the entire state of Madhya Pradesh.

Scaling up e-Choupal

ITC realized that soyabean was only a five million tonne crop in Madhya Pradesh while wheat in Uttar Pradesh (UP) was 14 times bigger. The company knew that if it had to be a player of long-term consequence it would have to enter the wheat business. But replicating the soya model for wheat was not easy. With soya, ITC could bring down costs from Rs.700 per tonne to around Rs.300 per tonne. In case of wheat, the company could only generate savings between Rs.55 to Rs.65 per tonne.[13] ITC realized that generating adequate returns would be a challenging task.

Farmers grew wheat of varying grades. Though these grades had the potential to meet diverse consumer preferences, the benefits never trickled down to the farmers, because all varieties were aggregated as one average quality in the mandis. Moreover, the high quality wheat that went into the making of bread and biscuits was available only in limited quantities. The other issue was that people's preferences for atta (wheat flour) varied depending on the region. The problem of inconsistent quality, had to be tackled at the source. If the wheat could be segregated at the origin, ITC could sell wheat that met the specifications of institutional buyers like McDonald's or Britannia. ITC itself could sell its Aashirvaad atta at various price points depending on the quality.

In the early 2000s, ITC began setting up e-Choupals across UP. ITC also introduced a new storage and handling system that helped preserve the identity of different varieties through the supply chain. ITC also scaled up its e-Choupal initiative to shrimp farming in Andhra Pradesh (AP) and coffee plantations in Karnataka. Aqua farmers suffered from contaminated soil, high levels of salinity in the water and killer viruses, any of which could wipe out an entire shrimp crop. ITC's aquachoupal site provided them the support and the knowledge to manage such risks. ITC also had a laboratory at Kakinada in AP that helped farmers detect the deadly 'White Spot' virus in the shrimp seed. Through the website, farmers could keep abreast of food safety norms to compete in the international market. These included parameters for antibiotic usage, hygienic washing, sanitized dressing and airtight packing.

Coffee planters in India had always been tossed between the highs and lows of the international coffee market. The information needed to manage risks in the volatile global coffee market, price updates and prevalent trends in coffee trading was not available to them. The launch of ITC's plantersnet.com in 2001 provided relevant information to India's coffee planters on:

- Prices of coffee (even as they were being traded) and news affecting those prices;
- Parity charts and technical analysis to help planters understand the logic behind price relationships and trends;
- Risk management tools to manage the price risk inherent in coffee a volatile commodity;
- Financing schemes against coffee stocks to supplement a planter's cash flow needs.

Tradersnet, a special link on the site, brought together a large number of coffee planters, traders and roasters, creating a virtual market for transparent price discovery.[14]

Selling through the e-Choupal Network

In the words of Y C Deveshwar, the Chairman of ITC,

> *"With the choupal infrastructure in place, we are hoping to create a system that allows a two-way flow of products and services to the rural economy".*[15]

With its infrastructure in place, ITC realized it made sense to expand the scope of activities. In Madhya Pradesh for instance, ITC tied up with Monsanto to sell high yielding seed varieties to farmers. ITC reckoned that it could sell a range of products from Fast Moving Consumer Goods (FMCG) to consumer durables through the network.

ITC planned to invite other companies to sell through the company's network. Not only was there an established infrastructure but also the sanchalaks being the closest link to the consumer, had the potential to pick up rural market signals first and transmit them back to the distribution channel. Thus came the idea of entering rural retailing in 2004.

ITC had already established a two-tier selling network where the sanchalak and samyojak played an important role. Farmers could buy fertilizers, seeds, herbicides, soyabean oil and other things from the company directly. After aggregating demand for products through orders placed by his neighbours, the sanchalak emailed the order to ITC. The items were either picked up by him at the ITC warehousing hub, or delivered by the samyojak at the village. The sanchalak then collected cash payments from his neighbours and remitted them to ITC.

The second tier did not involve any prior orders. Instead, the sanchalaks bought products based on estimated demand and stocked them in their homes. They were later sold to both the local grocer and village households. This system was most effective for consumer goods such as salt, matchboxes, soyabean oil, and confectionery items. So ITC brands like Aashirvaad salt and atta, Candyman and Minto confectionery, and Aim matchboxes were sold through this route.[16]

The last and also the most visible tier ITC wanted to add involved getting farmers to go 'shopping' outside their villages. ITC observed that every time sanchalaks and farmers visited its soybean factories in Madhya Pradesh to sell their produce, they also had the opportunity to spend their freshly earned cash. Encouraged by its image as a fair and reliable buyer of farm produce, ITC decided to invest in five acre malls, costing between Rs.3-5 crore each, across 15 states.

The company launched its first rural hypermarket at Sehore in Madhya Pradesh in August 2004. The initial response—footfall of about 700-800 people on weekdays and soaring to 1,000 on weekends with conversion levels of 35% was encouraging. ITC planned to open about 50 such stores, spread across rural Madhya Pradesh and Uttar Pradesh by the end of 2005. S Sivakumar, CEO, ITC – IBD commented on how ITC's rural distribution plans were different from that of other FMCG companies,

> *"The per capita income in rural India is just a fourth of that of urban India. In this context, there are two differences between the rural marketing infrastructure being created by ITC e-Choupal and the distribution channels of other FMCG companies. Firstly, unlike the traditional approach of engaging in competitive marketing, namely competing for a larger share of the same small wallet, ITC e-Choupal first enhances the incomes in rural India and then serves those consumers with appropriate products and services. Secondly, unlike the distribution channel of a typical FMCG company, ITC e-Choupal infrastructure carries the products of several companies besides ITC's. This enables active distribution right into the remote villages with less than 2000 people also, by amortizing costs across multiple companies. Given the expensive last mile, traditionally FMCG companies distributed products up to the feeder market towns only, which then served as passive wholesale channel"*[17].

Looking Ahead

E-Choupal's performance had been heartening for ITC. Farmers had seen a rise in their income levels because of higher yields, improved quality and reduced transaction costs. But ITC realized there were some challenges in scaling up:

- Developing entrepreneurial capacity among the rural community to take up the role of *sanchalaks* and *samyojaks* was difficult and required a lot of training. Also, there was a need to enhance the management capacity of ITC frontline by developing a new cadre of agricultural graduates.
- Lack of infrastructure, such as power and broadband in the villages.
- Slow policy reform (e.g., modification of the Agricultural Produce Marketing Act).

Was ITC's rural retailing model sustainable in the long run? A rural customer base was not just the number of villages multiplied by their population. The economic health of the area was a major factor. Unless malls were located in high-income agricultural zones, profits would not come soon. Industry watchers were also skeptic about once-in-a-while purchases like motorcycles and tractors because villagers would not mind going to the nearest big town for such purchases. This would be because ITC's offering would include just a couple of brands.

But ITC was confident that its formula would work. By 2005, 60 companies, including the likes of Nagarjuna Fertilizers, Monsanto, Eicher, TVS Motor, Hero Cycles, LIC (Life Insurance Corporation) and ICICI Prudential sold their products through the e-Choupal network. ITC earned a commission of anything between 3% and 40% on these. ITC was adding 7 new e-Choupals a day and planned to scale up to 20,000 by 2010 covering 100,000 villages in 15 states, servicing 25 million farmers. Transactions through the e-choupals were expected to rise to about US $2.5 billion by 2010[18].

(Nadarajan Gayatri Devi is a Faculty Associate at Icfai Knowledge Center (IKC), Hyderabad (India).)

Notes

1. *www.itcportal.com.*
2. Nidhi Nath, Srinivas. "The village people," *The Economic Times- Brand Equity*, 14th January 2004.
3. "Farmers e-nabled – Markets not antipathic to masses," *The Economic Times- Editorial*, 26th May 2004.
4. Mandi was a government mandated market yard.
5. The marketing of agricultural produce was one of the critical areas where the farmers were exploited. Each State Government enacted its own Agricultural Produce Marketing Committee Act to cover the marketing arrangements in the state. The marketing committees were autonomous entities representing growers, traders and local authorities. The government had a supervisory role to ensure that the market regulations are implemented properly. The objectives of the Act were: the creation of market areas and markets to ensure fair transactions; prohibition of collection of excess charges; the regulation of market prices; the licensing of market functionaries; and the dissemination and display of market information, *www.macroscan.com.*
6. Charles, Assisi and Indrajit, Gupta. "ITC's rural symphony," *www.businessworldindia.com,* 20th January 2003.

7. Indrajit, Gupta and Rajshekhar, M. "ITC vs HLL," *www.businessworldindia.com,* 2nd May 2005.
8. ibid.
9. Very Small Aperture Terminal. An earth station, used for the reliable transmission of data, video, or voice via geo-stationary satellite, with a relatively small dish-antenna (often 2.4m or 3.8m in diameter).
10. *www.worldbank.org.*
11. Charles, Assisi and Indrajit, Gupta. "ITC's rural symphony," *www.businessworldindia.com,* 20th January 2003.
12. ibid.
13. ibid.
14. *www.itcportal.com.*
15. Nidhi Nath, Srinivas. "The village people," *The Economic Times- Brand Equity,* 14th January 2004.
16. ibid.
17. In an email interview with Manas and Ravikanth of GITAM Institute of Foreign Trade, *www.indiainfoline.com.*
18. Moinik, Mitra. "Distribution's disruptive duo," *Business Today,* 18th January 2004.

Bibliography

1. Mohan, Padmanabhan. "ITC's drive for rural farm growth gets good response," *www.blonnet.com,* 2nd July 2002.
2. Charles, Assisi and Indrajit, Gupta. "ITC's rural symphony," *www.businessworldindia.com,* 20th January 2003.
3. Kuttayan, Annamalai and Sachin, Rao. "What works: ITC's eChoupal and profitable rural transformation," *www.bus.umich.edu,* August 2003.
4. Upton, David M and Fuller, Virginia A. "The ITC eChoupal initiative," *www.hbsp.harvard.edu,* January 2004.
5. Nidhi Nath, Srinivas. "The village people," *The Economic Times- Brand Equity,* 14th January 2004.
6. Moinik, Mitra. "Distribution's disruptive duo," *Business Today,* Issue 18th January 2004.
7. "Farmers e-nabled – Markets not antipathic to masses," *The Economic Times- Editorial,* 26th May 2004.
8. Rohit, Saran. "Call of the countryside," *India Today,* 11th December 2004, p-50.
9. Mohammed, Shaukat H. "ITC e-Choupals to touch more loves," *www.asianage.com,* 11th April 2005.

10. Indrajit, Gupta and Rajshekhar, M. "ITC vs HLL," *www.businessworldindia.com,* 2nd May 2005.
11. Sambit, Saha, "ITC hold out mall hope for villagers," *www.telegraph.co.uk,* 4th July 2005.
12. *www.iimahd.ernet.in*
13. *www.indiainfoline.com.*
14. *www.worldbank.org*
15. *www.itcportal.com*

Exhibit 1: Financial Performance of ITC over Ten Years

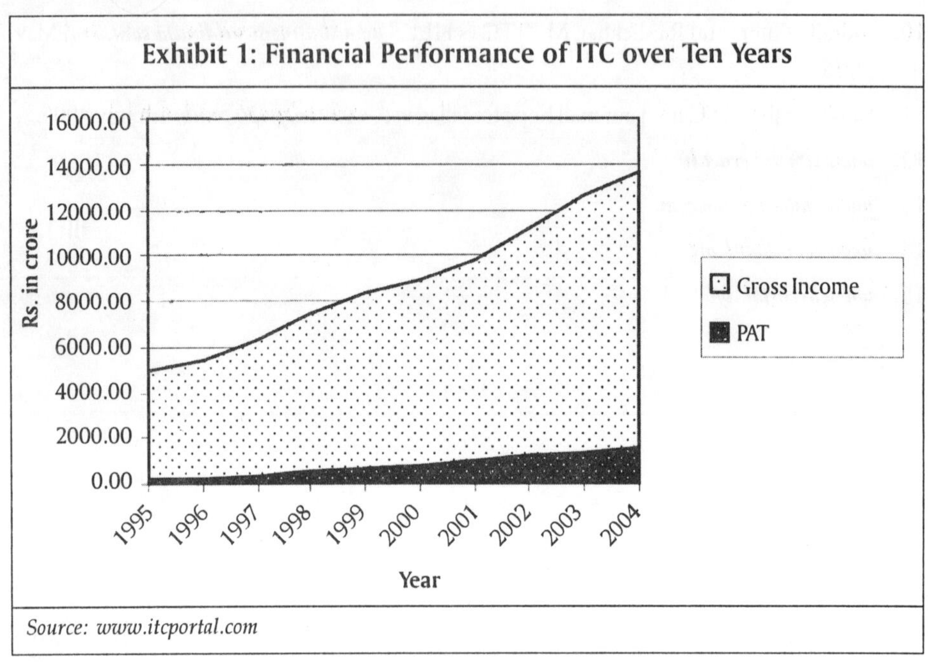

16000.00
14000.00
12000.00
10000.00
8000.00
6000.00
4000.00
2000.00
0.00
Rs. in crore
1995
1996
1997
1998
1999
2000
2001
2002
2003
2004
Year
Gross Income
PAT

Source: www.itcportal.com

Exhibit 2: Market Capitalization over Ten Years

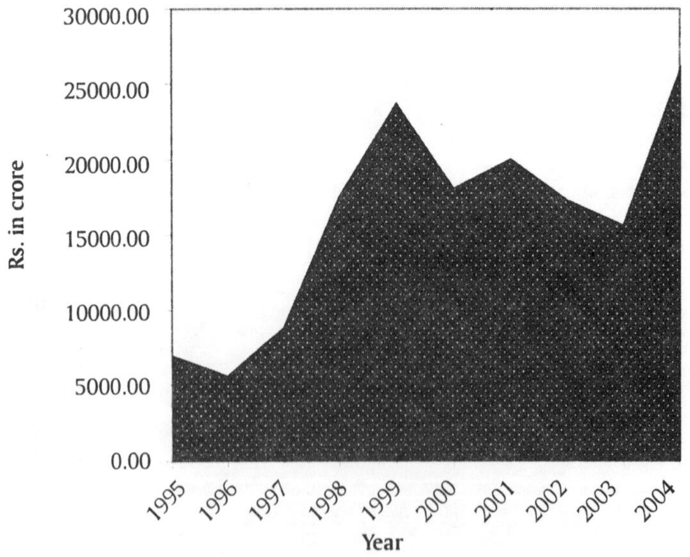

30000.00
25000.00
20000.00
15000.00
10000.00
5000.00
0.00
Rs. in crore
1995
1996
1997
1998
1999
2000
2001
2002
2003
2004
Year

Source: www.itcportal.com

Exhibit 3: E-Choupal at Work

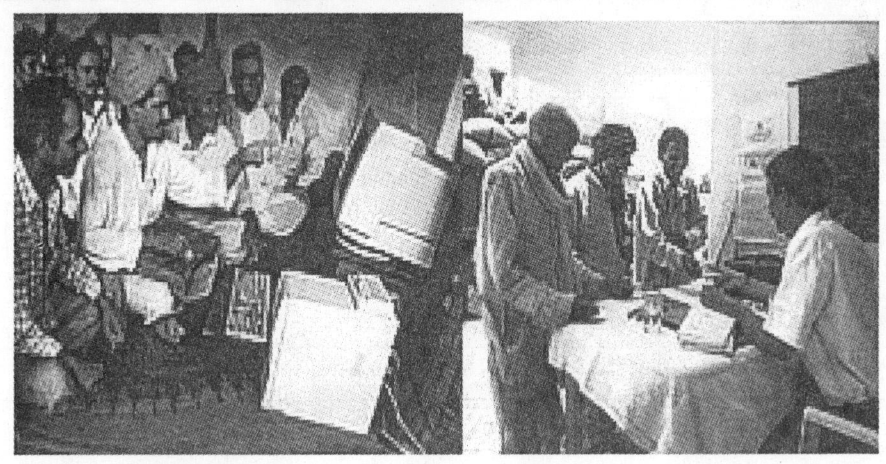

Source: www.itcportal.com

Exhibit 4: ITC's Rural Hypermarket – Choupal Sagar

Source: www.itcportal.com

Exhibit 5: Traditional Soyabean Supply Chain

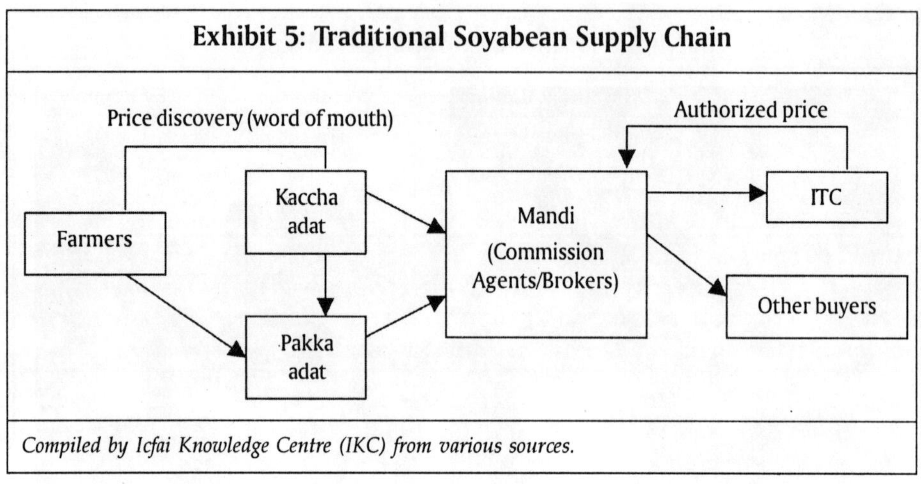

Compiled by Icfai Knowledge Centre (IKC) from various sources.

Exhibit 6: Re-engineered Supply Chain via E-Choupal

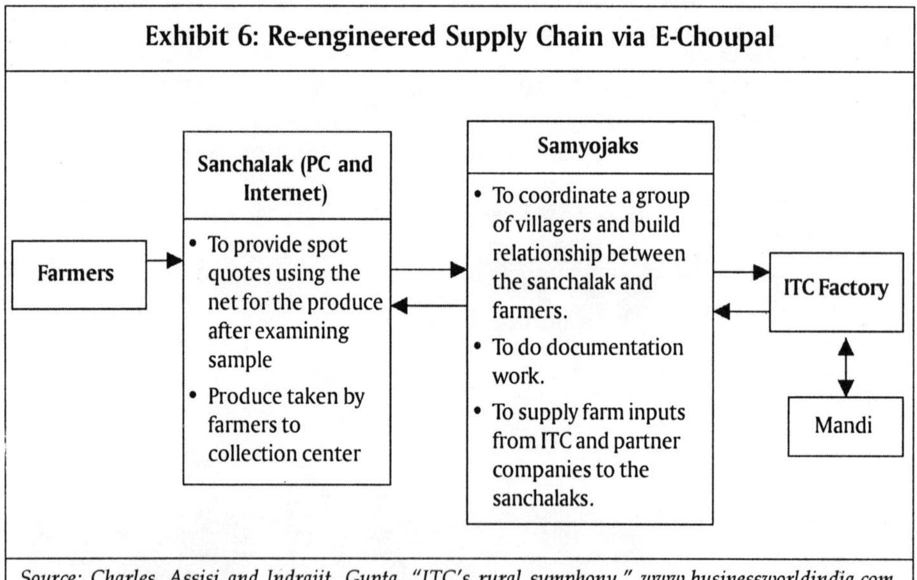

Source: Charles, Assisi and Indrajit, Gupta. "ITC's rural symphony," www.businessworldindia.com, 20th January 2003.

Exhibit 7: How E-Choupal Saved Costs

	Soyabean Trading	Mandi	E-Choupal
Cost incurred by farmer (Rs./tonne)	Trolley freight	120.00	120.00
	Labour	50.00	Nil
	Middlemen	150.00	Nil
	Handling loss	50.00	Nil
	Total	**370.00**	**120.00**
Cost incurred by processor (Rs./tonne)	Commission	100.00	50.00
	Gunny bags	75.00	75.00
	Freight to factory	120.00	Nil
	Storage and handling	40.00	40.00
	Disbursement cost	Nil	50.00
	Total	**335.00**	**215.00**
	Total chain	**705.00**	**335.00**

By shifting to e-Choupal farmers saved 68% of the costs and the processor about 36%.

Source: Rohit, Saran. "Call of the countryside," India Today, 11th December 2004, p-50.

Exhibit 8: E-Choupal at a Glance

Commencement of initiative – 2000

- States covered: 6 (Madhya Pradesh, Uttar Pradesh, Maharashtra, Andhra Pradesh, Rajasthan and Karnataka)
- Villages covered: 31,000
- e-Choupal installations: 5200
- Empowered e-farmers: 3.1 million

Agenda for the Decade

- States to be covered: 15
- Villages to be covered: 100,000
- e-Choupals to be installed: 20,000
- Farmers to be e-empowered: 25 million

Source: www.itcportal.com

10

Telemedicine in Rural India

Sanjit Bagchi

Basic health-care still eludes a majority of rural Indians. Although 70% of Indians live in rural areas, more than 75% of Indian doctors are based in cities. Telemedicine promises to be an effective alternative to reach healthcare services to rural areas – it may turn to be the cheapest as well as the fastest way to bridge the rural-urban health divide.

In a developing country such as India, there is huge inequality in healthcare distribution. Although nearly 75% of Indians live in rural villages, more than 75% of Indian doctors are based in cities[1]. Most of the 620 million rural Indians lack access to basic healthcare facilities[2]. The Indian government spends just 0.9% of the country's annual gross domestic product on health, and little of this spending reaches remote rural areas[3]. The poor infrastructure of rural health centers makes it impossible to retain doctors in villages, who feel that they become professionally isolated and outdated if stationed in remote areas.

In addition, poor Indian villagers spend most of their out-of-pocket health expenses on travel to the specialty hospitals in the city and for staying in the city along with their escorts[4]. A recent study conducted by the Indian Institute of Public Opinion found that 89% of rural Indian patients have to travel about 8 km to access basic medical treatment, and the rest have to travel even farther[5].

Can Telemedicine Bridge the Divide?

Telemedicine may turn out to be the cheapest, as well as the fastest, way to bridge the rural–urban health divide. Taking into account India's huge strides in the field of information and communication technology, telemedicine could help to bring specialized healthcare to the remotest corners of the country.[6,7]

The efficacy of telemedicine has already been shown through the network established by the Indian Space Research Organization (ISRO), which has connected 22 super-specialty hospitals with 78 rural and remote hospitals across the country through its geo-stationary satellites. This network has enabled thousands of patients in remote places such as Jammu and Kashmir, Andaman and Nicobar Islands, the Lakshadweep Islands, and tribal areas of the central and northeastern regions of India to gain access to consultations with experts in super-specialty medical institutions[8]. ISRO has also provided connectivity for mobile telemedicine units in villages, particularly in the areas of community health and ophthalmology[9].

A Telemedicine Program in Action at the Apollo Gleneagles Hospital, Kolkata, India

Photo: Nilmoni Debnath/Apollo Gleneagles Hospital.

This encouraging early success in reaching patients—together with recent technological advances in India, such as the proliferation of fiber optic cables, the expanding bandwidth, and the licensing of private Internet service providers—has encouraged ISRO to set up an exclusive satellite, called HealthSAT, to bring telemedicine to the poor on a larger scale. The proposed satellite would not only serve remote areas of India but also those in other poor countries in Asia and Africa. In the government of India's current budget, INR102.8 billion has been allocated for health[10]. HealthSAT is expected to cost only about 1% of this budget, that is, between INR600 million to INR1 billion. Each receiving terminal (where patients and rural doctors are present for audiovisual conferences) in the villages is expected to cost only about INR0.5 million[11]. This telemedicine service will save some costs, for example the money that patients would have spent on travel and accommodation.

A telemedicine system in a small health centre consists of a personal computer with customized medical software connected to a few medical diagnostic instruments, such as an ECG or X-ray machine or an X-ray scanner for scanning X-ray photos[12]. Through this computer, digitized versions of patients' medical images and diagnostic details (such as X-ray images and blood test reports) are dispatched to specialist doctors through the satellite-based communication link. The information, in turn, is received at the specialist centre where experienced doctors examine the reports, diagnose, interact with the patients (along with local doctors), and suggest appropriate treatment through video-conferencing. The entire system is relatively user-friendly, and only a short period of training is needed for doctors at super-specialty centres and rural health centres to handle the system. And hospital technicians can take care of the operation and maintenance of the equipment.

M N Sathyanarayan, Executive Director of Space Industries Development, and organising secretary of the 2005 International Telemedicine Conference, said: "In the pilot phase of the telemedicine project, ISRO is providing telemedicine equipment as well as making available the required bandwidth on INSAT satellites. The main criteria for funding by ISRO are that the hospitals have to be government-run—state or central—or belong to public sector industries. The hospitals have to provide infrastructure as well as doctors and technicians for operating the system."

"ISRO also provides the equipment and bandwidth to private specialty hospitals and hospitals run by Trusts, if these hospitals provide free service, including specialty consultation to rural hospitals that have been connected in the telemedicine network of ISRO. These hospitals have to provide follow-up treatment to teleconsulted patients at government rates."

In its telemedicine initiative, ISRO intends to connect different types of Indian healthcare centers in a series of phases. L S Sathyamurthy, Programme Director of Telemedicine at ISRO said: "There are 650 district hospitals, 3,000 taluk [subdistrict] hospitals, and more than 23,000 primary health centers in the country. We must aim to connect all these in phases—first the district hospital connected to speciality hospitals in major cities, then the taluk-level hospitals, and finally the primary health centers, so that nobody, irrespective of his location, is deprived of lifesaving specialty consultation." When the network grows, it may even include private hospitals as well as hospitals in Asia and Africa. Although the network will initially be used for teleconsultation and postoperative consultation, in the future it may accommodate even telesurgery and telerobotics.

The Impact So Far

Starting with pilot projects in the year 2001, together with a "proof-of-concept" technology demonstration, ISRO has established the facility in nearly 60 remote hospitals, which have been connected with 20 super-specialty city hospitals.[13] A report presented at the Rajya Sabha (the House of States, or Upper House) of the Parliament of India suggested that the initial results of India's telemedicine initiative are encouraging.[14] The report states that several telemedicine projects in India have been successfully interlinked—for example, the Andaman and Nicobar Islands telemedicine project links the G B Pant Hospital at Port Blair with Shri Ramachandra Medical College and Research Institute, Chennai, while in Karnataka, Narayana Hrudayalaya is connected to District Hospital, Chamarajnagar and Vivekananda Memorial Hospital, Saragur.

> *"There are inevitable difficulties associated with the introduction of new systems and technologies."*

Adding to these early reports of successful linkage, there are also reports that telemedicine has helped to save lives in crowded pilgrimage centres and military outposts connected with mobile telemedicine units. For example, the Amrita Telemedicine Programme reports that on 13 January 2003, the programme's first remote telesurgery procedure was performed.[15] The Amrita Emergency Care Unit at Pampa was able to save the life of a pilgrim by a telesurgical procedure using the local telemedicine facility. The cardiothoracic surgeon guided the procedure remotely, and the pediatric cardiologist at Pampa performed the procedure. Mobile telemedicine units were also rushed to the coasts and islands of India after the 2004 tsunami to provide medical consultation and relief to the affected people[16].

There are other indications that the telemedicine initiative may have had a positive impact. ISRO's annual report for 2004–2005 states: "More than 25,000 patients have so far been provided with teleconsultation and treatment. An impact study conducted on a thousand patients has revealed that there is a significant cost saving in the system since the patients avoid expenses towards travel, stay, and for treatment at the hospitals in the cities".[8] Dr. Devi Shetty, a cardiac surgeon and the Chairman of Narayan Hrudayalaya, a hospital that has served thousands through telemedicine, said: "We have treated 17,400 patients using telemedicine connectivity in various parts of India, mainly from rural India, and [a] few patients from outside India. We use both satellite as well as ISDN connectivity. Now, with the Indian Space Research Organisation, which is our associate in this project giving us the satellite connection free of cost, we have a [larger] game plan of offering healthcare to African and other Asian countries."

The Challenges and Controversies

The telemedicine initiative in India has not been free of challenges and controversies. "There are inevitable difficulties associated with the introduction of new systems and technologies," according to Sathyamurthy. "There are some who needlessly fear that they will lose their jobs. Although the systems are user-friendly, there are others who are affected by the fear of the unknown in handling computers and other equipment. There is a feeling that the initial investment is high and hence financially not viable." In addition, there may be technical hitches, such as low bandwidth and lack of interoperability standards for software.

Discussing HealthSAT, Dr. D Lavanian, an Indian expert in telemedicine affiliated with the Apollo Telemedicine Networking Foundation, Apollo Hospitals, Hyderabad, India, said: "[HealthSAT] is excellent, but some questions remain. Presently HealthSAT connectivity is expected to be given free of charge to certain government entities. This is unsatisfactory as a large percentage of healthcare in India is by private entities." Dr. Lavanian added: "On my requesting to ISRO to open up the same to the private health industry, of course for a fee, I have not received any positive answer. This means that a large percentage of the population of India will be denied healthcare via telemedicine."

These difficulties can probably be surmounted. In the late 1980s, when computers came to India, similar kinds of problems were seen in different parts of the country. That is, people showed technophobia and expressed their fears that computers would cause unemployment and would also be prohibitively expensive. But the country overcame these challenges and fears, and eventually became a superpower in the field of knowledge and information technology.[17]

Conclusion

With the aid of HealthSAT, India's telemedicine initiative has the potential to provide specialized healthcare to millions of poor Indians. This potential was well summed up by Dr. Devi Shetty: "In terms of disease management, there is [a] 99% possibility that the person who is unwell does not require [an] operation. If you don't operate you don't need to touch the patient. And if you don't need to touch the patient, you don't need to be there. You can be anywhere, since the decision on healthcare management is based on history and interpretation of images and chemistry… so technically speaking, 99% of healthcare problems can be managed by the doctors staying at a remote place—linked by telemedicine."

(Sanjit Bagchi is a medical practitioner and medical journalist based in Calcutta, India.)

References

1. Agence-France Presse (2005 March 17) India to launch satellite exclusively for telemedicine. Available: *http://servesrilanka.blogspot.com/2005/03/india-to-launch-satellite-exclusively.html*. Accessed 27 January 2006.
2. Krishnakumar A (2003 January 18–31) Healing by wire. Frontline. Available: *http://www.hinduonnet.com/thehindu/thscrip/print.pl?file=20030117007309400.htm&date=fl2001/&prd=fline&*. Accessed 27 January 2006.
3. Rajalakshmi TK (2004 December) India confronts AIDS. Multinational Monitor. Available: *http://multinationalmonitor.org/mm2004/122004/front.html*. Accessed 26 January 2006.

4. Sharma DC (2000) Remote Indian villages to benefit from telemedicine project. Lancet 355: 1529 Available: *http://www.thelancet.com/journals/lancet/article/PIIS0140673605745931/fulltext*. Accessed 22 June 2005. Find this article online.

5. Rao R (2005 May) Taking healthcare to rural areas. i4d. Available: *http://www.i4donline.net/May05/satellitetech.asp*. Accessed 26 January 2006.

6. Ganapathy K (2004) Telemedicine in the Indian context: An overview. Stud Health Technol Inform 104: 178–181. Find this article online.

7. Pal A, Mbarika VW, Cobb-Payton F, Datta P, McCoy S (2005) Telemedicine diffusion in a developing country: The case of India. IEEE Trans Inf Technol Biomed 9: 59–65. Find this article online.

8. Indian Space Research Organization (2005) ISRO Annual Report 2004–2005: Space Applications. Available: *http://www.isro.org/rep2005/SpaceApplications.htm*. Accessed 27 January 2006.

9. The Hindu (2005 July 17) IT-based healthcare systems launched. Available: *http://www.hindu.com/2005/07/17/stories/2005071702321000.htm*. Accessed 27 January 2006.

10. BBC News (2005 February 28) India unveils anti-poverty budget. Available: *http://news.bbc.co.uk/2/hi/business/4303507.stm*. Accessed 27 January 2006.

11. Asian Tribune (2004 February 12) Satellite to enable telemedicine in rural India. Available: *http://www.asiantribune.com/show_news.php?id=9193*. Accessed 27 January 2006.

12. Wootton R (2001) Recent advances: Telemedicine. BMJ 323: 557–560 Available: *http://bmj.bmjjournals.com/cgi/content/full/323/7312/557*. Accessed 27 January 2006. Find this article online.

13. Indian Space Research Organization (2004 November 29) International telemedicine conference to be held in Bangalore [press release]. Available: *http://www.isro.org/pressrelease/Nov29_2004.htm*. Accessed 27 January 2006.

14. Parliament of India (2002) 108th report of action taken by the Department of Space. Available: *http://rajyasabha.nic.in/book2/reports/science/108threport.htm*. Accessed 27 January 2006.

15. Amritanandamayi Devi SM (2005) Telemedicine at Amrita. Available: *http://www.amritapuri.org/health/aims/telemed.php*. Accessed 27 January 2006.

16. Indian Space Research Organization (2005 January 4) Tsunami disaster: ISRO deploys its resources [press release]. Available: *http://www.isro.org/pressrelease/tsunami.htm*. Accessed 27 January 2006.

17. New Scientist.com (2005 February 19) India special: The new knowledge superpower. Available: *http://www.newscientist.com/special/india/mg18524876.800*. Accessed 27 January 2006.

Section IV

Rural-Urban Scenario: Country Profiles

11

The Rural-Urban Divide and the Evolution of Political Economy in China

John Knight, Li Shi and Lina Song

China accounts for about 20% of the world's population, and is the fastest growing economy in the world. Despite the urbanization that goes along with economic development, the rural population in China has grown in absolute terms, and a majority of the country's population lives in rural areas. Considerable disparities exist in rural and urban China with respect to incomes, access to education and healthcare, and housing. This article examines the extent of the rural-urban divide in China, which is extreme; why and how it arose and persists till this day; whether it will be eroded; and views it from a political economy perspective.

1. Introduction

China's is an important economy. It accounts for about 20% of world population and for nearly 20% of the world's poor. Moreover, it is becoming more important. During the period of economic reform – roughly the last 20 years – it has achieved a remarkable rate of economic growth: something like 8% per annum. By comparison with other communist or ex-communist countries, it has so far made

Source: John Knight, Li Shi and Lina Song (2006), 'The rural-urban divide and the evolution of political Economy in China', in James K Boyce, Stephen Cullenberg, Prasanta K Pattanaik and Robert Pollin (eds), Human Development in the Era of Globalization: Essays in Honor of Keith B Griffin, Chapter 2, Cheltenham, UK and Northampton, MA, USA: Edward Elgar, 44-63 (18 pages). Reprinted with permission.

a smooth transition from a planned economy towards a market economy. The Chinese economy presents fascinating challenges to economists, and Keith Griffin was one of the first Western development economists to accept the challenge (for instance, Griffin and Saith, 1981, Griffin and Griffin, 1983).

As a group we first teamed up with Keith Griffin as members of an international project on income distribution in China, which he led with Zhao Renwei. The project was based on a very detailed and representative national household survey, designed by the team. It was an improvement on official surveys because it permitted empirical analysis at the micro (household and individual) levels, and because it used a broader definition of income, including the various forms of payment in kind which were important in China. The main output of the project was the book edited by Griffin and Zhao (1993). One of the most startling figures to emerge from it was the ratio of urban to rural household income per capita, which had a value of no less than 2.4 to 1. Recognising that this rural-urban divide deserved further study, we decided to accept the challenge (Knight and Song, 1999).

There has always been a strong political economy element to Keith Griffin's writings. Our contribution to this festschrift takes its cue from that. The explanation for the rural-urban divide in China – its creation, its maintenance, its ups and downs – requires a political economy approach, complemented in the reform period by the analysis of market forces.

The paper has the following structure. In section 2 we describe the rural-urban divide in China, and in section 3 we attempt to explain it: why and how it came about and has been maintained to this day. In section 4 we pose the question: will the rural-urban divide be eroded? To examine this issue we provide a framework of endogenous government responding to various pressures and interests. In particular, we examine three forces now driving economic policies: rural-urban migration, rising income inequality, and state-owned enterprise reform. The rural-urban divide is a common phenomenon, although China represents an extreme case. Section 5 places China first in empirical perspective and then in theoretical perspective. Section 6 concludes.

2. Describing the Rural-Urban Divide

In 1949 almost 90% of the Chinese population was classified as rural. This census definition of rural and urban corresponds closely to the administrative division. In 1999 the rural population accounted for 69% of the total. Despite the urbanization that goes along with economic development, the rural population has grown in absolute terms and the great majority of Chinese people continue to live in rural areas. Almost all of China's arable land was already in use in 1952, and yet over the next 50 years the rural population was to grow by over 350 million. This growing pressure on the land posed a threat to both rural and urban living standards.

Figure 1 shows rural and urban income, and also consumption, per capita, expressed in constant prices, from 1952 to 2000, taken from official sources. Both rural and urban income rose very slowly until the process of economic reform began in 1978. Figure 2 shows the ratio of urban to rural income, and consumption, per capita over the same period. Throughout the central planning era, the ratios exceeded 2 to 1, and they were particularly high (over 3) in the mid-1950s. The ratios narrowed over the years 1978-1985, when rural economic

Figure 1: Urban and Rural Real Income and Consumption per annum at 1985 Prices

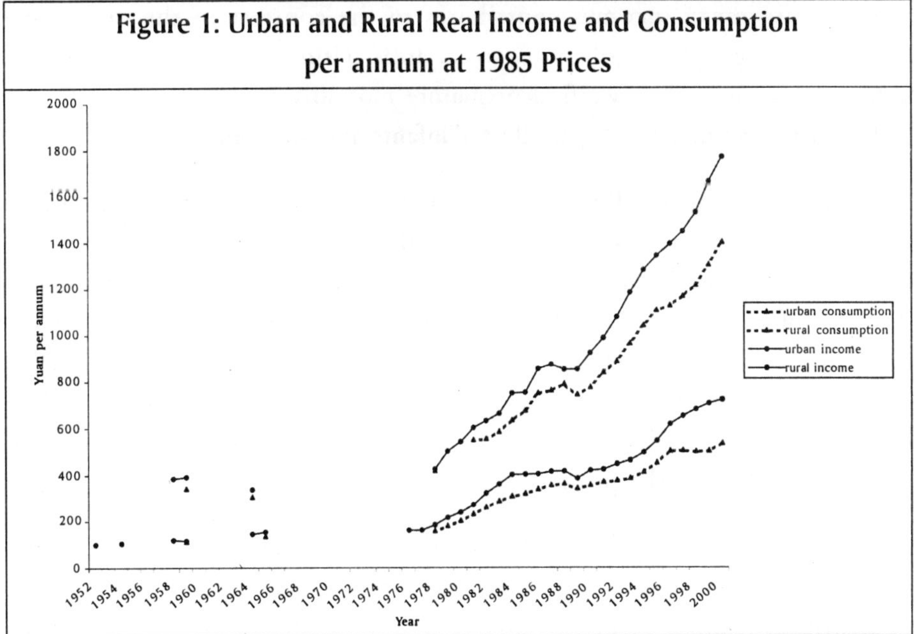

reforms – the disbanding of the communes and the restoration of household production – took place. As urban reforms began and accelerated after 1985, urban incomes grew rapidly. The rural-urban divide actually increased, and in the year 2000 the ratios (2.8 for income and 3.0 for consumption) were higher than they had ever been throughout the economic reform era.

The rural-urban divide is not confined to conventionally measured income. It is apparent also in education, health care and housing (Knight and Song, 1999, chs. 4, 5 and 6 respectively). The most important factor influencing a person's educational attainment, or enrolment, after his age, is whether he lives in a rural or urban area. The standardised mean difference in educational attainment is no less than 4.6 years in favour of urban-dwellers. Moreover, school cost per pupil, public subsidy per pupil, and the average quality of teachers, are all far higher in urban than in rural areas.

There is a considerable gap between urban and rural provision of, and access to, health services. The rural population is at a disadvantage in both quality and quantity of health care. Moreover, urban services are much more heavily subsidised, so that rural people have to pay no less than urban people for health care. Yet the difference in mean incomes contributes to the contrast in the underlying healthiness of people in urban and rural areas. Using the extreme measure of unhealthiness, mortality, we find premature mortality rates to be considerably higher in the countryside, especially for infants and children.

There are too many dimensions, with their valuation problems, to decide whether urban- or rural-dwellers are better off in terms of housing. Urban people live in cramped conditions but the quality of their housing is generally higher than that of peasants. Peasants have to build and improve their own houses, and must do so without the help of mortgages, whereas until recently urban-dwellers have paid only minimal rents and have thus enjoyed heavy subsidies of their housing. The recent sale of much urban housing to occupiers at low prices has effectively capitalised the previous rental subsidies.

Even the addition of education, health and housing to income yields too narrow a concept of well-being. There are also the relative degrees of freedom and of security that different people enjoy. Perhaps the greatest difference between

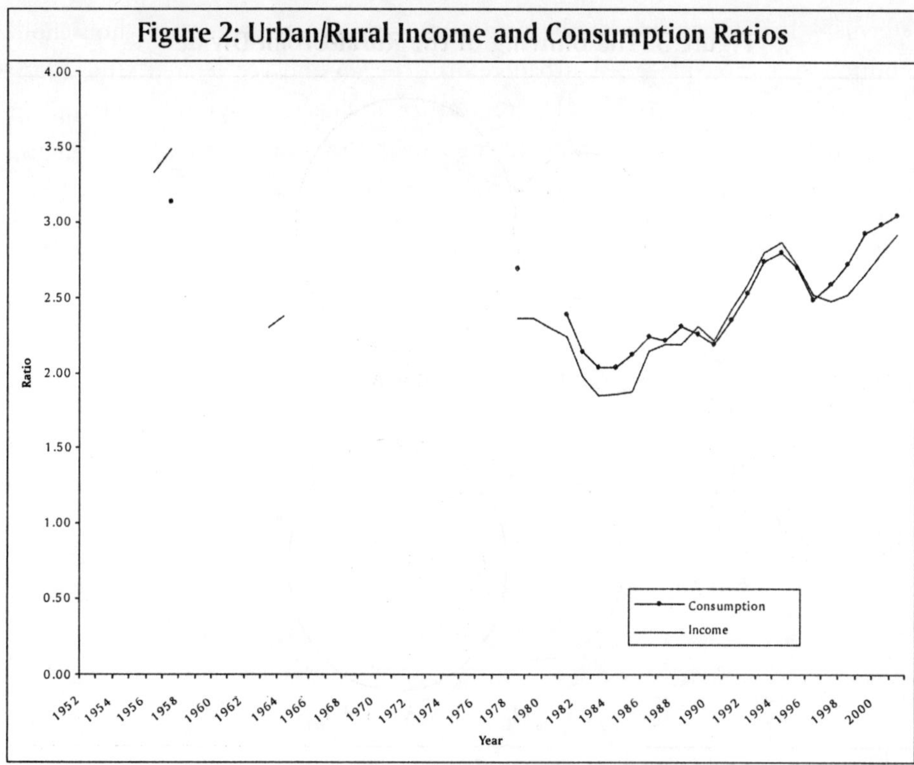

Figure 2: Urban/Rural Income and Consumption Ratios

rural and urban people is that they have different forms of security. Peasants have secure access to farming and housing land, whereas urban workers have until recently had their iron rice bowls guaranteeing secure jobs and pensions. Peasants had more, and earlier, freedom to pursue their economic self-interests locally, but they were in the past prevented from migrating to the cities, and they are still prevented from settling in the cities.

3. Explaining the Rural-Urban Divide

So far we have described the rural-urban divide: now to explain it. Why, and how, did it come about? The Communist Party, when it came to power, proceeded to build an institutional framework in which the State, dominated by the Party, divided China into rural and urban compartments, separated in terms of administration, finance and resources. The State either prevented or controlled the flow of funds and resources between the sectors. Rural residents, forming the great majority of the population, were governed by the urban representatives of

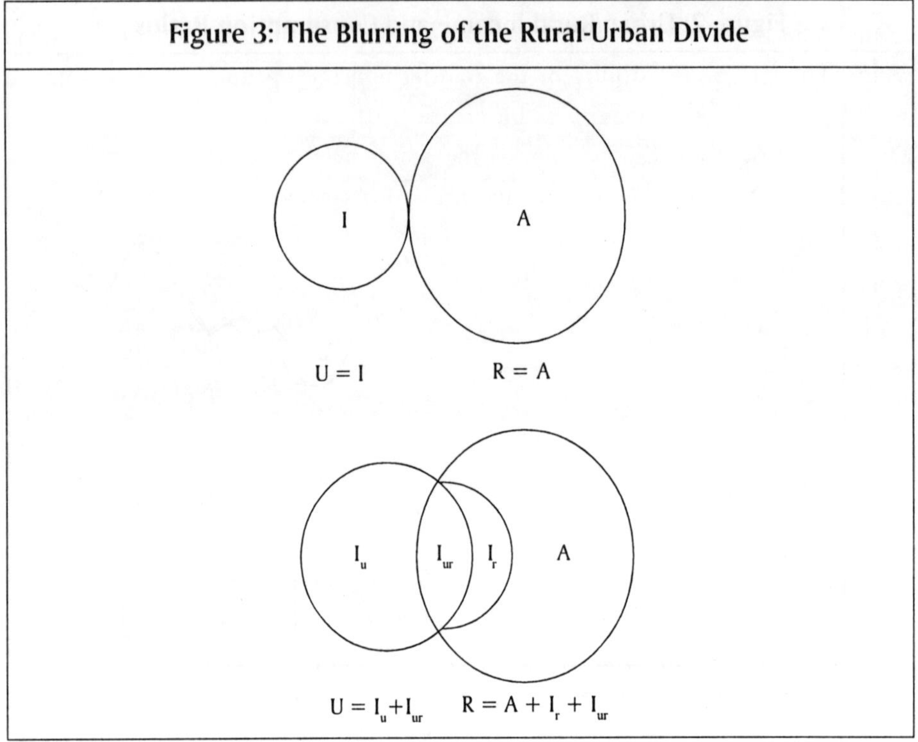

Figure 3: The Blurring of the Rural-Urban Divide

the State. During the period of economic reform the policies of decentralization and marketization contracted the role of the State and expanded the role of market forces. However, the institutional framework remained in place, and the urban-rural income ratio did not decline. The invisible Great Wall which separates rural and urban China remained standing.

Consider the policies of government as they evolved. The first tasks of the Communists, when they came to power, were the elimination of the landlord class, land reform, and the introduction of centralized economic planning. Recall that it was a peasantbacked revolution. Nevertheless, the main economic objective was rapid industrialization, and this meant urbanization. The terms of trade between agriculture and industry were an important policy variable to this end. Following the example of the USSR, the government depressed the terms of trade in order to provide cheap food in relation to manufactures, and thereby to secure high industrial profits for reinvestment. This was the so-called price scissors policy (Knight, 1995, Knight and Song, 1999, ch. 7). The hand that wielded the price scissors effected a transfer of income and resources from the rural to the urban sector. The relative invisibility of the transfer and the opaqueness of the burden added political attractiveness. The creation of the communes and enforced procurement of food can be seen as the States need to extract a surplus from agriculture in the absence of price incentives for farmers. In fact, it led to rural stagnation up to 1978. The peasants bore most of the sacrifice in consumption, and effectively paid for industrialization.

The real wages of urban workers were set at a level which enabled households to enjoy a higher standard of living than their rural counterparts. Thus, part of the investable surplus was diverted to the support of urban workers and their iron rice bowls. It was not only future generations that gained from the price scissors: urban workers also benefited. There is a fine line between the so-called efficiency wage and political pressure explanations of the relatively high urban wage. Worker discontent, low morale, and threat to political stability are all aspects of the latent power – latent rather than overt in the Chinese case – which residentially concentrated, interacting workers appear to possess.

The period of decollectivization, 1978-1985, was one of rapid growth in peasant incomes. The changes reflect a shift in the concerns of the Chinese leadership from the ideological to the economic. The rural reforms were that rare event, a Pareto improvement with hardly any losers. It is interesting that the reforms, which began at the grassroots level, went further and faster than was intended. A process of atomised peasant behaviour and cumulative causation pulled the leadership along behind.

In the mid-1980s government attention turned from rural to urban reform policies. The once-for-all nature of the gains from decollectivization and the policy reluctance to raise food prices produced agricultural stagnation for some years thereafter. However, this was ameliorated by rapid rural industrialization and an increase in temporary migration of rural workers to the cities and towns.

Government policy with regard to procurement, producer prices of grain and other necessities provides a good test of the relative political influence of workers and peasants. Government came to recognise the need to raise producer prices in order to elicit more farm production. However, when producer prices rose, government was also concerned to protect the living standards of urban workers. This necessitated a sharp increase in food subsidies. The budgetary expenditure on urban food subsidies actually came to exceed budgetary expenditure on agriculture in the early 1990s. The tardy and tortuous dismantling of the price scissors policy suggests that the urban minority were politically more important to government than the rural majority.

Urban real wages rose rapidly over the period of urban reform. This occurred despite the abundant supply of rural labour that was potentially available. It was made possible by the shielding of urban workers from the competition of rural labour, and the decentralization of power to enterprises. Managers appeared willing – possibly for efficiency wage reasons – to share profits with their employees.

It is of course misleading to speak of the urban-rural income ratio. There is considerable inequality within rural and within urban China. Much of the inequality of rural income per capita is spatial in character, reflecting the vast size and diversity of China. Spatial inequality existed even under the egalitarian policies of the pre-reform period, but both spatial and household inequalities increased during the reform period. We have found reasons to expect that processes of cumulative causation are at work, increasing inequality at the province, county, village and household levels (Knight and Song, 1993, Knight and Li, 1997). In some areas rural industrialization has proceeded rapidly, labour shortages have emerged, and rural incomes have risen towards urban incomes. In other areas rural development remains limited, surplus is chronic, and the potential economic gain from rural/urban migration is very great.

Spatial variation in urban real wages and incomes is not large across urban China, although it has increased (Knight, Li and Zhao, 2001). Urban incomes have been standardised by the institutional element in pay determination whereas rural incomes reflect regional disparities in natural resources and economic opportunities. This means that the urban-rural gap is greater in poor provinces.

The reasons for the superior provision of education in urban areas is to be found mainly in the separate administrative and funding arrangements for rural and urban education. However, it also reflects the opportunity costs and the lower perceived economic returns to education for rural households. The educational attainment of a rural area is strongly related to its income per capita, on account of the decentralised funding of rural public expenditures. There is no such urban relationship, owing to the more centralised funding arrangements.

China has a good health record, even in rural areas, by comparison with most poor countries. The emphasis on preventive medicine has borne dividends. It is probably the high quality of health care in urban China that is the real international outlier. The disparity between rural and urban China is the result of the institutional divide in health care arrangements, which in turn stems from the separate administration of rural and urban areas. Urban residents have widespread access to state-supported health care. The rural co-operative health schemes that operated during the commune period collapsed during the reform period. Especially in the poorer villages, which cannot afford collective insurance schemes, rural households face user charges for curative care and medicines. Other than for preventive care such as the vaccination of children, peasants' access to state-subsidised services is limited.

The general stance of the State with regard to education, health care and housing is that the rural sector should be self-reliant. The peasants have had to take care of themselves and not to be a burden on the State. There are large differences in urban and rural tax revenue per capita, reflecting the industry-centred tax base, and these differences are not offset by fiscal transfers.

It is arguable that a large urban-rural income gap should not survive the impact of equilibrating market forces. As the Chinese economy became more marketised, why were the returns to factors not equalised across space? Why did the income gap not get competed away? The answer to the question is: the continued rigid control of rural-urban migration. Without this, the income disparity would have served as a magnet to rural people wanting to better themselves, and it would not have survived. The invisible Great Wall has become more permeable during the period of economic reform. However, central and local governments have attempted to control the flow of temporary rural-urban migrants. Their objective has been to meet the needs of the growing urban economy while avoiding giving preference to urban residents. Moreover, it remains very difficult for rural-born people to acquire the right to permanent urban residence.

4. Will the Rural-Urban Divide be Eroded?

4a. Endogenous Government

The policy implications of this analysis can be approached in two ways. One is to assume that government formulates its objectives exogenously, i.e., independently of the pressures arising from the economic interests of various groups in society. We might, for instance, assume that government possesses a given social welfare function which makes no distinction between rural and urban people *per se*, and that the poorer the person, the higher the value placed on additional income. By this criterion, various Chinese government policies are difficult to understand, and might be regarded as errors, attributable to imperfect knowledge or imperfect control. A government with the social welfare function posited above would share our vision for the future elimination of the rural-urban divide. The more complete marketization of the economy would help to achieve this vision. Even more important would be the elimination of the administrative and institutional boundaries between rural and urban China.

The second approach is to recognise the endogeneity of government, i.e., that government is itself an economic agent, whose objectives are determined by the political economy. The government's social welfare function is in principle predictable from the relevant model, and government – more realistically, different segments and tiers of government – responds in predictable ways to dangers, threats and pressures. Government may be self-interested, in that it is ultimately concerned with staying in power. On this view, the apparent policy errors are in fact chosen correctly in the pursuit of government objectives. For instance, there may be good political reasons to favour urban people over rural. The remedy therefore lies in changing those objectives. The issue becomes one of understanding the balance of pressures that mould government policy.

It is necessary to form a view of the factors that shape economic policy in China. In the early years the Communist Party was securely in power, having won over almost all the population. Ideological objectives were therefore a luxury that could be pursued with little hindrance. Later on, particularly after the Cultural Revolution, the State became more sensitive to threats to political stability. Concern about the retention of power acquired an influence on economic policy.

It is possible to analyse certain policy outcomes by reference to the interests of various institutions and groups in society, and the pressures that they could exert on a government whose underlying objective was to stay in power. However, these pressures were normally implicit rather than explicit, passive rather than active. Underlying the urban bias often observable in State policies and institutions was State bias, to be explained in terms of the concerns and objectives of the Chinese leadership.

In the early years pressures on government were weak. The process of economic reform gave rise to clearer economic groups and perceptions of group interests. The rural-urban divide has become more apparent because the two sectors now communicate and interact directly, whereas they previously interacted only through the intermediation of the State. Conflicts of interest have come more into the open. A good example is the huge discrepancies that for some years existed between the producer prices, the market prices, and the rationed consumer prices of staple goods.

What are the prospects for the erosion of the rural-urban divide, bearing in mind current changes and trends in the economy and society? It has been argued that, as South Korea and Taiwan developed, their governments switched from urban bias to rural bias policies (Moore, 1993). The explanation is in terms of the changing structure of the economy, which reduced the need to extract a surplus from the agricultural sector and increased the political threat from rural-urban migration. Similarly, some of the changes taking place in the Chinese economy may assist the peasants. For instance, the price scissors policy has become less important for the accumulation of capital. Also, the diminishing share of food in urban household budgets makes urban real incomes less sensitive to the price of food. The voice of rural people may be enhanced by the greater awareness of their relative position that better education, greater mobility and improved communications can foster. The increased marketisation of the economy may itself reduce the degree of urban bias in government policies insofar as it accords greater weight to market-based allocation of resources and income and less weight to location-based allocation.

The future of the rural-urban divide depends to a great extent on the forces driving economic policies in urban China, in particular those relating to rural discontent, rural-urban migration, rising income inequality, and state-owned enterprise reform. Moreover, the evolution of Chinese political economy is well illustrated by these four important phenomena. We consider each in turn.

4b. Rural Discontent

To begin with the rural sector, what is the prospect for the peasant voice to be strengthened, so that peasant interests can acquire a greater weight in government policy objectives? In the 1980s the State's power to govern the countryside was eroded. To cope with this crisis of legitimacy, government decided to rejuvenate grassroots institutions and to encourage peasant participation. It gave legal recognition to village committees and encouraged elections to them, and it encouraged village representative assemblies. This has improved village governance and political consciousness. However, it has not given peasants political influence at higher levels of governance – county governments sometimes resisted the reforms – nor has it impacted significantly on the underlying conflict between the peasants and the State on account of its urban bias policies.

The process of economic reform has assisted the development of civil society in rural China, as various social organisations have emerged. These can be seen as intermediaries between government and people and, in principle, can articulate peasant interests. In practice, however, the influence of rural social organisations is weak, nor are they concerned with the central issue, i.e., peasant feelings of relative deprivation and of unfair treatment.

4c. The Evolving Policy on Migration

Before the start of rural economic reform in 1978, rural-urban migration of any sort was tightly restricted and indeed, with only minor exceptions, prohibited. The introduction of the household responsibility system in farming meant that surplus labour, previously disguised by commune work rules, became available for new farm and non-farm activities. In the 1980s peasants began to sell their products in the reopened urban food markets and new grassroots rural industries responded to the demand for consumer goods. The growth of rural industry was the outstanding phenomenon of the 1980s. TVE employment grew by 13 percent per annum in the 1980s in response to a market disequilibrium, but by less than 3 percent per annum in the 1990s as equilibrium was established and competition from the reforming urban economy intensified. Instead, rural-urban migration was the outstanding phenomenon of the 1990s. This redirection of rural labour absorption was assisted by the abolition of urban food rationing, the acceleration of the urban reforms that had commenced in 1985, and – as the one-child family policy took lagged effect – a deceleration of urban labour force growth. The rapid growth of the urban economy compared with the slow growth of the urban-born labour force meant that there was an increasing need for rural workers in the urban economy. Temporary migration expanded to meet that need.

Rural-urban migration should be viewed from three perspectives – those of the migrants themselves, their prospective employers, and government – any one of which might wish to promote or resist migration (Knight, Song and Jia, 1999). Consider each in turn. Many rural people have a strong economic incentive to migrate, having few productive opportunities in the village. Some are put off by the transaction costs involved, including lack of information and contacts as well as the costs of movement. Hence the importance of the village and of migrant networks in facilitating migration.

Many urban employers have a profit incentive to employ more migrants – essentially because migrants are willing to work for lower pay than are residents, and to accept jobs that urban residents reject. Different parts of government have different objectives. Central government is most concerned to ensure that flows of migrants are orderly and do not threaten social stability. Governments of sending areas – at the province or county level – encourage out-migration and operate recruitment agencies to assist it. As rural-urban migration began to burgeon in the 1990s, city governments, concerned to protect their citizens against the influx of migrants, introduced systems of control over in-migration. Their objectives were to allow temporary migrants into jobs unfilled by urban residents but to protect their residents against undercutting competition.

The late 1990s saw an increase in the number of migrant settlers in the big cities. They were commonly found in distinct migrant communities from a particular sending area, often semi-autonomous and well-structured. These migrants continued to be at a blatant disadvantage with respect not only to jobs but also to housing and schools, whereas access to medical care was now a matter of ability to pay. However, they were becoming urbanised: their reference groups were switching from rural to urban. The late 1990s also witnessed increasing conflict for urban jobs between rural migrants and urban workers. City governments responded to the widespread redundancies by restricting the recruitment and reemployment of rural migrants, and urban job centres gave priority to unemployed and *xia gang* urban *hukou* residents. Out-migration from rural China, which had grown rapidly in the early 1990s, was constant in the late 1990s (Du, 2001).

4d. Rising Income Inequality and Social Instability

Except in respect of the rural-urban divide, China was an egalitarian society before economic reform. The Gini coefficient was estimated to be below 0.20 in urban areas and about 0.25 in rural areas in the late 1970s (Adelman and Sunding, 1987). A national household survey for 1988 revealed that, a decade after rural reform had commenced, the Gini coefficient (based on micro data) had risen to 0.23 and 0.34 in urban and rural China respectively; the rural-urban divide meant that the national Gini coefficient was higher than either, at 0.38 (Griffin *et al,* 1993, pp.41, 45, 48). By 1995, a decade after the start of urban reform, the comparable urban and rural Gini coefficients were 0.28 and 0.42 respectively, and the national figure 0.46 (Gustafsson and Li, 2001, p.54). An urban household survey for 1999 showed a further sharp rise in the urban Gini coefficient, to 0.40. China was no longer an egalitarian society by international standards.

How important is the income gap between urban and rural areas in the context of overall income inequality in China? A decomposition of the Theil index shows it to have been a major contributor (Li and Gustafsson, 2001, p.66). In the 1988 household survey, the urban-rural income gap accounted for 43 percent of overall inequality. This proportion declined to 35 percent in the corresponding 1995 survey owing to the increase in within-area inequality, but the absolute contribution of the urban-rural income gap to the Theil index actually increased, by over 20 percent. Thus, overall income inequality in China would be reduced considerably if the urban-rural income gap could be eliminated.

How is the sharply rising inequality of incomes to be explained? Here we must look to government objectives in the post-Mao period. Because the Communist Party's grip on power has been firm by international standards, its concern to remain in power can be viewed more as an underlying influence on policy-making than as an over-riding objective. In the reform period the objectives of government have been primarily economic. These can be interpreted as the rapid growth of the economy and of government revenue, the former objective being stressed by central government and the latter by local governments.

The pursuit of growth objectives has generated rising income inequality – among the important mechanisms being the creation of markets, including markets offering initial high profits; the provision of incentives for enterprise and accumulation, including the lucrative transfer of state assets; and the application of efficiency rather than equity criteria in public decision-taking, including the demise of egalitarian regional policy. Rising inequality may threaten government if it leads to social instability. Moreover, social instability may in turn put at risk the continuation of rapid economic growth. Are these signs of growing social instability? If so, does the rural-urban divide play a role in this growth?

There is evidence that slow growth of rural incomes – partly due to increases in the taxes and fees charged by local governments – has induced a rise in conflicts between peasants and local officials in recent years (Liu, 2001) and in peasant refusals to pay local taxes and fees (He, 2001). The effect of increased rural-urban migration has been to destabilise the cities. Observing their economic disadvantage, migrants may regard themselves as second class citizens. The weakness of mechanisms of social control among migrants and the relative deprivation that they feel is said to contribute to rising crime in the cities (Liu and Fan, 2001). The number of criminal cases registered in public security organs rose by 127 percent between 1996 and 2000, with robberies and larceny rising even more rapidly.

4e. The Evolving Policy on State-owned Enterprise Reform

A further source of greater social instability was the policy of reforming the state-owned enterprises, which began in earnest in the mid-1990s. The policy is worth examining in some detail because it appears to be the most serious discrepancy in our explanation of the rural-urban divide.

The remarkable development of rural industry over the economic reform period was a response to extreme market disequilibrium. Supernormal profits were there to be earned by competing against the inefficient, high-price, state-owned enterprises. Township and village cooperatives and private entrepreneurs responded to these opportunities, and the number of workers engaged in rural non-agricultural activities rose remarkably, by 100 million over 20 years. State-owned firms were affected also by private sector development under the urban reforms, and by the tendency for local governments to over-invest. This increased competition for the state-owned sector depressed its profitability severely, and consequently government revenue also suffered. By the mid-1990s the reform of the state-owned enterprises had become a crucial issue which the government could no longer ignore.

One of the problems of the state sector has been overmanning: estimates suggest that about 20% of urban employment has been superfluous (Knight and Song, 1999b). Until recently, government had a political preference for disguised unemployment within enterprises rather than open unemployment on the streets. The reforms involved the withdrawal of subsidies, and state directives to lay off surplus labour. Few young people were recruited, many middle-aged workers were retired early, and many previously protected employees became *xia gang* workers, i.e., they continued to be nominally employed by the relinquishing enterprise while receiving a low wage, but they did not have to attend the workplace. Over 24 million redundancies were created in the period 1995-99. For many who continued in their jobs, employment was no longer guaranteed, their iron rice bowls were now made of cardboard, and feelings of insecurity were rife. Even the creation of *xia gang* status for laid-off workers did not protect them from hardship. A survey conducted early in 2000 showed that over half of the workers made redundant since 1992 were still unemployed, that the expected average duration of unemployment was about four years, and that they suffered a considerable loss of income during their period of unemployment (Appleton et al, 2002). There are journalists reports of social unrest among the unemployed, especially in cities where unemployment is high.[1] When, in a survey conducted in 2000, urban people were asked to rank the most important social problems, unemployment was ranked first, corruption second, and increasing income inequality third (Project Team of the Academy of Macroeconomics, 2001).

1 See, for instance, *Newsweek*, March 4, 2002, pp.24-5.

Does the new determination to reform the state-owned enterprises signify the end of the policy of urban bias? Perhaps the most plausible interpretation runs as follows. The reform was forced on government by the declining profitability and the rising incidence of loss-making in the state-owned sector, with adverse implications for both government revenue and prospects for continued rapid growth. Faced with a threat to the achievement of its main objectives, government was willing to risk a degree of political threat inherent in the erosion of urban-dwellers privileges.

The risk was worth taking given that there were three safety valves. First, to some extent unemployment could be exported to rural China, through tighter restrictions on the recruitment and renewed employment of migrants in cities. Second, as a result of the reform, the state-owned sector should become more efficient; and more difficult, therefore, for rural industry to compete against. In these ways the burden of the reform could be transferred from urban to rural people. Third, the majority of urban workers continued to be employed, and their real wages continued to rise despite the increase in urban unemployment. Standardised real wage growth for non-retrenched workers averaged 9 percent per annum over the period 1995-99 (Appleton et al, 2004). The fact that wages were sensitive to profits, and became more so between 1995 and 1999, suggests that managers were willing to share rents with their remaining workers (Knight and Li, 2002). Rent-sharing and efficiency wage explanations are difficult to distinguish, both conceptually and empirically: the wage increases might be viewed as payments for maintaining the morale, goodwill and effort of urban workers. According to the official household surveys, the real income per capita of urban *hukou* residents rose by almost 6 percent per annum between 1995 and 2000; the ratio of urban to rural income per capita thus actually rose, from 2.71 to 2.79. The new urban hardship was borne unevenly, and by a relatively small minority.

5. The Chinese Case in Perspective

The Chinese case can be viewed from two perspectives, the empirical and the theoretical. First, we make comparisons with other countries, so as to establish whether the rural-urban divide in China is ordinary or extraordinary.

5a. Empirical Perspective

Table 1 presents results for twelve countries on which we could obtain data. Only Zimbabwe and South Africa exceed China in their ratios of urban to rural income per capita. These two southern African countries have in the past been subject to powerful class and race bias in government policies, for which rural-urban distinction serves as a proxy. Their rural households, reliant on farming and labour migration, possess very little land and resources, and have been powerless and neglected. China's successful neighbours, Taiwan and South Korea, report extremely low urban-rural ratios; indeed, in South Korea there appears to be no difference between urban and rural living standards. The ratios in Sri Lanka, Egypt, Iran and Turkey are all well under 2 to 1. In terms of size, resources, structure and

Table 1: The Ratio of Urban to Rural Income, and Consumption, Per Capita, Selected Countries, Recent Years

Country		Ratio of urban to rural:	
	Year	income per capita	consumption per capita
China	1995	2.72	3.41
Taiwan	1995	1.32	1.43
South Korea	1994		1.03
India	1987/8		1.49
Iran	1991		1.82
Turkey	1994		1.71
Philippines	1991	2.26	2.17
Thailand	1990	2.23	2.66
Sri Lanka	1990/1	1.79	1.33
Egypt	1990/1		1.50
Zimbabwe	1990/1	3.57	
South Africa	1993	3.14	

Notes: 1. In South Korea the ratio is per household, not per capita; in Taiwan, Iran and the Philippines the per capita figure is derived from the household figure and the average number of members per household.

2. In Taiwan, Thailand, South Africa and Zimbabwe, aggregation into urban and rural categories was necessary, based on population weights.

Source: Knight and Song (1999a, p.338).

level of development, the economy of India is most similar to that of China. However, the Indian ratio of consumption per capita is only half the Chinese. This may be because in India markets operate more freely, factors of production can move unhindered, there is a wealthy landlord class, and there is a more democratic form of government. All but one of our countries has a sizable urban-rural income gap. China is not unique but it is unusual, at least by Asian standards. State institutions and government policies are responsible for China's artificially great rural-urban divide.

Rural-urban inequalities are not only to be found in poor countries of the late twentieth century: they are a more general phenomenon. For instance, in *The Wealth of Nations* (1776, ch.10), Adam Smith argued that... the inhabitants of a town, being collected into one place, can easily combine together... to prevent free competition, whereas... the inhabitants of the country, dispersed in different places, cannot... Throughout Europe, townspeople incorporated themselves, that is they regulated to restrict entry to industries, trades and occupations so as to increase their profits and wages, whereas rural people did not. The latter... have not only never been incorporated, but the corporation spirit never has prevailed among them. The effect was to... break down that natural equality which would otherwise take place in the commerce which is carried on between (town and country). Stock and labour naturally seek the most advantageous employment. They naturally, therefore, resort as much as they can to the town, and desert the country. The forms, mechanisms and degree of rural-urban division may vary from one nation or one era to another, but there are underlying reasons why it is often to be found.

5b. Theoretical Perspective

Consider the relevance to the Chinese case of four possible models of the relationship between the rural and urban sectors of a developing economy. These are the Lewis model, the price scissors model, the urban bias model, and the state bias model. Any interpretation of government policy, or of changes in policy, invites the criticism that the beneficiaries of the policy are too readily assumed to have been responsible for it. It is difficult to adduce direct evidence of the influences that govern policy, but all too easy to infer them. We recognise this methodological problem. Nevertheless, the four models provide a framework for a plausible and consistent account of policymaking.

We begin with the well-known Lewis model. Recall that this envisages economic development proceeding as a transfer of labour from the rural (identical to agricultural) sector to the urban (identical to industrial) sector. The industrial sector accumulates capital through the reinvestment of profits. In conditions of surplus labour the industrial real wage – being determined by the rural supply price – remains low and constant until rural labour becomes scarce. At first sight, the Lewis model applies well to China, with its abundant labour and its urban industrialization policy, especially during the period of central planning. However, it requires qualification.

Economic reform did not simply accelerate the transfer of labour from the rural to the urban sector, in line with the Lewis model. Rather, it led to the growth of the third sector – non-urban, non-state, non-agricultural – the rural industrial sector. The relationship of the new sector to the existing two sectors is mainly complementary in one case and competitive in the other. It was promoted by agricultural development and it in turn promoted agricultural development. Although it diverts resources from agriculture, the opportunity cost of rural labour is low. Rural industry competed with urban industry, particularly for raw materials in the early stages of the reform process, and for markets in the later stages. It contributed to the falling profitability of state enterprises, which occurred as a result of the price reform and the opening up of competition.

The new sector developed in the rural rather than the urban areas largely because of the institutional divide between rural and urban China that the State had created. Only in the rural areas could economic agents respond to the supernormal profits available in light industry. Moreover, the policy of rural fiscal self-reliance created a strong incentive for rural authorities to promote the industrialization of their localities. In this sense the institutional divide generated a degree of rural bias, in contradistinction to the more familiar urban bias in State policies. The fact that the most dynamic industrial growth in recent years took place in the rural sector should in itself have reduced the urban-rural income ratio. However, as this development was more than offset by other changes, the ratio actually rose after the mid-1980s.

The evolution of policy and the economy can be illustrated in Figure 2. The circles represent the rural and urban sectors, with their areas proportional to population. The upper part of the figure shows the situation in the pre-reform period, with the rural (*R*) and urban (*U*) sectors separate and coinciding with the agricultural (*A*) and industrial (*I*) sectors. The lower part shows the situation after the development of the third sector, rural industry (I_r). This is located within *R*. However, the figure shows a degree of overlap between the rural and urban areas, representing a semi-industrialized, semi-urban, grey area. This contains people who are generally not accorded urban privileges but some of whom are reported by the census of population as living in newly classified urban locations. Part of industry (I_{ur}) is to be found in the grey area and part (I_r) in the purely rural area.

Our argument is that the rural-urban divide has become more porous and less tidy in recent years. The rural-urban distinction is being blurred, and it is no longer equivalent to the agriculture-industry distinction. The main reason for this is rural industrialization – itself a product of the institutional divide – and the socioeconomic changes that it brought about. Although it was trivial at the start of the economic reforms, the overlap between the rural and urban frequency distributions of household income per capita has gradually increased. Some rural people in some parts of China are now better off than most urban people.

The Lewis model of the transfer from agriculture to industry is indeed relevant, but within rural China. The model depicts well the process that operated within the rural sector after 1978. The basic elements of the model are present in rural China: an elastic supply of labour from agriculture to industry, and the rural industrialization which was achieved through the reinvestment of profits within that sector. The Lewis model is a rather less appropriate description of the relationship between the rural and the urban sector. Government set the urban industrial wage at a level which greatly exceeded the supply price of rural labour, and it was necessary for government therefore to restrict and control rural-urban migration. Moreover, the funds for industrial investment, although nominally derived from industrial profits, were extracted from agriculture by means of government pricing policy. The relationship between the rural and the urban sector therefore requires a model that incorporates both the price scissors and the urban bias policies.

The theory of price scissors can be readily applied to China. Moreover, some government policies such as the formation of the communes, compulsory procurement of food, and urban rationing of food can be seen to flow from the price scissors policy. Government intervention on prices effected a transfer of resources from the rural to the urban sector. These were used for capital accumulation in urban industry, in accordance with the price scissors model of industrialization. However, they were also used to raise the consumption of urban workers. Thus the Chinese experience does not correspond precisely to the price scissors model: it also requires a role for the urban bias model.

It is likely that urban bias does exist in China, in two senses. First, government allocates fewer resources to the rural sector than it would if it were concerned only with improving economic efficiency, as determined by shadow prices. Second, rural-dwellers receive less priority than they would if the government social welfare function made no distinction between rural and urban residence *per se,* and placed a greater value on additional income, the poorer the person. The urban bias model has perhaps been most forcefully propounded by Lipton (1999). As Lipton put it: the rural sector contains most of the poverty, and most of the low-cost sources of potential advance; but the urban sector contains most of the articulateness, organization and power. Bates (1993) summarized the urban bias displayed by the state in socialist countries in the following terms. Socialist governments create large bureaucracies, forge strong ideological ties with urban labour, and are committed to industrialization and to public ownership; hence their concern to ensure low food prices and high industrial profits. Socialist governments accordingly adopt policies against the interests of their poorest citizens – the peasants. The Chinese case corresponds well to this general account.

Although the policies of the Chinese government can be accurately described as involving urban bias, the underlying reason for the policies is better described as state bias. An underlying motivation was the preservation of government by the Chinese Communist Party. The failure to close, or even to diminish, the rural-urban gap in income and welfare stems from the need to stave off potential political threats to the regime. Even during the early years of economic reform, when the rural sector received priority, the motive was to restore political legitimacy with the peasants and to relax the most serious constraint on the growth of the economy. We do not claim that the State entirely understood or controlled economic events. Take, for instance, the issue of promissory notes instead of money to peasants for their produce in the late 1980s and the early 1990s. This was clearly not a policy objective for central government – indeed, it tried in vain to outlaw the practice. However, it was the outcome of its other policies, such as that requiring rural local governments largely to raise their own revenue and the set of policies making investment in industry more profitable for local government than investment in agriculture.

The Chinese political process should not yet be viewed as the outcome of conflicting articulated pressures from various organized interest groups. The Communist Party remains too dominant for that. Rather, the urban bias policies reflect the latent political power of urban-dwellers. The government purchases an insurance policy to ensure that urban workers will refrain from political protests which could challenge it, and that they will not threaten production and therefore state revenue. The erosion of the economic security of urban households in the late 1990s – associated with reform of the state-owned enterprises – can be viewed as a risky but necessary response to the financial deterioration of that sector, which posed a threat to the public finances and to continued rapid economic growth.

It is apparent that no single model of rural-urban economic relationships is sufficient to describe the Chinese experience. In fact, all four models that we considered are relevant in at least some respect. They were therefore combined to produce an encompassing model with Chinese characteristics.

6. Conclusion

It appears from the evidence that the Chinese Government is more concerned to promote economic growth, and to alleviate poverty through growth, than it is to prevent the sharply rising inequality that is taking place in China. Moreover, the Government's social welfare function seems to accept two classes of citizenship – one class for urban-dwellers and another, inferior, class for rural-dwellers.

These priorities may alter in response to the various pressures and threats that the changing economy throws up. In an increasingly well-informed society, widening, or even continued, economic disparities – among households, across regions, between city and countryside, and between urban residents and rural migrants – are likely to generate feelings of relative deprivation, expressions of discontent, and outbreaks of social instability. The likely response of Party and Government to these developments could help to bring inequality issues onto the policy agenda and also to erode the rural-urban divide.

(John Knight is Professor of Economics at Department of Economics, University of Oxford;

Li Shi is a professor and senior research fellow at the Institute of Economics, Chinese Academy of Social Sciences, and a research fellow at the University of Oxford;

Lina Song is a Reader in China Studies at the School of Sociology & Social Policy, University of Nottingham.)

References

Adelman, Irma and David Sunding (1987). Economic policy and income distribution in China, *Journal of Comparative Economics*, 11, 3, September, 444-61.

Appleton, Simon, John Knight, Lin a Song and Qingji Xia (2002). Labor retrenchment in China: determinants and consequences=, *China Economic Review,* 13, 252-75.

Appleton, Simon, John Knight, Lina Song and Qingji Xia (2004). 'Contrasting paradigms: segmentation and competitiveness in the formation of the Chinese labour market', mimeo.

Bates, Robert H (1993). Urban bias: a fresh look, *Journal of Development Studies*, 29, 4, 219-28.

Du Ying (2001). Research on employment issues of out-migrants, Beijing: Ministry of Agriculture of P R China (in Chinese).

Griffin, Keith and and Ashwani Saith (1981). *Growth and Equality in Rural China*, Singapore: Maruzen (for ILO).

Griffin, Keith and Kimberley Griffin (1983). 'Institutional change and income distribution in the Chinese countryside'. *Oxford Bulletin of Economics and Statistics*, 45, 3, August, 223-48.

Griffin, Keith and Zhao Renwei (eds) (1993). *The Distribution of Income in China*, London: Macmillan.

Gustafsson, Bjorn and Li Shi (2001). A more unequal China? Aspects of inequality in the distribution of equivalent income, in Carl Riskin, Zhao Renwei and Li Shi (eds), *China's Retreat from Equality: Income Distribution and Economic Transition*, New York: M E Sharpe.

He Xuefeng (2001). Peasants burden and rural governance: a survey of Dai village in Hubei, *Management World*, 2 (in Chinese).

Knight, John (1995). Price scissors and intersectoral resource transfers: who paid for industrialization in China?, *Oxford Economic Papers*, 47, 1, 117-35.

Knight, John and Li Shi (1997). Cumulative causation and inequality among villages in China, *Oxford Development Studies*, 25, 2, 149-72.

Knight, John, Li Shi and Zhao Renwei (2001). A spatial analysis of wages and incomes in urban China: divergent means, convergent inequality, in Carl Riskin, Zhao Renwei and Li Shi (eds), *China=s Retreat from Equality. Income Distribution and Economic Transition,* Armonk, New York: M.E. Sharpe, 133-66.

Knight, John and Lina Song (1993). The spatial contribution to income inequality in rural China, *Cambridge Jou rnal of Economics,* 17, 195-213.

Knight, John and Lina Song (1999b). *The Rural-Urban Divide. Economic Disparities and Interactions in China,* Oxford: Oxford University Press.

Knight, John and Lina Song (1999b). Employment constraints and sub-optimality in Chinese enterprises, *Oxford Economic Papers,* 51, 284-98.

Knight, John, Lina Song and Jia Huaibin (1999). Chinese rural migrants in urban enterprises: three perspectives, *Journal of Development Studies,* 35, 3, February, 73-104.

Knight, John and Li Shi (2002). How does firm profitability affect wages in urban China?, May mimeo.

Lipton, Michael (1977). *Why Poor People Stay Poor. Urban Bias in World Development,* Cambridge, Mass: Harvard University Press.

Liu Renwen and Fan Zaiqin (2001). Public security in 2000', in Ru Xin, Lu Xueyi and Shan Tianlun (eds), *Analysis of the Social Situation in China 2001*, Beijing: Social Sciences Documentation Publishing House (in Chinese).

Lu Xueyi (2001). Problems in rural China, in Ru Xin, Lu Xueyi and Shan Tianhin (eds), *Analysis of the Social Situation in China 2001*, Beijing: Social Sciences Documentation Publishing House (in Chinese).

Moore, Mick (1993). Economic structure and the politics of sectoral bias: East Asian and other cases, *Journal of Development Studies,* 29, 4, 79-128.

Project Team of Academy of Macroeconomics, State Commission of Planning and Development (2001). Analysis of the impact of income inequality and its acceptability, *Management World,* 5 (in Chinese).

Smith, Adam (1776). *The Wealth of Nations,* London: Everyman's Library (1910 edition).

12

Rural and Urban Development Case Study – Bangladesh

Tim Ruffer and Nadia Masud

Bangladesh is one of the least urbanized countries in South Asia with densely populated rural areas composed of clustered villages. Poverty is predominantly rural – 93% of the very poor and 89% of the poor reside in rural areas. This article covers a number of aspects relating to rural and urban development in Bangladesh, which includes the agriculture sector, livelihood sources, migration and remittances, rural and urban policies of the government, and policy implications.

1. Introduction

Bangladesh faces many challenges in alleviating poverty. A large population and high population density, a high vulnerability to natural disasters and slow economic growth all contribute to slow poverty reduction in the country. According to 1995 measurements, half of the total population was considered poor, and over a third very poor. Poverty is still predominantly rural, remaining at twice the levels of that in the urban areas. Inequality has increased, while poverty alleviation

Source: Oxford Policy Management. *This document is an output from a project funded by the UK Department for International Development (DFID) for the benefit of developing countries. The views expressed are not necessarily those of DFID. Reprinted with permission.*

programs have had difficulty in achieving a direct impact on the poorest groups in both rural and urban areas.

2. Key Trends

Although one of the most densely populated countries of the world, Bangladesh is still an agrarian society – three quarters of the population live in rural areas. It is one of the least urbanised countries in south Asia and features densely populated rural areas composed of clustered villages that develop near roadways.

In Bangladesh, as in many other developing countries, rural and urban economies overlap considerably, and the two sectors are highly interdependent and complementary. Although Bangladesh is still predominantly rural, its urban population growth has been unprecedented. Currently, the country faces an urban crisis and a process of rural transformation that has uprooted or impoverished many rural communities. Rapid rural-to-urban migration has been an important contributor to the urbanization process.

Bangladesh's overall population has more than doubled since 1970 and currently stands at around 140 million. Industrial development and agrarian distress has drawn migrants to a number of urban areas and due to urbanization, it is estimated that by 2020 about 40% of the population will live in urban areas.[1] Urban population has grown consistently at a higher rate than the growth rate of rural population. The urban population is currently growing at 4.0%, compared to rural population growth of 1.0%. Urban population growth peaked in the 1980s before slowing down since 1991.

Table 1: Population Data

	1985	1990	1995	2000	2002
Rural population	80.1	88.3	93.4	98.3	100.2
Rural population (% of total population)	82.5	80.2	77.7	75.0	73.9
Rural population growth (annual %)	1.9	1.8	1.1	1.0	1.0
Urban population	17.0	21.8	26.7	32.8	35.5
Urban population (% of total)	17.5	19.8	22.3	25.0	26.1
Urban population growth (annual %)	5.8	4.8	4.1	4.1	4.0

Source: World Development Indicators.

Urban areas in Bangladesh were classified into four distinct classes for the 1991 population census on the basis of their functions and sizes. These include: (1) Megacity – the metropolitan area having population more than 5 million. Dhaka metropolitan area is the only megacity of Bangladesh; and (2) Statistical Metropolitan Area – the city corporation and the adjacent areas having urban characteristics have been defined as metropolitan areas; they have a population between 500,000 and 5 million. Table 5 summarises the trends in the spatial distribution of the urban population. At the time of the 1991 census, there was one megacity and three metropolitan cities with a population of more than 500,000. These were Dhaka, Chittagong, Khulna and Rajshahi. 47.7% of the total urban population lived in these cities at the time of the 1991 census. This share increased to 54.2 % in 2000. Dhaka alone accounts for over one third of the urban population.[2] Table 3 presents a summary of some key trends of the urbanization trend in Bangladesh.

The largest city of Bangladesh is the capital Dhaka with a population of 12,519,000 in 2000, followed by Chittagong with a population of 3,651,000.[3] Squatter settlement is common in Dhaka City. A large number of people have no access to land in the city. The land ownership pattern is extremely skewed and unequal – almost 70% of people do not have any. Despite this, migration to the city is continuously increasing. Low income peasants, victims of natural disasters, together with a vast number of rural unemployed and under-employed comprise the bulk of the migrants of the city's population but share only a tiny portion of the city's land.

Under present circumstances, neither rural nor urban economies are fully "rural" or fully "urban" in the strict sense. The tertiary sector has grown significantly in rural areas, while rural-urban social and economic interaction has intensified. Most of the urban areas in the country are small, and many of the economic activities taking place within their established boundaries are not strictly urban. The main metropolitan areas (Dhaka and Chittagong), have deconcentrated and become vast economic regions including rural and semi-rural areas and agricultural activities.

Population density and socio-demographic profiles of rural settlements have been changing steadily, demanding continuous redefinition of the boundary between urban and rural. In 1981, in particular, the definition of urban areas was extended in the census to include small administrative townships and economically significant production and marketing centres in the rural areas that have certain significant "urban" characteristics.

The "graduation" from rural to urban settlements is likely to accelerate because there are powerful incentives for rural settlements to change their designation to urban. Besides becoming administratively autonomous, the newly incorporated areas are entitled to lump-sum grants, which are more generous on a per capita basis than the funds that the area would receive as part of a rural decentralised government unit.

According to most projections, Bangladesh will in the near future assume a more "peri-urban" look than at present. A process of axial densification is in full force: a clearly distinguishable NW-SE corridor is emerging to include some of the fastest growing cities and most of the largest cities, vast peri-urban areas, and prosperous agricultural zones.

As shown in Table 2, poverty in Bangladesh is still predominantly rural and it remains at twice the levels of urban poverty. The rural sector concentrates 93% of the very poor and 89% of the poor. While almost 40% of the total rural population was below the lower poverty line (thus categorised as 'very poor') in 1995-96, the urban population under this threshold was 14%. When the upper poverty line is considered, about 57% of the rural population and 35% of the urban population classify as 'poor'.

Table 2: Headcount Indices of Poverty with the Cost of Basic Needs Method (1995-96)

	Very Poor (Lower Poverty Line)	Poor (Upper Poverty Line)
National	35.55	53.08
Rural	39.76	56.65
Urban	14.32	35.04

In general, most of the urban population in the country is comprised of recent rural migrants. Currently, about 60% of urban growth is due to migration and reclassification (the rest stems from natural increase). It is estimated that about 5,000 rural poor migrants arrive daily to Dhaka in search of work. Rural hardcore poor have increasingly joined the ranks of the urban absolute poor. According to recent estimates, 72% of heads of urban poor households are migrants (in Dhaka alone the figure is 85%).

3. Characteristics of the Agriculture Sector

With the great majority of poor people living in rural areas, a situation that will persist over at least the next two decades, substantial reductions in poverty will require improvements in rural livelihoods. This in turn will need diversification of livelihood sources (from both stronger urban linkages and diversifying rural sources) and sustained increases in productivity (especially poor people's productivity) in agriculture which underpins much of the growth of the non-farm rural sectors.[4]

The need for a focus on productivity for poor people is sharpened by the structural changes under way in Bangladesh's agriculture. The achievement of rice self-sufficiency in the past few years has stepped up pressure for diversification towards higher value enterprises, pressure reinforced by longer-term trends of urbanization, rising incomes, increased consumption levels, and diet diversification.

Agriculture and the rural economy in Bangladesh have undergone a process of reform and structural changes in recent years. The country embraced a process of reform in the 1980s under which liberalisation of agricultural inputs and outputs took place. With a few exceptions, rural areas have become increasingly integrated with urban areas through physical infrastructure, communications, markets and institutions.

During the last three decades there has been a significant structural change in agriculture, both in terms of its contribution to the national economy and employment. Agricultural value added as a percentage of GDP declined from about 60% in 1972 to around 50% in 1980, 29% in 1990, and 23% by 2001. The share of agricultural employment in total employment declined slowly from 77% in 1974 to 61% in 1981 and 53% in 1991. Agriculture remains the main source of rural employment in Bangladesh. Among the four sub-sectors within agriculture (crop, livestock, fisheries and forestry), the crop sector has experienced the greatest decline. Its contribution to agricultural output declined from more than 71% in 1972/1973 to 57% by 2000/01.[5] Table 7 shows the volume of production over time of key agricultural crops in Bangladesh.

The non-farm sector grew at a much faster rate than the farm sector between 1987 and 2001. The average annual growth rate of income from the farming sector was around 1.4% during this period whereas the average income per year from the non-farm sector grew at a rate of 6.8%. The non-farm sector now accounts for over 50% of total rural household income.[6]

Bangladesh is a land scarce country. With growing urbanization and infrastructure development taking land away from agriculture use, as well as continuing population growth, arable land on a per capita basis is declining. In 2000 among the poorest of the poor (20% of the population), four out of five owned less than half an acre of land. Other surveys suggested that nearly half of the country's rural population are effectively landless, owning at most 0.05 acres (just homesteads). This is making it harder to achieve significant reduction of poverty, especially in rural areas.

This is one of the main forces driving rural-urban migration. Although most rural out-migrants are poor and uneducated, the most likely to succeed in the cities are the best educated who are city-bound, creating a rural-to-urban "brain drain". Nonetheless, urbanization in Bangladesh is still much more the reflection of rural despair than of urban opportunity. The agricultural sector is overpopulated, and sub-division and fragmentation of land have contributed significantly to the main rural "push factors" in rural-to-urban migration. Frequent and crippling natural disasters, famine, loss of the family breadwinner and long periods of unemployment and underemployment have also been identified as significant factors in this massive exodus process.

Besides owning land, poor people can have access to land under the evolving land tenure system. Here also the poor have not fared well. The two most recent censuses provide a useful picture of systems of tenancy in Bangladesh. Key information is summarised in Table 3. About 40% of holdings report some kind of tenancy arrangement in both periods, covering about 17% of area in 1983-84 and 22% of area of 1997.

Sharecropping remains the dominant form of tenancy arrangement, accounting for about 12% of area in 1983-84 and 13% in 1997. Sharecropping is the most common form of tenurial system for the poor (among landless and smallholders) to gain access to land. The proportion of sharecropping has not changed much despite the fact that there has been a 10 percentage point increase in landlessness.

Other arrangements have become correspondingly more frequent over the same period. Not surprisingly, sharecropping area is lowest in importance on larger farms, and by 1997 other forms of tenancy accounted for nearly as much area as sharecropping. All size classes have seen pronounced growth in alternative arrangements; especially noteworthy is the taking of land on mortgage amongst the small holdings.

Table 3: Percentage Area Under Various Contractual Arrangements, 1983-84 and 1997 (As a Percentage of Total Land Operated)

	All		Small		Medium		Large	
	1983-84	**1997**	**1983-84**	**1997**	**1983-84**	**1997**	**1983-84**	**1997**
Sharecropping	12.4	13.4	15.3	15.4	13.9	13.6	6.7	7.5
Total Other	4.9	8.2	7.1	10.1	4.1	7.3	3.2	6.1
Fixed rent	1.7	2.5	2.3	2.8	1.6	2.4	1.2	2.0
Lease	0.2	0.6	0.2	0.5	0.2	0.7	0.2	0.8
Mortgage	2.0	4.4	3.0	5.9	1.8	3.6	1.2	2.7
Others	1.0	0.7	1.5	0.9	0.6	0.5	0.6	0.5

Source: Rabbani.

Looking at operated land by tenancy status, 58% of land is operated by owners (i.e., those who cultivate the land they own), 40% by owner-tenants (i.e., their operational holding include some land that they do not own), and just 2% by pure tenants. This again confirms that overall the landless poor does not gain much access to land through pure tenancy. However, the small holders who own some land do increase their operational holding under the evolving tenurial system.

It is also important to review poor households' access to common property. In Bangladesh, there is not much common or community land. The only common properties left are water bodies and some forest land. Some poor people do depend on these common properties. For example, some fishermen depend on fishing in rivers and common water bodies and similarly some poor people in selected areas (e.g., Chittagong Hilltract) depend on forests for livelihood. But the overall availability of these common properties for the poor is declining and in the absence of well-defined and enforced common property rights, poor people's access to these common properties is becoming extremely limited.

The sum total of the effects of a complex land administration system – faulty and fraudulent land titling, and inordinate delays in updating land records – has led to high costs in land transactions. This has resulted in serious imperfections in the rural land market, which restricts the access of the poor but efficient farmers to land. Also, it is generally recognised that problems of land administration and land records constitute a key source of governmental corruption and failure of governance in the rural areas.

4. Livelihoods Sources

The sectoral composition of the workforce over the last two decades is shown in Table 8. The share of agriculture in employment fell substantially in the early 1980s and rose later in the decade. Since then, fluctuations have been moderate. Employment in the manufacturing sector has also experienced a notable decline whereas the share of services in employment has increased. One reason behind the decline in the share of manufacturing in employment is the closing down of loss making state owned enterprises and the retrenchment of excess labour in privatised state owned enterprises.

There has been an expansion in employment opportunities outside the agricultural sector in rural Bangladesh. A case study of a rural area indicates that in the mid-1970s, there were few job opportunities outside agriculture. In several of the better-off households, sons with an education were employed as teachers, and some households had diversified into trading in buffaloes and rice. Some other occupations like petty trade, tailoring and carpentry were also present. Migration of both a seasonal or permanent nature was limited.

However, following the Green Revolution and introduction of high yielding crop varieties and fertilisers, there has been an increase in agricultural productivity. The positive effects manifested themselves in both the agricultural and non-agricultural sector. With an increase in the demand for agricultural labour, wages in the sector increased, causing income to increase and employment opportunities in the non-farm sector to expand. The service and trade sectors received a boost, with an increase in catering/restaurants and modern shops for stationary, bicycles, etc. There has also been an expansion in the informal sector with a growth in rickshaw pulling and petty trading, including milk vending. Women especially have been prominent in selling cow-dung cakes for cooking. The improvement in infrastructure which allows for these to be supplied to neighbouring areas is one factor responsible for the growth in this activity. Embroidering pillows and blankets is another activity rural women engage in.

Rural non-farm activities account for over 40% of rural employment. The sector grew at 5% per annum between late eighties and mid-nineties and in 1995/96, it contributed 36% to the country's total GDP compared to about 31% for agriculture.

Rural non-farm activities outside agriculture include livestock, fisheries and forestry. They can be classified into three categories: mostly manual labour-based, human capital-based occupations, and physical and human capital intensive activities. Manual labour-based activities include self employed subsistence oriented cottage industries, wage employment in rural business enterprises, transport operation, and construction labour. Human capital-based occupations include salaried service in public and private organisations, teachers and imams, village doctors, and various types of personal services. Physical and human capital-intensive activities include commercial type rural industries, including agro-processing, shop-keeping, peddling, petty trading, medium and large scale trading and contractor services.[7]

In many cases, landless workers with income from the informal sector have been able to save on their salaries and have used their savings for investment in money lending. There is also evidence to suggest that expansion in employment opportunities over time has led to increases in the real incomes of the landless.

Tables 10-12 show employment by occupation and major sources of people's income, employment and composition of household income. They show that there has been an increase in the importance of the trade and business and service sector. There has been an expansion in the share of the urban informal sector in employment, growing from 26.5% in 1999, to 27.9% in 2000 to 29.4% in 2001.[8] This expansion is partly a result of the inability of the urban formal economic systems to absorb the flow of rural unskilled migrants. Informal sector activities include petty trade, quack doctors, cycle rickshaw repairing, food processing, selling fruit, rice cakes snacks and main meals. Head load hawkers sell fruits, vegetables, fish and household goods like floor and wall cleaning accessories, rugs etc. Shoulder load hawkers sell pottery goods, aluminium-cooking pots and plastic wares and sometimes fruits.[9]

The composition of the economy in designated rural and urban areas have many common characteristics that make rural-urban sectoral delineation difficult. Specifically, the tertiary sector has grown significantly in rural areas. Small businesses catering to the surrounding rural population abound in small and medium-sized towns. A large number of seasonal migrants go to these towns seeking temporary employment, and as a result, rural and urban economies become more integrated. Most urban areas in the country are physically small, and a large part of economic activities that take place within their administrative boundaries are not strictly speaking "urban activities".

Simultaneously, as the few large cities have grown, they have tended to deconcentrate and become vast economic regions, including rural and semi rural areas and agricultural activities. Dhaka has thus been categorised as "one of the most ruralised megacities of the world."[10] According to a 1991 survey of land uses, only 39% of the Dhaka metropolitan area was considered to be under urban land uses (i.e., residential, industrial and commercial), while 61% was considered to be under non-urban rural or semi-rural agricultural uses. Specifically, agricultural land uses were estimated to cover 45% of the total metropolitan area. 28% of total urban employment is composed of so-called peri-urban agro-enterprises such as poultry and other livestock raising, agro-processing (i.e., husking, food preservation), fisheries and forestry.

5. Migration and Remittances

Historically, most migration from rural to urban areas was undertaken by men who travelled for temporary non-agricultural work. By the 1990s, however, a lot of migrants sought to settle permanently in the urban areas, and there was also an increase in the flow of women migrating independently to work in urban areas, especially in the garment factories. Migration can be a result of changes in land use patterns. Rising population density, proportional inheritance rules and highly liquid markets have reduced average plot sizes and margins of profitability. The fragmentation and division of land leaves many households without enough land to earn a living, encouraging migration or involvement in non-farm activities. A study on migration in Dhaka[11] shows that most migrants belong to one of three categories: students (37%), day-labourers (10%) or the unemployed (15%). There are few studies analysing the economic activities of migrants, although research has shown that 21% of those unemployed migrated while only 5% of students did. Unemployment therefore seems to be a more powerful factor in determining migration than continuing education. Better economic conditions, greater freedom for women and better education were identified by surveys as reasons for migration. Average wage rates in urban areas tend to be higher than in rural areas both in the agricultural and non-agricultural sector, which may be one reason for the rapid growth of urban population. A vast majority of rural-to-urban migrants are poor and very poor.

However, not all urban migrants are permanent. Many are seasonal or may have settled in for a long-term stay, with the intention of returning. For example as many as 40% of rural dwellers look for work in a neighbouring town or city, during the lean agricultural season or during flooding.[12]

From an urban perspective, although this may help rural households cope with year round employment, seasonal migration can harm the livelihood of the urban poor who must compete with these temporary migrants for jobs at the same time as food price increases.

6. Government Policy

Despite being aware of the rapid urbanization in the country and the associated physical, economic and social problems, the government has not yet adopted an explicit urban policy. However, a number of government documents and other initiatives have indicted the direction of policy thinking with regard to urbanization and urban development. In the 1970s, the UN recommended that various planning regions be identified and in each region, one medium sized town be chosen as the focal point of regional growth, in order to create spatially balanced urban development. The First Five Year Plan of the early 1980s envisaged that infrastructure and service facilities would be extended from 100 urban centres to 1,200 growth centres throughout the country. The Third Five Year Plan incorporated the idea of upazilla growth as a method of decentralisation whereas the Fourth Plan talked about drawing up master plans for developing townships. The Fifth Five Year Plan did not provide any comprehensive urban planning guidelines.

The government has created a number of institutions to boost the rural non-farm sector. These include the Bangladesh Small-Scale and Cottage Industries Corporation, the Handloom Board and the Sericultural Board. However, they are under-resourced. There is a need for implementation of proposals from previous plans, such as the development of rural growth centres in market places, especially in the case of rural transport equipment and agricultural equipment. The Third Five Year Plan had proposed to set up employment and resource centres for the promotion of rural non farm employment. The centres would have training and demonstration units for the development of local crafts and new product lines. The plan also included proposals to strengthen the technology development and extension work of the Bangladesh Small and Cottage Industries Corporation and other institutions geared to promote rural non-farm employment. Measures to promote the growth of the rural non-farm sector in the Fourth Plan include appropriate reform in exchange rates and tariff policies to remove bias against rural industries, restructuring of licensing system to benefit small scale enterprises, providing credit with training and technology extension programme.

Several programmes were initiated in the past to reform land legislation, tenancy, and land taxation. These programmes emerged from the political system but implementation on the ground has far lagged behind the expressed goals of the reforms. The problem is a familiar one in any reform process: implementation relies on the cooperation of groups with a vested interest in the status quo.

7. Consequences

An increase in employment opportunities, especially non-farm activities in rural areas, have allowed modest increases in income for landless workers. A high natural population growth rate, high population densities in rural areas, increased loss and fragmentation of land, frequent natural disasters and long periods of underemployment all exert pressures on the rural economy. In such a situation, increased urbanization expands the employment possibilities of rural inhabitants who can migrate on a temporary or permanent basis to urban areas. Urban areas also offer better job opportunities, higher wages, relatively better access to education and health care.

Serious poverty has accompanied urbanization. The formal economy is not able to keep pace with the growing population of unskilled labour. In many states with high levels of urbanization, the share of urban population below the poverty line is greater than in rural areas. Poor entrepreneurs in the urban informal sector are extremely vulnerable to macroeconomic changes, more so than their rural counterparts as they tend to rely almost completely on the cash economy for production inputs. Inequality is higher in urban than in rural areas.[13] Higher inequality in urban areas may be related to the fact that first and second generation rural migrants are finding it increasingly difficult to access local economy, even the informal and the "non-urban" activities. Urban poverty has assumed alarming proportions, under a situation where the poor (recently arrived from rural areas, or belonging to the second and third generations) have hardly any access to land, shelter and services.

Only around 50% of the urban population has access to any safe water. The situation with regard to toilet facilities and sewage systems is very limited, causing serious environmental problems of surface and ground water contamination. The urban population also suffers from health problems including high child immortality.[14]

The pressure on urban land is also extremely high. The supply of serviced land or land suitable for urban development is limited and is greatest in the metropolitan cities. Historically, and increasingly, the distribution pattern of land ownership in urban areas is highly skewed and unequal. In the major cities, such as Dhaka, as much as 70% of the population (being largely very poor) do not own any land. Among those who are owners, the richest 8% own 40% of the land and the 50% small land owners hold 20% of the land in the city. This has resulted in low density development in high income areas very high densities in low income areas.

The urban poor who do not own land in urban areas, get access to land mainly as renters in private slums or as free dwellers in squatter settlements. In either case the shelter and environmental conditions in these settlements are extremely poor. In the squatter settlements the situation is obviously much worse. In the slums rents are extremely high and there is always problem of insecurity.

8. Policy Implications

Urbanization, if combined with greater education and access to financial capital, can help improve the circumstances of the urban poor. They must also be given the resources necessary to take full advantage of the economic opportunities that liberalisation can offer. Attention also needs to be paid to private sector participation to close the infrastructure gap and improve management of urban services. Active community participation in solid waste management is required. Slums need improved access to health services, both curative and preventative. There is also a need to improve the access of rural dwellers to shelter, water sanitation and other environmental services.

The generation of employment opportunities and adoption of measures for the diversification of rural livelihoods, would assist in slowing down the transfer of population from rural to urban areas. This would provide some relief to the urban infrastructure and economy as well as help improve economic conditions of the rural population. Although government policy recognises the need for the development of rural non-farm employment, there is the need to properly implement the initiatives proposed. There is also a need for special allocation to rural areas in more general development programmes such as secondary education, road and other transport network, rural electrification, infrastructure for telecommunication and information technology.

The labour force is growing at twice the rate of population growth. To achieve a substantial reduction in unemployment and underemployment, over 50 million jobs will have to be created in the next 25 years. On the basis of a high growth scenario, it is projected that urban and peri-urban centres will employ about 40% of the 100 million employed workforce by 2020 (today is only 20%, a trend that parallels the current and future distribution of the population). Existing level of skills of the urban workforce is very poor and this is a serious constraint to the efficiency of the urban sector to act as the engine of growth and drive the economy forward.

(Tim Ruffer is Senior Economist in the Economic Policy Programme of Oxford Policy Management, a UK-based international consultancy firm. He works predominantly in Africa, Asia, and the Caribbean, where he has provided consulting services for a number of governments and multilateral and bilateral development agencies. His work covers the economics and political economy of development, international trade policy, public finance management, and aid policy.

Nadia Masud is a PhD candidate at the University of Oxford, UK.)

Notes

1. Garrett James, Chowdhury Shyamal, *Urban-Rural Links and Transformation In Bangladesh: A Review of the Issues*, IFPRI.
2. Ibid.
3. Bangladesh, Making Cities Work, August 2002.
4. 'The transition to market-oriented agriculture: achieving a poverty focus,' by Alastair Orr, Working Paper prepared for the PETRRA project (Poverty Elimination through Rice Research Assistance).
5. Garret, James and Chowdhury Shyamal, (2004) *Urban-Rural Links and Transformation In Bangladesh: A Review of the Issues,* IFPRI.
6. Ibid.
7. Hossain, Mahbub, (2002), Promoting Rural non farm economy of Bangladesh, Centre for Policy Dialogue, Bangladesh.
8. Labour Economic Data on CAPE website, *www.cape-emp.org/useful/labor/Bangladesh.htm*
9. *http:/Bangladesh.search.com.bd/HT/H_0090.htm*
10. See N Islam (1996). Dhaka: From City to Megacity. Urban Studies Program, University of Dhaka.
11. Bhuyan, A R, H Khan, and S U Ahmed 2001, Rural Urban Migration and Poverty: The Case for Reverse Migration in Bangladesh. MAP Focus Study Series 10. Dhaka: Centre on Integrated Development for Asia and the Pacific.

12. Hossain, M and U Deb. 2003, Moving Forward Looking Behind: Creation of Livelihood Options through Migration, Livelihoods of the Extremely Poor Study. Research Report 3. Dhaka PROSHIKA.
13. The factor contributing most to inequality in urban areas is education of the household head, while in rural areas it is land ownership. In both urban and rural areas, the second largest determinant of inequality is location.
14. South Asia Brief, Urban Fact sheets, 2002, USAID.

References

Bangladesh, Making Cities Work, August 2002.

Census of Bangladesh, various issues.

Economic Trends Statistical Department, Bangladesh Bank, 1998.

Garrett James, Chowdhury Shyamal, Urban Rural Links and Transformation In Bangladesh: A Review of the Issues, IFPRI. *www.bbsgov.org/ana_vol1/urbaniz.htm*

Hossain, Mahbub, (2002), Promoting Rural non-farm economy of Bangladesh, Centre for Policy Dialogue, Bangladesh.

Labour Economic Data on CAPE website: *www.capeemp.org/useful/labor/Bangladesh.htm*

Oxford Policy Management (2002), Bangladesh: Supporting the Drivers of Pro-Poor Change, June.

South Asia Brief, Urban Fact sheets, 2002, USAID.

Rahman, Rushidan; Islam K M, (2003) Employment Poverty Linkages: Bangladesh.

Rouf, M A and Jahan, S (2000), Urban Centres in Bangladesh: Trends, Patterns and Characteristics.

Various Labour force survey reports.

ANNEXURES

Annexure 1: Maps of Bangladesh

Map 1: Bangladesh Population Density, 1991

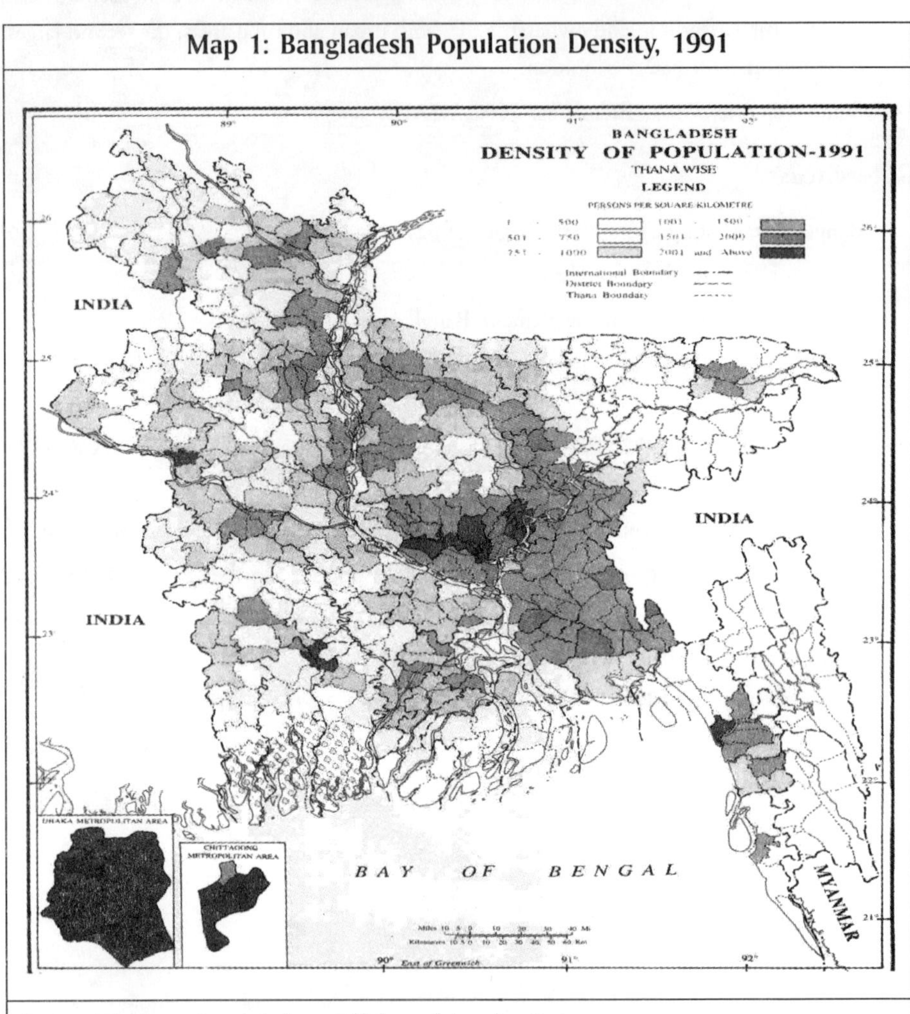

Source: http://www.bangladesh.gov.bd/bdmaps/bdpopdensity.jpg.

Map 2: Bangladesh Transportation Network

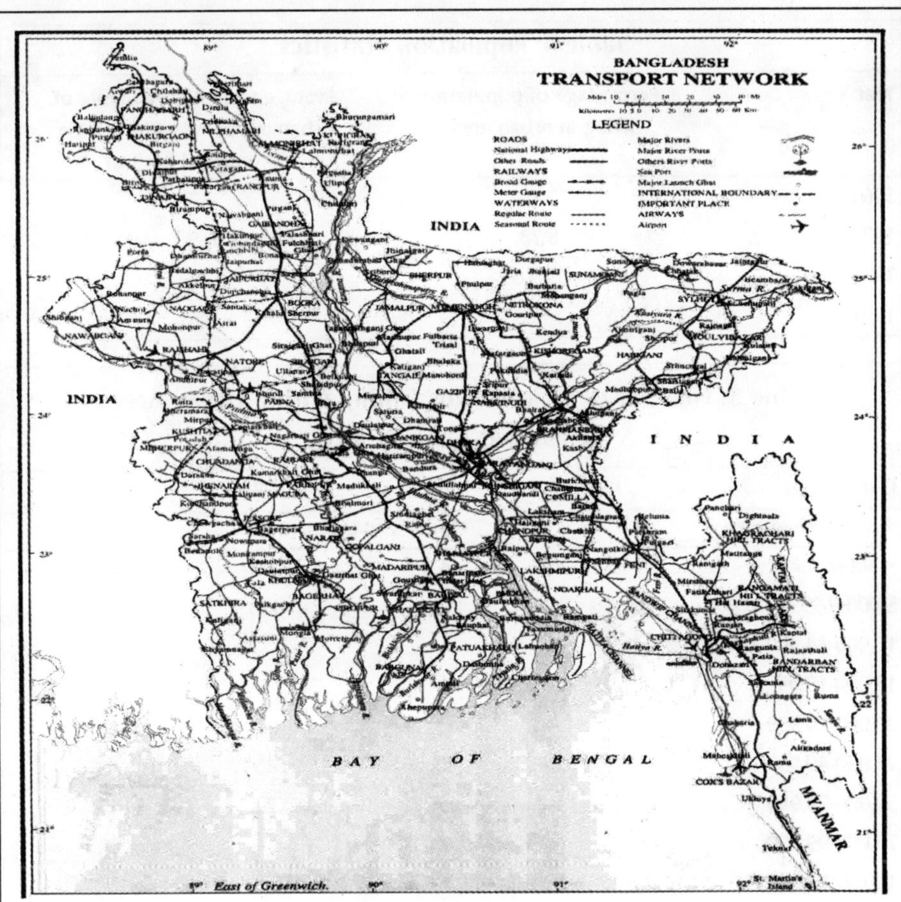

Source: http://www.bangladesh.gov.bd/bdmaps/bdtransport.jpg.

Annexure 2: Statistical Appendix

Table 4: Population Statistics

Year	Percentage of population living in urban areas	Average annual growth rate of urban population (during the intercensal period)
1961	5.19	3.75
1974	8.78	6.62
1981	15.18	10.63
1991	19.63	4.67

Table 5: Number of Cities/Towns Falling within Urban Areas Classified by their Size

Census Year	1961	1974	1981	1991
Size of urban area	Number of urban areas			
<5000	10	4	168	325
5,000-9,999	20	12	129	74
10,000-14,999	-	-	-	-
15,000-19,999	2	4	8	10
20,000-24,999	23	49	114	44
25,000-49,999	16	20	45	13
50,000-74,999	5	17	23	17
75,000-99,999	-	-	-	-
100,000-199,999	-	-	-	-
200,000-299,999	2	1	8	14
300,000-399,999	1	1	1	-
400,000-499,999	-	1	1	-
500,000-999,999	1	1	1	1
1,000,000-1,999,999	-	1	1	1
2,000,000-2,999,999	-	-	-	1
3,000,000-4,999,999	-	-	1	-

Sources: Census of Bangladesh. www.bbsgov.org/ana_vol1/urbaniz.htm

Table 6: Urbanization in Bangladesh, 1970-2020 ('000)

	1970	1980	1990	2000	2010	2020
Urban Population	5,059	12,713	21,750	34,354	52,223	74,432
Rural Population	61,420	72,725	88,275	103,085	115,703	123,209
Total	66,476	85,438	110,025	137,439	167,926	197,642
Percent Urban	7.6	14.9	19.8	25.0	31.1	37.7
Urban Growth Rate Annual	7.8	5.8	4.7	4.3	3.7	3.0
Rural Growth Rate Annual	2.1	1.9	1.7	1.3	0.8	0.2
Chittagong	693	1332	2265	3651	5389	na
Dhaka	1,474	3,257	6,621	12,519	19,393	na
Khulna	325	632	973	1,442	2,081	na
Rajshahi	108	238	517	1,035	1,676	na
Percent of urban population in:						
Chittagong	13.7	10.5	10.4	10.6	10.3	na
Dhaka	29.1	25.6	30.4	36.4	37.1	na
Khulna	6.4	5.0	4.5	4.2	4.0	na
Rajshahi	2.1	1.9	2.4	3.0	3.2	na
Total	51.3	43	47.7	54.6	54.6	na

Source: Garrett James, Chowdhury Shyamal, Urban Rural Links and Transformation In Bangladesh – A Review of the Issues, IFPRI.

Figure 1: Growth Trend of Urban Centres

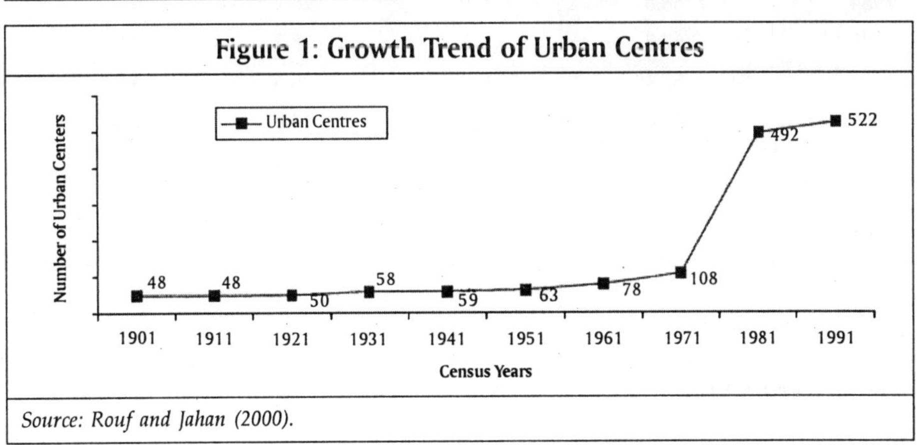

Source: Rouf and Jahan (2000).

Table 7: Production of Major Agriculture Commodities ('000s of tonnes)

	1990	1992	1993	1994	1995	1996	1997	1998
Aus Rice	2487	2199	2075	1850	1791	1676	1871	1875
Aman Rice	9202	9269	9680	9419	8509	8790	9552	8850
Boro Rice	6167	6804	6587	6772	6538	7221	7460	8137
Wheat	890	1065	1176	1131	1245	1369	1454	1803
Sugar Cane	7423	7446	7507	7111	7446	7165	7520	7379
Rape and Mustard	217	243	244	239	245	246	249	254
Moong	31	32	31	30	32	32	34	34
Masur	148	153	163	168	168	170	171	163
Tobacco	38	34	36	38	38	175	38	37
Tea	39	45	49	51	52	48	53	51
Jute and Mestha	4639	5317	4956	4489	5355	4105	4906	5872
Cotton	-	14	16	26	13	13	14	14

Source: Economic Trends Statistical Department, Bangladesh Bank, 1998.

Table 8: Sectoral Composition of Labour Force

Year	Sectoral Composition of Employed Workforce (%)			
	Agriculture	Manufacturing	Service	Household Work
1981	70.1	19.6	8.7	1.6
1984	58.8	9.0	26.2	6.0
1985	57.7	9.3	28.2	4.8
1986	57.4	11.8	26.6	4.3
1989	65.0	15.5	14.8	4.8
1991	66.3	12.7	16.1	4.6
1991	63.2	9.5	25.1	2.2
1996	62.1	10.3	24.8	2.8

Source: Various Labour Force Survey Reports.

Table 9: Income per Hour from Wage and Self-Employment (Taka)			
Sector		**Wage**	**Self-Employment**
Agricultural sector	Rural	8.2904	19.2813
	Urban	9.8925	22.4131
Non-Agricultural sector	Rural	11.7188	16.008
	Urban	12.2124	20.2919
Total	Rural	8.8481	17.8676
	Urban	11.5552	20.5711

Source: Rahman, Rushidan; Islam K M, (2003) Employment Poverty Linkages: Bangladesh.

Table 10: Employment by Occupations (Percent of Workers)		
Year	**1987-1988**	**1999-2000**
Farming	41	35
Trade and Business	10	14
Services	15	21
Agricultural Labour	22	11
Non-agricultural Labour	11	18

Table 11: Major Sources of Income		
Year	**1987-1988**	**1999-2000**
Farming	47	49
Trade and Business	10	14
Services	12	16
Wage Labour	31	21

Table 12: Composition of Household Income		
Year	**1987-1988**	**1999-2000**
Rice Farming	32	16
Non-rice Farming	15	24
Trade and Business	14	24
Service	21	26
Wage Labour	18	10

Source: Hossain Mahabub, (2002) Promoting Rural non-farm economy of Bangladesh, CPD.

Figure 2: Composition of Household Income

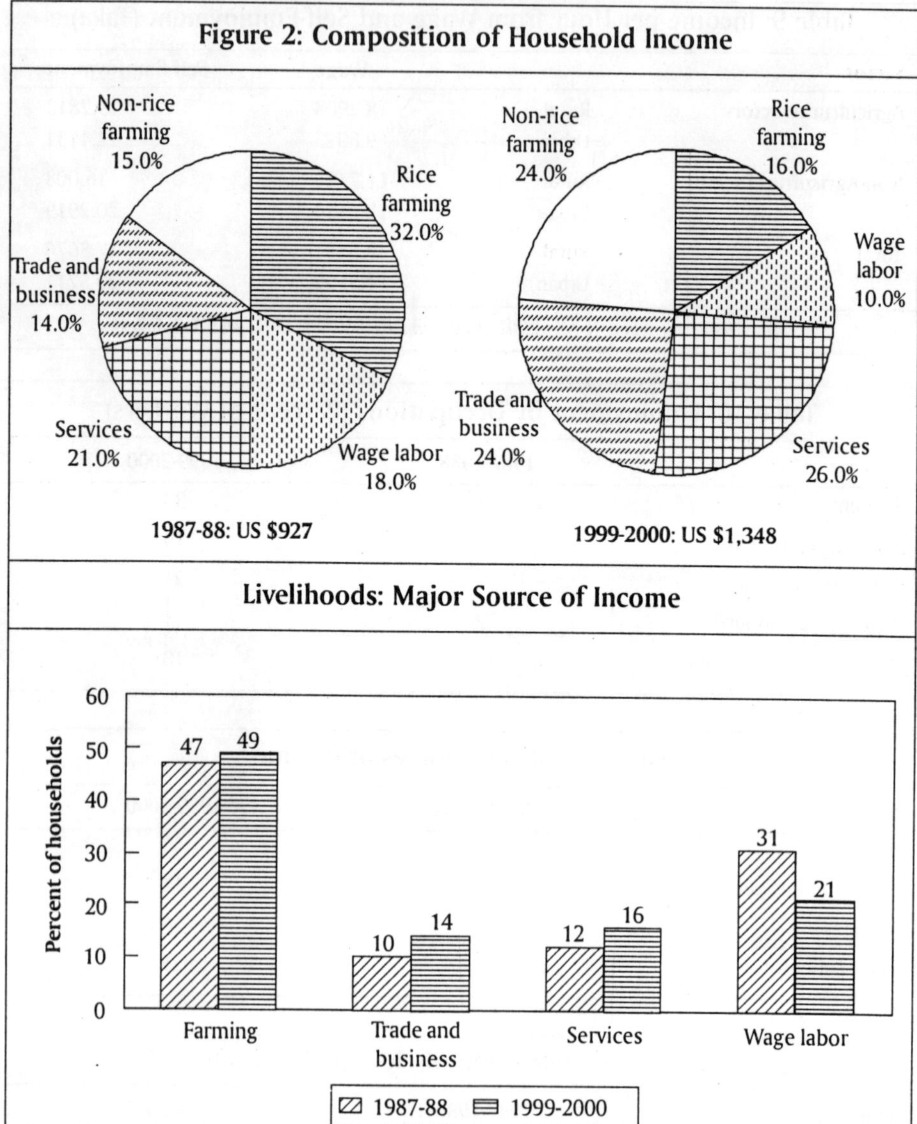

13

Rural and Urban Development Case Study – Nigeria

Tim Ruffer

With a population of 125 million, Nigeria is Africa's most populous country, and has the highest urban population among sub-Saharan African countries. Poverty is higher in rural than in urban areas, and per capita incomes in urban areas are roughly a third higher than in rural areas. This article, like the previous one on Bangladesh, covers a number of aspects relating to rural and urban development in Nigeria.

1. Introduction

In Nigeria, population has been a rather sensitive and controversial issue because of its implications for shaping regional (now geopolitical), state and ethnic relations, the distribution of oil revenues between states, and the balance of power in the country. It is the attitude towards the population question, in terms of its absolute size, as it affects the states and the sub-regions, that constitute the background to the census controversies which the country has been associated with. This means that reliable data on population movements is impossible to come by – even estimates of Nigeria's total population are subject to a margin of error of 20%.

Source: Oxford Policy Management. © Oxford Policy Management. This document is an output from a project funded by the UK Department for International Development (DFID) for the benefit of developing countries. The views expressed are not necessarily those of DFID. Reprinted with permission.

Time series data on rural-urban change is made even more difficult by the fluidity in defining communities as rural or urban. The common exercise of creating new local government areas (LGAs), which begun in 1963, has meant that each LGA must have a capital or headquarters, which has been declared an urban centre by administrative fiat – many erstwhile rural settlements were elevated overnight to an urban status to fit their new designation, regardless of their population size or level of infrastructural development.

Given the lack of relevant survey data and unreliability of the data that does exist, much of the analysis in this paper is based on the results of case study material which provides suggestions of trends taking place in the country.

2. Key Trends

With a total population of around 125 million, Nigeria is the most populous country in Africa. Although Nigeria does not have the highest proportion of urban population in sub-Saharan Africa (in several of the countries of francophone Central Africa, for example, close to 50% of the population lives in the major city or cities), it has more large cities and the highest total urban population of any sub-Saharan African country.

Migration from the rural areas to urban centres is a common livelihood activity. Although young males are the predominant category of rural-urban migrants, young females are increasingly joining this movement to take advantage of greater educational and occupational opportunities in the cities. Spurred by the oil boom prosperity of the 1970s and the massive improvements in roads and the availability of vehicles, Nigeria since independence has become an increasingly urbanised and urban-oriented society. Estimates of urban dwellers reveal this shift: in 1952, 11% of the total population was classified as urban; this figure had grown to 28% by 1985 and to 46% by 2002.

It is not only the increase in urban population that has been dramatic but also the geographical spread has been spectacular in recent times. It is estimated that in 2002, some 18 cities had a population of more than 500,000. The 1991 population census indicated that about 359 settlements have at least 20,000 people. Estimates for the year 2000 put the figure at more than 450. Thus unlike most African countries where one or two cities dominate the urban network, almost all corners of the Nigerian land space have large centres of human agglomeration.

Table 1: Key Data

	1985	1990	1995	2000	2002
Population growth rate (National) (%)	2.8	2.9	3.0	2.8	2.7
Population growth rate (Urban) (%)	5.7	5.5	5.4	4.5	4.0
Population growth rate (Rural) (%)	1.9	1.5	1.4	0.8	0.7
Poverty rate (Urban) (%)	38	-	37	-	-
Poverty rate (Rural) (%)	41	-	51	-	-
Urban population as % of total	31	35	40	44	46

Migration was strongly stimulated by the oil boom of the 1970s, which provided a rapid growth in income generating opportunities in cities such as Lagos, Port Harcourt, and Warri, as well as others that were indirectly affected by the oil economy. In the late 1980s, many young people were compelled by the sharp downturn of the economy and the shortage of urban employment to return to their home villages. As a longer-term phenomenon, however, migration from the rural areas, especially by young men, is a continuing social process.

Lagos, Nigeria's largest city, which also contains 85% of the country's industrial activity, is one of the fastest growing cities in the world – its annual growth rate was estimated at almost 14% during the 1970s, when the massive extent of new construction was exceeded only by the influx of migrants attracted by the booming prosperity. Its current population is estimated at around 10 million. By 2020, it will be the third biggest city in the world.

Five other cities have populations of more than one million. Aside from Lagos, the most rapid recent rates of urbanization have been around Port Harcourt in the Niger Delta region, which was at the heart of the oil boom, and generally throughout the Igbo and other areas of the southeast.

Despite the recent dramatic pace of urbanization, the incidence of poverty remains higher in rural than urban areas – in 1995, poverty rates were estimated at 51% in rural areas and 37% in urban areas. Per capita incomes in towns and cities are roughly a third higher than in rural areas.

Wage differentials alone do not fully explain the reasons for migration to urban areas. Another major factor leading to rural-urban migration has been the neglect of infrastructure in rural areas. Many people have moved to urban areas for better economic or educational opportunities due to a lack of markets, good transportation facilities, schools, and health facilities. Difficulties in agricultural areas, including scarcity of land, declining crop yields, poor harvests and soil erosion, also partly explain rural-urban migration.

Projections suggest that the number of people living in Nigeria's towns and cities will reach 100 million by 2020. Although the urban population growth rate is now declining (it has fallen steadily from 5.7% in 1985 to current rates of 4.0%), it is still far higher than Nigeria's overall population growth rate.

As well as rural-urban migration, other forms of population movement observed in Nigeria have included the following:

- Rural to rural migration is an important feature linking different areas of the country. Some activities, such as palm or rubber tapping, lumbering, trading in farm produce, or working as hired labour, require regular movement between rural areas. Improvement of country's road networks has been important in stimulating the scale of seasonal labour migration. For example, it has become feasible for Hausa and other northern workers to come south to work as hired labourers in the cocoa belt and elsewhere at the onset of the rains and later return to their home villages in time to plant their own crops.
- Yunusa (1999) found that in the 1960s and 1970s, many of the youth moved from the middle belt to the booming cocoa producing areas and cities in the north. On their return, they set up non-farm activities, with farming remaining a secondary activity – migration took people out of household farm labour and out of the farm.
- Surveys have found that even though rural-urban migration may be on the increase, the simultaneous growth of urban-type income generating activities in the rural areas has succeeded in reducing the volume of migration to the cities. As well as trends of rural-urban migration, there is also growing evidence of increasing urban-rural migration – including not only returned people, but also younger people. A number of factors, many of which were exacerbated

by the Structural Adjustment Programme (SAP), initiated in 1986, account for return migration, including disillusionment with urban conditions, declining business fortunes, loss of work, serious ill-health, congestion, as well as increasing returns to agricultural production brought about by the liberalisation of agricultural prices. In the Nasarawa State, Yunusa (1999) found that many urban informal sector workers moved to rural areas with their businesses to avoid the increasingly stiff competition in the cities. In a study of a northern Kaduna State village, Meagher (1999) reported a trend towards return migration in a significant number of rural households. She noted however that '*this process does not appear to be bringing skills and capital back into the community. On the contrary, return migration has involved a retreat from collapsed opportunities outside*'. Such re-ruralisation has in many cases led to land tenure disputes as a result of migrants returning to homelands to reclaim land now taken over by others.

3. Characteristics of the Agriculture Sector

Climatic and soil conditions allow Nigeria to produce a wide variety of agricultural products, including many food and cash crops. Although past economic conditions have not favoured the agricultural sector, prices of agricultural commodities are generally no longer subject to price controls. Considerable seasonal price fluctuations are frequent, reflecting the problems of inadequate storage, processing, marketing, and distribution facilities. Some estimates suggest that post-harvest losses reach 25% in cereal production, and up to 50% in horticultural production.

The contribution of agriculture to GDP stood at 21% in 1980. It increased to 41% in 1988 after a collapse in oil prices and growth in the agriculture sector following the liberalisation of agricultural prices. It has since fluctuated between a low of 24% in 1992 and a high of 39% in 1998.

In the past decade, growth in production of staple foods has exceeded population growth, a considerable achievement in view of the country's large and growing population and the relatively minor official support for such production. Less than 3% of the value of food consumed is imported.

More than 70% of the working adult population of Nigeria are employed in the agricultural sector directly and indirectly. Small farm-holders, account for about 81% of total farm holdings. They are usually subsistence farmers lacking in capital and in modern techniques of farming. They are constrained by many problems, including those of poor access to modern inputs and credit, poor infrastructure, inadequate access to markets, land and environmental degradation, and inadequate research and extension services. Only 10% of agricultural production is further processed industrially in Nigeria. Infrastructural factors, including energy and water shortages, credit constraints, poor knowledge of potential markets, and transport and telecommunications problems are important impediments to increasing this share.

Over the past couple of decades, successive governments have initiated numerous policies and programmes to revive agricultural performance. During the pre-structural adjustment period, agricultural policies were designed to facilitate agricultural marketing, reduce the cost of agricultural production and enhance agricultural product prices as incentives for increased production. Major policy instruments included those targeted to agricultural commodity marketing and pricing, input supply and distribution, input price subsidies, agricultural extension and technology transfer, agricultural cooperatives, and agricultural water resource and irrigation development.

Since the structural adjustment period, the state has withdrawn completely from involvement in certain agricultural sectors and the incorporation of private sector involvement in the provision of these services has scarcely begun. However there are active private trader networks (Okorua and Bedford, 2001) on which the agricultural sector depends, particularly in urban food supply, although their activities are often regarded as exploitative and based on cartel arrangements, with a dominance of marketing systems by particular ethnic groups. The relatively strong growth of the sector since the mid-1990s does however suggest the marketing system is functional despite its constraints, though little progress has been made in reviving agricultural exports except in limited cross-border trade and in the cocoa sector. The state's withdrawal from an active role in agricultural marketing has been positive in its impact on the marketing system, but the state is failing to provide key services or effectively to support research or other forms of technology support.

Land tenure systems in Nigeria have been confronted with problems resulting from rapid population growth and the advances being sought towards the modernisation of agriculture through investment, market orientation, technology and attempts to increase size in order to achieve economies of scale. Customary land tenure systems are breaking down under the impact of cash cropping, population pressure and non-agricultural enterprises and there has been a growing individualisation of land tenure. As a result there is a need to modify the existing tenure systems in order to solve the complex and dynamic sets of problems affecting resource management, the adoption of new technologies, and farm income levels. Population growth has led to a fragmentation of farm plots with a more intensive use of the land for agricultural practice. Depletion of soil fertility and reduced production levels invariably result.

An important form of government intervention in the agriculture sector, now that it has largely withdrawn from involvement in output marketing, has been related to fertiliser. Between 1990 and 1996, government heavily subsidised fertiliser use. Liberalisation of the government monopoly from 1997 and its withdrawal from fertiliser procurement and subsidy led to a sharp drop in fertiliser use. Nagy and Edun (2002) argue that the way in which liberalisation was implemented limited the private sector response, particularly "ad hoc procurement/ subsidy policies of the FGN in 1999, 2001 and 2002." They note that most stakeholders identify the quality and availability of fertiliser as the main constraint on use, while government policies have justified subsidy on the grounds that farmers cannot afford the free market price.

Cities represent the largest and fastest growing market for farmers, in a context where over 90% of total agricultural production is used for domestic consumption. But the influence of urban demand for food and labour is unevenly spread in the country, resulting in different dynamics:

- In areas fully exposed to the influence of urban markets, agriculture is in competition with non agricultural activities for land use, employment as well as investment. These areas, often characterised by high population density and high density of exchanges, concern a growing proportion of the rural population.

- In a second belt, market influence is growing, but is not regular enough to have generated new regulation systems, giving rise to fierce competition over resources.

- Some areas of Nigeria are still barely connected to markets. Most of these areas have had to adapt to out-migration to better endowed areas.

The distribution of the rural population is more and more determined by the size and location of the urban markets and by infrastructure, with the rural population density decreasing with the distance from the markets. Agricultural output per hectare and per rural inhabitant as well as the surplus per farmer of farm products available for marketing tend to become a direct function of population density. The areas of dense rural settlement, located in the proximity of the major markets, are therefore those which generate the highest farm surpluses per farmer, despite the constraints imposed by their higher rural population densities.

Marketing and purchasing can be a problem for poor farmers who may not have resources to either transport their produce to the market during harvest, or patronise the market to purchase food during hungry season. This is especially so with those living in villages that are less accessible due to the poor road network. Farmers in such villages transport their produce to the market as head loads, on bicycles, motorcycles or lorries. 37% of the households are living in villages that are easily accessible, while others are less accessible (Obamiro et al 2003).

4. Livelihoods Sources

A series of case studies undertaken in different parts of Nigeria provide important evidence of the diversification of livelihoods sources in rural areas.

In a study of non-farm activities in the Nigerian savannah from the start of colonialisation, Meagher (1999) found that the majority of households across all income strata are involved in several non-farm activities, whose importance has increased over the last 25 years. Non-farm activities are diverse, partly seasonal and often performed within the family compound. They include agro-processing, snack and food production, transport, retail and household trade, and tailoring. Some are based on investment in grinding machines, sugar cane crushing machines and sewing machines. Non-farm activities accounted for 60% of cash income and an average of 36% of adult working hours in the course of a year. Farm and non-farm activities are more complimentary than competitive activities. Meagher found that agricultural growth is essential for a productive expansion of the non-farm rural sector. The major source of start-up capital for non-farm activities is profits from agriculture or livestock. Other sources include relatives, informal credit, bank loans and the sale or mortgage of land.

Meagher also found that the process of deagrarianisation was not constant, but that there is a tendency to shift in and out of agriculture depending on the shifting profitability of agricultural production, which is affected by policy shifts and terms of trade – this is particularly the case with the upper stratum of farming households who have the resources to make timely and profitable changes. She and Yunusa (1999) both underline that the existence of non-farm activities in rural areas is not a new phenomenon – historically both farm and non-farm activities complemented each other in meeting the needs of the rural family in Nigeria.

Okali *et al,* (2001) found that income diversification is increasing in the rural areas through the sub-urbanization of industrial activities like paper mills, packaging and intensified home construction activities. The latter has brought a significant shift in occupations from farming to working on construction sites. The continued spread of urban areas, coupled with improved transportation and higher literacy levels has facilitated the incidence of commuting from peri-urban rural sites to towns and cities for employment.

There are also a number of case studies providing evidence of trends in livelihoods sources in urban areas.

Meagher and Yunusa (1996) estimated that informal activities have increased in importance as livelihoods sources from approximately 50% of the urban workforce in the late 1970s to 65% by the late 1980s, as rising urban wages encouraged migration to the cities. However, expansion was linked to increasing differentiation and a trend towards income stagnation at the lower end of the informal economy. Women and informal labourers were particularly affected by this dynamic. The study highlights new patterns of entry into Nigeria's informal sector:

- First, entry has intensified from the traditional sources of participation, particularly low income wage earners and the unemployed.

- Second, the category of unemployed now includes not only retrenched workers and civil servants, but secondary school and university graduates.
- Third, there is an increase in female participation as part of a household level survival strategies.
- Finally, a growing number of employed civil servants are becoming very active in the informal economy.

A study of Zaria, a northern Nigerian town, found that 67% of low income entrepreneurs were involved in at least one low income activity, including farming (52%) and/or other petty informal activities (32%). The study found that involvement in these activities is significantly lower among high income actors. Studies have also established the significance of urban and peri-urban agriculture which has been a response to rapid inflation of food prices and a general lack of employment opportunities in the formal sector. For this reason, urban people often turn to horticultural crop production on open sites as a direct means of improving their livelihoods. Farmers in urban areas are generally a relatively homogeneous group: mostly males, with little formal education, resource poor and with few other income-earning opportunities.

Case studies point to a long-term trend of growing dependence of rural dwellers on remittances from relatives residing in urban areas. However survey evidence from Okali *et al,* (2001) suggest that remittances have declined in recent years in line with decreasing incomes and increasing urban hardship.

Gifts and cash are also sent from rural to urban areas, particularly in the form of food to urban relatives and assistance with the expense of family members moving to the city. Interaction is also facilitated by the strong social support network transcending rural and urban areas. Members of the extended family living in both localities provide a base from which their relatives can move back and forth. Increasing transportation costs in recent years, however, have reduced the frequency of home visits for many people, particularly the poor.

While it is difficult to summarise the varied rural settlement patterns of a country as large as Nigeria, a few key points can be made. First, the household is the main social unit of the rural village or town. Another important point to note about rural villages is that they serve commercial functions. Depending on the size of the settlement, most rural towns and villages have markets that serve as a place of exchange for the settlement and its surrounding trade area. The size of the market is also typically related to the frequency with which it meets. The smallest rural markets in Nigeria may only meet once every two weeks, while the largest meet daily. In the market one can find all kinds of daily and specialised goods for sale: meats, grains, oils, nuts, and fruits. Most towns also serve as service centers. Here one is likely to find a health clinic, a "barbing salon", a car mechanic, and a police station.

While there is some variance in rural communities' access to collective infrastructure, most rural areas lag behind cities in the development of these services. There are often no electricity connections to rural towns. Many rural settlements are also poorly connected by transport links to their surrounding region. This is the case for at least two reasons. First, construction and upkeep of roads has not been sufficient to afford all rural peoples easy access to an efficient, well-maintained highway network. Second, many rural people have limited access to motor vehicles. While taxis are abundant in the cities, those without cars in the countryside are severely constrained.

5. Government Policy

A National Urban Development Policy was launched in 1997. Its stated goal is to develop a dynamic system of urban settlements that will foster sustainable economic growth, promote efficient urban and regional development and ensure improved standard of living and well being for all Nigerians. The 1992 Urban and Regional Planning Law of Nigeria provides the legal framework for the implementation of the policy. The law specifies the urban limit for any settlement and the planning and development parameters guiding such development. Thus it holds a good promise for the protection of rural agricultural lands in peri-urban areas.

Necessary institutional frameworks have been established to implement the policy. At the local level, Urban Planning Authorities are being set up to administer the policy, while Urban Planning Boards are located at the State level and a National Urban Development Commission has been set up at the Federal level. The decree setting up the Commission is now being reviewed.

The recently published National Economic Empowerment and Development Strategy (NEEDS) highlights evidence that suggests that the rural sector has been facing "a relatively more serious poverty situation than the urban" and explains this as being due to a variety of factors which include:

- "Sharp seasonality in the flow of production, income and employment opportunities in the rural sector.
- Relative shortage of social and economic infrastructure in the rural areas, as compared to the urban.
- Migration of the (educated) workforce to the urban areas and the consequent ageing of the rural population.
- Low productivity of rural (and especially agricultural) production, due partly to limited access to credit, pesticides, extension services support, and modern technology for agricultural production, processing and preservation."

NEEDS further states that "with partly rural-fed increases in population putting pressures on limited resources in the urban areas, the latter centres continue to face serious problems of unemployment, under-employment, housing and other environment-related problems, which contribute to persistent seriousness of the urban poverty situation".

Furthermore, constraints inhibiting private sector participation in the transformation of agricultural production highlighter by NEEDS include "The rapid shift of population from rural to urban areas and the perceptible shift in consumption patters from local to imported food items" and a "land tenure system that inhibits the acquisition of land for mechanised farming".

Policy thrusts in NEEDS that aim to address these issues include the "creation of more agricultural and rural employment opportunities to increase the income of farmers and urban dwellers through the modernisation of production and creation of an agricultural sector that is responsive to the demands and realities of the Nigerian economy" and the "promotion of integrated rural development involving agricultural and non-agricultural activities including the provision of physical infrastructure such as feeder roads, rural water supply and rural communications".

6. Consequences

In rural areas, the vast increase in food demand generated by the growth of cities and expansion of transport capacity were amongst the major driving forces of agricultural production and modernisation through the 1990s. Urbanization has played an important role in reducing pressures on scarce land and rural environmental resources and allowing the remaining rural population to develop viable production. Unless there is a considerable increase in the country's dependence on food imports, farm output per worker will need to grow by two-thirds and farm surplus per worker will need to double by 2020 in order to feed Nigeria's growing urban population (Club du Sahel 2000). If this growth does occur, it has the potential to provide for a significant increase in the standard of living of farmers.

Migration between rural and urban areas in Nigeria has had a significant impact on both rural and urban areas because of the number of people involved and the fact that most migrants have been the young, often male, most productive members of the rural population. This has meant that the rural areas from which they came have often been left with a demographically unbalanced population of women, younger children, and older people. This process has affected the rural economy in the areas of migration by creating marked changes in the gender division of labour.

Agricultural labour was traditionally specified by gender: men had certain tasks and women had others, although the specific divisions varied by culture and ethnic group. As working-age men have left the rural areas, the resulting labour gap has normally been met by others, usually wives or children, or by hired labour. In other cases, the tasks have been modified or not performed.

The departure of men has helped to generate a lively market for rural wage labour. In many areas, male and female labourers are commonly hired to perform agricultural tasks such as land preparation, weeding, and harvesting, which in the past were done either by household labour or traditional work parties. In turn, the growth in demand for hired labour has fostered an increase of seasonal and longer term intra-rural migration.

In more remote areas, however, finding hired workers is often difficult. The absence of men has led to neglect of such tasks as land clearing and heavy soil conservation work, which they generally performed. Thus, in forest areas from which there has been much male migration, thickly overgrown land that has been left as fallow for extended periods is often not cleared for cultivation; instead, the same areas of land are used repeatedly, leading to rapid declines in soil fertility and yields. As a result, land degradation has occurred in these low density areas.

Intra-rural migration has led to increasing land disputes. Migrants can be allocated land but they lack security of tenure and the host community can in theory reclaim land at will. Many long running conflicts in Nigeria are rooted in the disputes over the property rights of migrants (such as the Tiv/Jukun and Ife/Modakeke conflicts).

The rapid growth of urban populations has created the following challenges in Nigeria's largest cities:

- Congestion leading to urban squalor, housing shortages, invasion of urban open spaces and green belts with low quality housing.
- A rapid accumulation of urban waste and a breakdown of urban infrastructure (including transport, water, and electricity).
- Atmospheric and groundwater pollution.
- Lack of adequate infrastructure for housing, sanitation, water, and open space amenities. Much of this is due to the absence of land planning statutes that encompass the evolving functions and responsibilities of urban areas.

7. Policy Implications

- Since rural-urban interactions are a significant part of livelihood strategies, they should always be taken into account by development policy makers in designing interventions for policy alleviation in both urban and rural development – rural and urban areas should be seen as two ends of a continuum of the urbanization process.
- As agriculture is shown to be the engine of growth in the rural economy, prioritisation of agricultural development is an important rural development

and poverty reduction strategy, despite the declining importance of agriculture in livelihoods and GDP.

- The government faces immense challenges in improving urban infrastructure and related public services. Continued privatisation of public utilities and policies that promote private funding of some ventures, such as urban water and electricity supply, refuse collection, and housing is one way in which service provision can be improved.
- Although highly controversial in Nigeria, reform of the 1978 Land Use Act has the potential to significantly improve the efficiency of land use in both rural and urban areas.

(Tim Ruffer is Senior Economist in the Economic Policy Programme of Oxford Policy Management, a UK-based international consultancy firm. He works predominantly in Africa, Asia, and the Caribbean, where he has provided consulting services for a number of governments and multilateral and bilateral development agencies. His work covers the economics and political economy of development, international trade policy, public finance management and aid policy.)

References

Bamire, A S and Y L Fabiyi (1999), Economic implications of property rights on smallholder use of fertilizer in southwest Nigeria.

Club du Sahel (2000), Urbanization, rural-urban linkages and policy implications for rural and agricultural development: Case study from West Africa: Understanding rural-urban linkages and rural non-farm economies for growth and poverty alleviation, SAH/DLR(2000)1.

Government of Nigeria (2004), National Economic Empowerment and Development Strategy.

Max Lock Centre (2003), Mapping Urbanization for Urban and Regional Governance, Final Report: September 2003 – DFID Research R8130, University of Westminster in London.

Magobunje, A (1970), A typology of population pressure on resources in West Africa, in: W Zelinsky, L A Kosinsky & R M Prothero (eds) Geography in a Crowding World, Oxford University Press.

Meagher, K and Yunusa, M (1996), Passing the buck: Structural adjustment and the Nigerian urban informal sector, UNRISD Discussion Paper, May.

Meagher, K (1999), If the drumming changes, the dance also changes: de-agrianisation and rural non-farm employment in the Nigerian savannah. Africa Study Centre Working Paper 40. Leiden.

Nagy, J G, and O Edun (2002), Assessment of Nigerian Government Fertilizer Policy and Suggested Alternative Market-Friendly Policies, Report to IFDC.

Obamiro, E O, W Doppler, & P M Kormawa (2003), Pillars of Food Security in Rural Areas of Nigeria, FoodAfrica, Internet Forum 31 March–11 April.

Odaman, O (1988), Migration and social-economic aspects of homeward remittances in Nigeria, Migration World Magazine, January 1; 16(1):16-20.

Okali, D, Okpara, E and Olawoye, J (2001), The case of Aba and its region, southeastern Nigeria, Working Paper Series on Rural-Urban Interactions and Livelihood Strategies, Human Settlements Programme, IIED, October.

Okoruwa, V and A Bedford (2001), Rural Livelihoods Programme – Agricultural Marketing Survey, DFID Abuja.

Oxford Policy Management (2004), Nigeria: Economic Growth Analysis, June.

Tiffen, M (2001), Profile of Demographic Changes in the Kano-Maradi Region, 1960-2000, Drylands Research Working Paper 24.

World Bank (1996), Restoring Urban Infrastructure and Services in Nigeria, Findings No.62.

Yunusa, M (1999), Not farms alone: a study of rural livelihoods in the middle belt of Nigeria, Africa Study Centre Working Paper 38. Leiden.

ANNEXURES

Annexure 1

Map of Nigeria

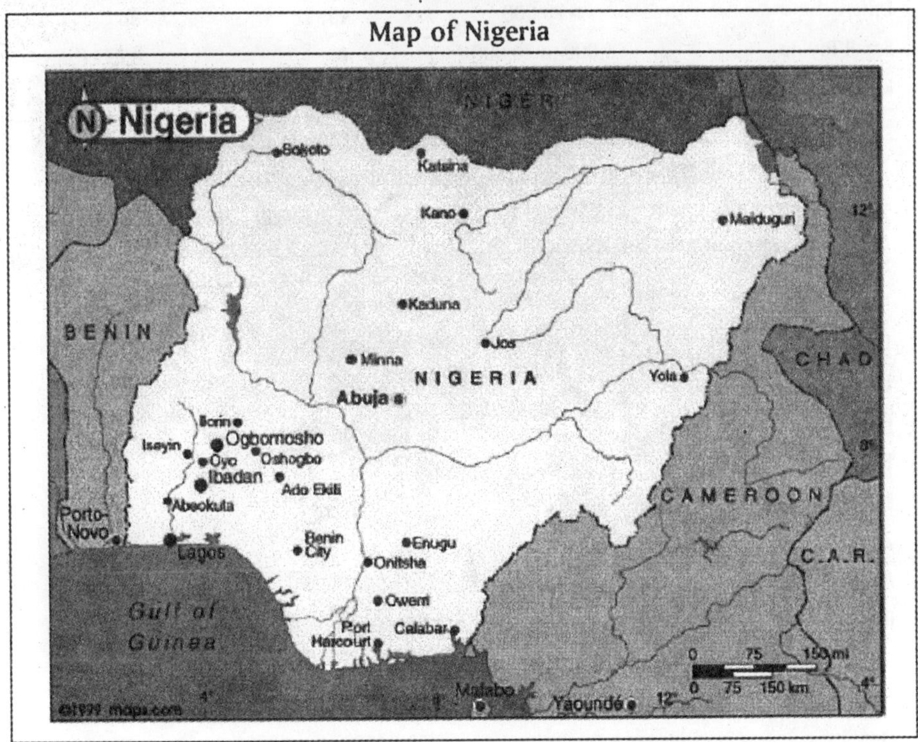

Annexure 2: Statistical Appendix

Table 2: Rural and Urban Population Statistics 1985-2002

	1985	1990	1995	2000	2001	2002
Rural population	57,623,210	62,490,580	67,201,520	70,985,840	71,590,480	72,097,340
Rural population (% of total population)	69	65	60	56	55	54
Rural population growth (annual %)	1.9	1.5	1.4	0.8	0.9	0.7
Urban population	25,572,790	33,712,420	44,068,480	55,924,160	58,284,520	60,687,660
Urban population (% of total)	31	35	40	44	45	46
Urban population growth (annual %)	5.7	5.5	5.4	4.5	4.1	4.0

Source: World Development Indicators.

Table 3: Population Distribution

Type	Community Size	Population (million)	% of Total
Urban	>20,000	45	38
Small Towns	5,000 to 20,000	40	33
Rural	<5,000	35	29

Table 4: Largest Cities in Nigeria (2002)

City	City Population	Urban Area Population
Lagos	8,029,200	9,123,200
Kano	3,248,700	3,519,500
Ibadan	3,078,400	3,6,0,400
Kaduna	1,458,900	1,458,900
Port Harcourt	1,053,900	1,190,600
Benin	1,051,600	1,051,600
Maiduguri	971,700	971,700
Zaria	898,900	898,900
Aba	784,500	899,100
Ilorin	756,400	756,400
Jos	742,100	742,100
Ogbomosho	726,300	985,600
Oyo	620,400	620,400
Enugu	593,300	662,800
Abeokuta	529,700	698,100
Onitsha	509,500	1,001,000
Warri	500,900	500,900
Sokoto	500,500	500,500
Okene	444,900	444,900
Calabar	431,200	431,200
Oshogbo	421,000	1,309,900
Katsina	387,000	387,000
Akure	369,700	369,700
Ife	313,400	313,400

Contd...

Contd...		
Bauchi	291,600	291,600
Iseyin	286,700	286,700
Minna	270,600	270,600
Makurdi	249,000	249,000
Owo	243,000	243,000
Ado	241,200	523,300
Ilesha	233,900	561,200
Gombe	230,900	230,900
Umuahia	230,800	230,800
Ondo	225,800	225,800
Damaturu	223,000	223,000
Jimeta	218,400	218,400
Ikot Ekpene	209,400	209,400
Gusau	201,200	201,200
Mubi	198,700	198,700

Source: The World Gazetteer.

Table 5: Agricultural Production Index 1985-2002

	1985	1990	1995	2000	2001	2002
Crop production index (1989-91 = 100)	60.8	97.1	134.5	156.1	153	159
Food production index (1989-91 = 100)	70.2	97.4	132.3	155.5	153.2	158.8

Source: World Development Indicators.

Table 6: Output of Major Agricultural Commodities ('000 tonnes)

Year	Staples													
	Maize	Millet	Sorghum	Rice	Wheat	Agha	Beans	Cassava	Potato	Yarns	Cocoyams	Plantain	Vegetable	Total
1970	1443.0	3106.0	4053.0	280.0	19.0	18.0	884.0	5224.0	24.0	12033.0	1381.0	985.0	1098.0	30548.0
1971	1274.0	2834.0	3794.0	279.0	20.0	18.0	801.0	4516.0	26.0	9766.0	880.0	1008.0	1136.0	26352.0
1972	639.0	2391.0	2298.0	447.0	20.0	14.0	408.0	2573.0	27.0	6900.0	1357.0	994.0	1175.0	19243.0
1973	808.0	3794.0	3125.0	487.0	15.0	14.0	530.0	2912.0	27.0	6935.0	1106.0	996.0	1211.0	21961.0
1974	528.0	5554.0	4738.0	525.0	18.0	17.0	1097.0	3582.0	27.0	7160.0	480.0	1018.0	1259.0	26003.0
1975	1332.0	2550.0	2920.0	504.0	18.0	16.0	858.0	2324.0	28.0	8620.0	504.0	1016.0	1303.0	21993.0
1976	1068.0	2893.0	2950.0	218.0	18.0	14.0	727.0	1786.0	30.0	6470.0	532.0	1022.0	1134.0	18562.0

Contd...

Contd...

1977	650.0	2579.0	3286.0	410.0	20.0	14.0	408.0	1656.0	32.0	6376.0	345.0	1026.0	1025.0	17828.0
1978	658.0	2386.0	2409.0	280.0	20.0	16.0	498.0	1620.0	34.0	5866.0	182.0	1032.0	976.0	15977.0
1979	488.0	2366.0	2604.0	160.0	22.0	16.0	624.0	1446.0	38.0	5256.0	132.0	1038.0	931.0	15121.0
1980	612.0	2354.0	3346.0	105.0	24.0	18.0	510.0	942.0	40.0	5248.0	208.0	1042.0	972.0	15421.0
1981	720.0	2682.0	3354.0	158.0	26.0	20.0	560.0	620.0	38.0	5212.0	270.0	1048.0	986.0	15704.0
1982	766.0	2666.0	3740.0	212.0	26.0	20.0	616.0	592.0	40.0	5385.0	280.0	1054.0	1048.0	16445.0
1983	594.0	2783.0	3292.0	145.0	26.0	18.0	553.0	513.0	38.0	4047.0	224.0	1068.0	909.0	14240.0
1984	2058.0	3349.0	4608.0	157.0	27.0	23.0	477.0	11500.0	42.0	4600.0	205.0	1086.0	1120.0	29552.0
1985	1190.0	3634.0	4911.0	195.0	113.0	25.0	611.0	13500.0	43.0	4738.0	223.0	1113.0	1254.0	31501.0
1986	1336.0	4111.0	5455.0	283.0	132.0	27.0	732.0	12388.0	46.0	5209.0	373.0	1127.0	1293.0	32512.0
1987	4512.0	3905.0	5455.0	808.0	139.0	26.0	686.0	13876.0	45.0	4886.0	354.0	1071.0	1241.0	37106.0
1988	5258.0	5136.0	5162.0	2081.0	565.0	30.0	657.0	15540.0	44.0	9132.0	693.0	1103.0	1354.0	47015.0
1989	5008.0	4770.0	7255.0	3303.0	554.0	35.0	1232.0	17404.0	50.0	9609.0	649.0	1413.0	1480.0	62772.0
1990	5768.0	5136.0	4155.0	2500.0	554.0	39.0	1354.0	19343.0	54.0	13624.0	731.0	1215.0	1761.0	55964.0
1991	5810.0	4109.0	5357.0	3226.0	455.0	43.0	1352.0	26304.0	66.0	15956.0	829.0	1339.0	2025.0	57581.0
1992	5840.0	4501.0	5909.0	3260.0	515.0	47.0	1411.0	29148.0	73.0	19781.0	940.0	1417.0	2243.0	75085.0
1993	6290.0	4602.0	5051.0	3065.0	33.0	50.0	1576.0	30128.0	80.0	21633.0	1066.0	1623.0	2494.0	78591.0
1994	6902.0	4757.0	5197.0	2427.0	35.0	55.0	1545.0	31005.0	90.0	23153.0	1128.0	1565.0	2843.0	51802.0
1995	6931.0	5563.0	5997.0	3203.0	44.0	58.0	1751.0	31404.0	95.0	22818.0	1182.0	1532.0	2608.0	54286.0
1996	6217.0	5803.0	7514.0	3122.0	47.0	54.0	1847.0	32950.0	99.0	23928.0	1295.0	1588.0	3506.0	88080.0
1997	6285.0	5997.0	7954.0	3230.0	49.0	57.0	1957.0	33510.0	101.0	24713.0	1380.0	1758.0	3816.0	90817.0
1998	6435.0	6328.0	8401.0	3485.0	51.0	70.0	2054.0	34192.0	105.0	25102.0	1450.0	1809.0	4018.0	93401.0
1999	6515.0	6423.0	5524.0	3522.0	53.0	73.0	2180.0	35960.0	109.0	25017.0	1491.0	1541.0	4151.0	96769.0
2000	6491.0	9743.0	5824.0	3841.0	55.0	78.0	2251.0	36750.0	118.0	25421.0	1592.0	1995.0	4480.0	102546.0
2001	6592.0	7088.0	9508.0	3989.0	57.0	81.0	2409.0	37949.0	128.0	27589.0	1702.0	2163.0	4788.0	104043.0
2002	6598.0	7231.0	9667.0	4085.0	59.0	88.0	2612.0	39410.0	138.0	28979.0	1912.0	2378.0	4992.0	108269.0

Source: Central Bank of Nigeria.

Table 7: Working Population by Economic Activity ('000)

	1999	2000	2001	2002	2003
Agriculture	23,912	23,431	25,050	25,789	26,519
Mining and Quarrying	209	204	223	210	216
Manufacturing	2,903	2,852	3,056	3,146	3,235
Production and Dist. of Utilities	489	479	522	537	552
Construction	409	401	438	451	464
Commerce and Hotels	6,532	6,379	6,867	7,061	7,261
Others	5,646	5,534	5,944	6,148	6,322

Sources: National Population Commission, Federal Office of Statistics, National Manpower Board.

14

A Portrait of Rural America – Challenges and Opportunities

LaStar Matthews and William H Woodwell, Jr.

Rural America, which covers 80% of US land, is home to about 59 million, or 21% of the population. This is in sharp contrast to the 70% and above proportion of population that reside in rural areas in developing countries. This article gives a picture of the rural sector in the US, a developed country, and provides comparisons with its urban sector.

Overview

America's rural communities are at a crossroads. In some respects, they face many of the same challenges and choices going forward as the nation's metropolitan areas. But many of the issues rural communities are dealing with are unique to them – and require unique strategies and solutions.

Rural America, covering more than 2,000 counties and 80 percent of US land area, is home to about 59 million people, or 21 percent of the US population. Like their metropolitan counterparts, America's rural, or non-metropolitan, areas are home to an increasingly diverse population, including a surging population of Hispanic residents. There is also remarkable diversity among rural communities

Source: National League of Cities (NLC). November 2005. © NLC. Reprinted with permission. The article can be found online at http://www.nlc.org/content/Files/05_RuralAmericaBrief.pdf

themselves, as seen in an analysis of their economies and the unique challenges they face in areas from transportation and poverty to economic development.

The People: Between April 2000 and July 2003, "non-metro" America added 580,000 people, averaging 0.4 percent population growth per year. This was lower than the growth rate for metropolitan areas (1.3 percent) and half the non-metro average during the "rural rebound" of the 1990s.

The rate of population growth or decline varies among rural areas. Some non-metro counties, especially those adjacent to metropolitan areas, have been experiencing rapid population growth, while others have seen steep declines. Population loss affects non-metro areas in all regions of the country but is particularly widespread in the Great Plains.[1]

The 2000 census counted 17 percent of rural residents as racial and ethnic minorities. The portion of rural residents who are minorities grew by 3 percent between 1990 and 1997[2], with much of the growth due to a surge in the rural Hispanic population. Growing numbers of Hispanics settling in rural America accounted for more than 25 percent of non-metro population growth during the 1990s. Hispanics are no longer concentrated in the rural Southwest; nearly half of the non-metro Hispanic population lives in other parts of the country, with the highest levels of growth occurring in the Southeast and Midwest.

Figure 1: Non-Metro Population Growth Rates by Race and Ethnicity, 1990-2000

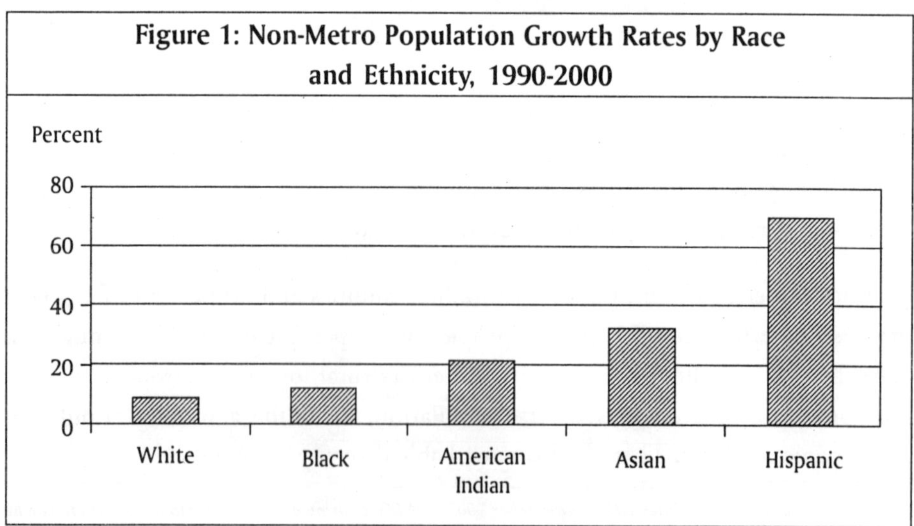

Nearly half of the population of America's rural areas and small towns lives within commuting distance of a metropolitan center or a community with at least 50,000 people. The other half of America's rural residents lives in geographically isolated areas.

Figure 2: Farm Earnings are Growing Less Important to Rural Economies

In 1969, farming accounted for 20 percent or more of earnings in 935 non-metro countries.

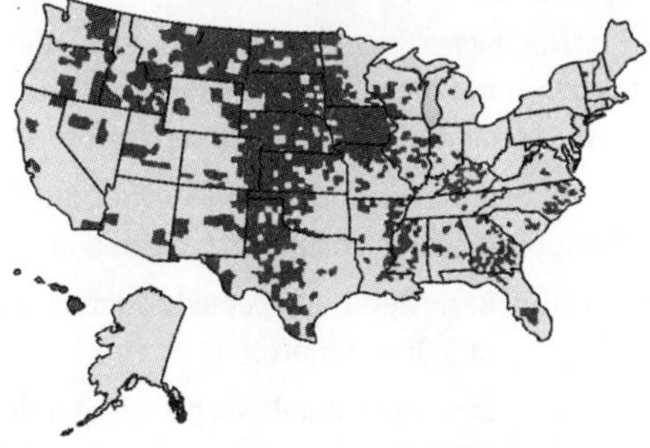

... versus just 262 non-metro countries in 1999.

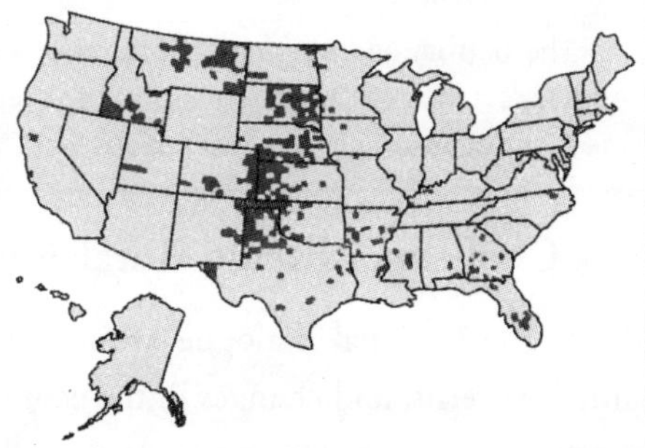

Source: Rural America: Opportunities and Challenges, Amber Waves, February 2003 (Economic Research Service).

The Economy: Agriculture no longer anchors the rural economy as it did through the middle of the twentieth century. Today, seven out of 10 rural counties are dominated by manufacturing, services, and other employment not related to farming.[3] Over the last 20 years, the percentage of the rural workforce employed in farming has dropped from 14.4 percent to 7.6 percent.[4] Rural residents today are working primarily in manufacturing and service jobs, although employment in manufacturing has been declining since 1970, mirroring national trends.

Today, an increasing portion of the rural workforce hold jobs in consumer services such as retail trade, education, and health care. In these jobs, rural residents are providing services primarily to other rural residents. This contrasts with economic trends in urban areas, where "producer services" tend to dominate the jobs picture, with growing numbers of workers engaged in legal, financial, research and business services.

Average weekly earnings for non-metro workers were $543 in 2002, about 80 percent of the $685 average for the nation's metro areas.

Defining Rural America

Rural America usually is defined more by what it is *not* than by what it is. The Office of Management and Budget (OMB) divides American counties into two types: metropolitan and non-metropolitan. In 2003, OMB defined "metro areas" as: (1) central counties with one or more urbanized areas; and (2) outlying counties that are economically tied to the core counties as measured by work commuting.

"Non-metro" counties lie outside the boundaries of the nation's metro areas and are divided by OMB into two types: "micropolitan" areas centered on urban clusters of 10,000 or more persons; and all remaining "non-core" counties.

Other government agencies divide rural America in different ways. The Department of Transportation, for example, has created three categories of rural areas, as follows[5]:

1) Basic Rural – dispersed counties or regions with few or no major population centers of 5,000 or more.
2) Developed Rural – dispersed counties or regions with one or more population center(s) of 5,000 or more, and perhaps a metropolitan area(s) with 50,000 or more.
3) Urban Boundary Rural – counties or regions that border metropolitan areas and are highly developed.

The bottom line: Varying definitions of what "rural America" is highlight the diversity of America's rural areas, which can include isolated farming communities as well as communities on the fringe of major metropolitan regions.

Key Challenges Facing Rural America

While the national dialogue around issues such as poverty, housing, changing family patterns, and changes in the economy tends to focus on urban and suburban trends, these issues also pose clear challenges for the nation's rural communities.

Poverty: The rural poverty rate declined from 15.9 percent in 1996 to a record low of 13.4 percent in 2000.[6] From 2001 to 2003, the non-metro rate stayed steady at 14.2%. Nevertheless, the non-metro poverty rate remains significantly higher than the rate for metropolitan areas, which stood at 12.1 percent in 2003. By almost every measure of economic well-being—median household income, real per capita incomes, and earnings per job—rural residents are disadvantaged when compared to their counterparts in America's urban areas.[7]

Researchers cite many reasons for the disparity between non-metro and metro poverty rates, including lower-paying jobs in rural areas, the prevalence of part-time and seasonal work, historically lower educational achievement, and the presence of racial groups that have not enjoyed the same opportunities as most Americans.

In all, 9 million people are poor in rural America today.[8] Thirty five percent of rural blacks and 33 percent of rural Hispanics live in poverty; these figures include half of all rural black and Hispanic children. The rural South and West are the poorest regions in the United States. Most of the counties in Mississippi, for example, have poverty rates above 20 percent, and some are more than 40 percent poor.

Housing: The homeownership rate for non-metro households continues to hit record highs, reaching 77 percent in July 2004. This was well above the 67 percent rate for metro areas but only 1 percent above the rate for metro suburbs. As is true for minorities throughout the country, minority-headed households in rural areas have lower homeownership rates than non-minorities—61 percent versus 80 percent.

Figure 3: Poverty Rates

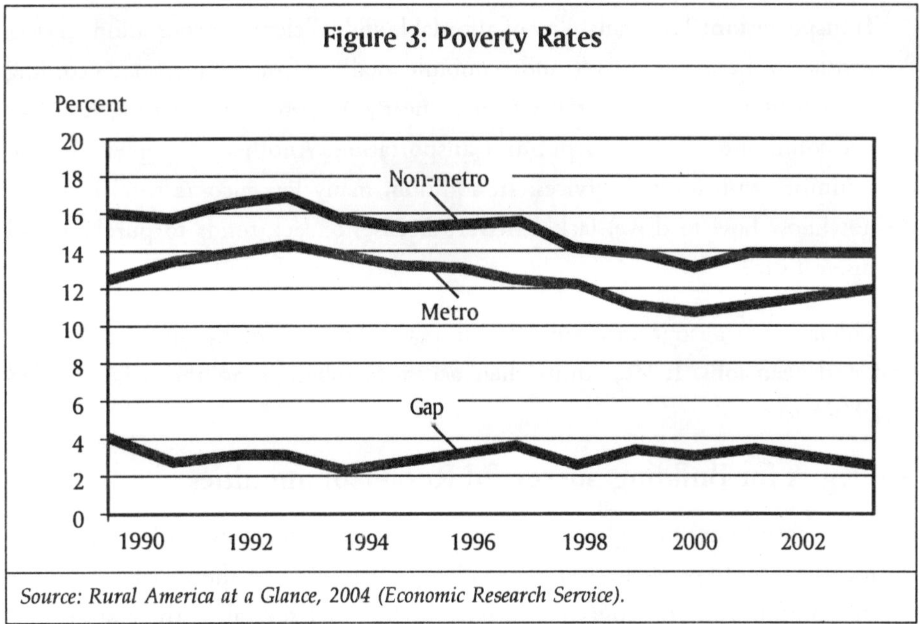

Source: Rural America at a Glance, 2004 (Economic Research Service).

Despite the relatively high level of homeownership in rural communities, many rural residents continue to struggle with inadequate housing and other problems. According to the Housing Assistance Council, nearly 30 percent of all non-metro households, or more than 6.2 million households, have at least one major housing problem.[9] Problems include affordability, quality, and crowding.

Most rural households with housing problems are cost-burdened, meaning they spend more than 30 percent of their incomes for housing. Many rural homeowners also lack access to credit and affordable mortgages. Approximately 10 percent of all non-metro mortgages, twice the proportion of metro loans, have an interest rate of 10 percent or more.

Despite dramatic progress in rural housing quality, 1.6 million non-metro housing units (6.9 percent) are substandard, meaning they lack complete plumbing, have exposed wiring, or have leaky roofs. Manufactured housing is twice as prevalent in rural areas as it is nationwide. And, although manufactured homes have improved in quality, many rural residents occupy older mobile homes that do not meet today's standards, particularly in the area of safety.

Transportation: The availability of affordable and efficient transportation services is essential to the quality of life and economic vitality of rural America. According to a report by the Rural Assistance Center, nearly 40 percent of all rural residents live in communities with no public transportation. Another 28 percent live in communities with limited services. In addition, many low-income rural residents do not know how to drive, lack a driver's license, or lack funds to purchase and maintain a car.

The lack of transportation options limits the ability of many rural residents to find and keep jobs. It also limits their access to job training and other needed social services.

Strategies for Building Successful Rural Communities

Rural communities throughout the country are experimenting with an array of strategies for addressing the unique challenges they face. In the course of NLC's Rural Communication Program, we have highlighted several of these strategies, along with examples of rural community initiatives.

Promoting Entrepreneurship: Rural communities rely on entrepreneurship as a cornerstone of economic development, bringing in new jobs, improving incomes and enlarging the local tax base. A number of organizations are looking at ways in which rural communities can get a bigger share of the entrepreneurial pie.

- The Small Business Administration (SBA) launched a Rural Initiative to assist rural businesses and promote rural development. The Rural Initiative included a pilot program to speed up the loan approval process and improve coordination with the US Department of Agriculture. *(http://www.usda.gov/da/smallbus/Federalpages.htm)*
- The US Treasury's Community Development Financial Institution (CDFI) Fund provides capital to community development banks, credit unions, venture capital funds, and microenterprise loan funds in distressed areas. Since 1994, the fund has awarded $300 million to community development organizations and financial institutions. *(http://www.cdfifund.gov)*
- The Entrepreneurship Initiative of the Appalachian Regional Commission (ARC) works to promote the creation and development of locally owned, value-adding firms that increase local wealth and provide employment opportunities for local residents. Under the initiative, ARC has funded 368 entrepreneurship projects that have created more than 1,200 new businesses and created or retained more than 5,000 jobs throughout the Appalachian region. These projects have leveraged over $45 million from other sources to support entrepreneurial activities in the region. *(http://www.arc.gov)*
- To help rural communities locate financial resources for entrepreneurship efforts, the Association for Enterprise Opportunity (AEO) publishes *Funding Sources for Rural Microenterprise Development. (http://www.microenterpriseworks.org)*

Investing in Telehealth: The expansion of telemedicine into rural health delivery systems has been dramatic over the last few years. Also referred to as telehealth, telemedicine relies on telecommunication technologies to provide health information, clinical care, health professions education, consumer health education, public health, and administrative services at a distance. Telemedicine has been instrumental in helping citizens living in rural or remote areas of the country to receive quality healthcare. Thirty states have developed telehealth systems to increase patients' access to specialists through video-imaging and real-time collaboration.

The State of Georgia has one of the largest telemedicine systems. Started in 1987, the network now involves 60 sites, including rural community hospitals, an ambulatory center, a public health facility, and correctional institutions. Along with interactive patient consultation, the system enables rural physicians to acquire continuing medical education. A future goal of the project is to examine patients with chronic illness via interactive cable television in their homes. Originally financed through telephone company rate overcharges, the system has been expanded and maintained through the joint efforts of the phone companies, a medical college, and the Governor's office.

Addressing Transportation Needs: States and localities can help rural residents resolve their transportation problems with the help of local councils of governments (COGs). In addition, there are various funding sources available to support the development of rural transportation programs. Examples include:

- Temporary Assistance for Needy Families (TANF). States can use TANF funds and state maintenance-of-effort funds to assist low-income, working families with transportation, including providing funds to purchase or lease cars and cover insurance costs. The assistance is not limited to welfare recipients. See *http://www.fta.dot.gov* for more information.
- The Job Access and Reverse Commute (JARC) program. Administered by the Federal Transit Administration (FTA), JARC authorizes funds annually for a national competition to support new or expanded transportation services that connect parents on welfare and other low-income workers to jobs and employment-related services.
- FTA's Elderly and Persons with Disabilities Formula Program. Also known as the Section 5310 program, this federal initiative provides formula funding to states to help nonprofit groups and certain public bodies meet the transportation needs of the elderly and persons with disabilities.
- Surface Transportation Funds. Funds from the Federal Highway Administration can be used for public transportation capital projects, including vehicle purchase for vanpools.

Bringing the Knowledge Economy to Rural America: Despite trailing metro areas in capturing "knowledge jobs," rural America can make use of a variety of resources to make knowledge-based growth possible. Among the recommended strategies: leveraging high-skilled labor, colleges and universities, vibrant business networks, and "world-class" infrastructure to transform rural economies.

The following examples were featured in an article in the May 2005 edition of *The Main Street Economist* by Jason Henderson and Bridget Abraham of the Center for the Study of Rural America at the Federal Reserve Bank of Kansas City.

- Oklahoma State University-Okmulgee is helping manufacturers in northeast Oklahoma gain capacity and certification for Defense Department (DOD) contracts by helping firms reengineer and reproduce parts for the department. As a result, Oklahoma vendors have increased their share of contracts at Tinker Air Force Base in Oklahoma City from 3 percent in 1995 to 20 percent in 2002.
- To stimulate economic activity, Garrett County, Md., in cooperation with Garrett County Community College, helped supply high-speed Internet access to the region's businesses and individuals through the Garrett Rural Information Cooperative. As a result, many businesses have chosen to locate in Garrett County because of the telecommunications capabilities in the county.
- In Maddock, N D, the Maddock Economic Development Council (MEDC) formed the Maddock Business and Technology Center in 1999 to create new businesses and high-paying jobs. MEDC also embarked on a telemedicine project to improve the delivery of rural health services.
- La Grande, in rural eastern Oregon, has a fiberoptic point of presence (POP) on an interstate cable running through the city. It acquired the POP by making city access to the cable a condition of granting a permit to the telecommunications company that was laying the cable. The city, county, and state spent $165,000 to install the POP. Because of the POP, an insurance claims company located its processing center in the town, immediately creating 50 jobs.

Reducing Poverty: The Northwest Area Foundation, through its newly established Great Strides Award program, awarded $100,000 to each of four organizations, which have developed important initiatives to reduce poverty. In addition to receiving the award, the organizations were invited to share lessons learned with other communities throughout their regions. The winners included initiatives in two rural communities:

- Heartland Community Action Agency, Willmar, Minn. Heartland Community Action Agency was selected for its implementation of the "Circles of Support" model, which builds relationships across class and race lines to bolster support and end the isolation of people living in poverty. Every participating family is matched with three "allies" who befriend the family. Along with staff support, the Circles provide intentional relationships that help people who are poor deal with practical matters of transportation, job searches, housing, childcare, and other challenges.
- The Lakota Fund, Kyle, S D The Lakota Fund is the first and only financial development institution on Pine Ridge Reservation. It was selected for developing a culture of entrepreneurship and nurturing a collaborative approach with other financial institutions on the reservation. The Lakota Fund is community-owned and promotes socioeconomic sustainability of the Oglala Lakota Oyate (people) through business loans, technical assistance, and targeted community and business development. In recent years, The Lakota Fund has helped with start-up costs of the Pine Ridge Chamber of Commerce and has developed an Individual Development Account (IDA) program, which helps people who are poor save money and receive matching federal funds for those savings.

Developing A World-class Workforce: In today's knowledge economy, the same holds true for rural as well as metropolitan areas: Worker skills and education are the key contributors to individual economic success, as well as the competitiveness of local and regional economies. However, many rural residents lack access to programs and services that can help them develop marketable skills.

In *Finding Funding: A Guide to Federal Sources of Workforce Development Initiatives,* the Finance Project discusses the range of resources available to rural and non-rural communities alike as they seek to build the skills and knowledge of local workers.[10] These resources include:

- Federal Investments. Federal workforce development initiatives include Workforce Investment Act (WIA) programs, Temporary Assistance for Needy Families (TANF), State Vocational Rehabilitation Services, and the Job Corps program.
- State Investments. States invest their own resources in workforce development, particularly in the area of skills development, to supplement federal programs and create their own state programs. Nearly all states have state-funded "incumbent worker" programs financed through general fund appropriations, funds tied to the Unemployment Insurance program or other funding mechanisms.

Other Strategies for Rural Communities

The Center of Rural Affairs has identified a number of strategies for revitalizing rural America. In addition to the strategies outlined in this brief, the Center's strategies include:

- **Expanding Access to Niche Markets.** This strategy focuses on ways to increase the ability of family farms and ranches to tap into high-value niche markets.
- **Supporting and Expanding Land Grant Universities.** Land grant universities have a critical role to play in revitalizing agricultural communities – for example, by providing training and technical assistance to small businesses and by supporting rural development initiatives.
- **Creating New Regional Cooperatives.** A new kind of regional cooperative could be a powerful force for revitalizing family farms and ranches.
- **Making Communities a Desirable Place to Live.** Rural communities can pursue an array of strategies for drawing young families and entrepreneurs who are likely to start new farms and businesses and revitalize existing enterprises. For example, communities that make a commitment to provide a quality education in small, community-based schools and invest in them will always have a powerful advantage in attracting young families with children.

For the full list of strategies, see *www.cfra.org/pdf/revitalization_strategies.pdf.*

- Local Investments. Supported by a combination of resources such as general funds and revenue from special taxes, cities and counties across the nation are working to improve the effectiveness of the workforce development system.

- Private Investments. Private foundations in recent years have paid increasing attention to workforce development issues and projects. The Annie E Casey Foundation, for example, launched its Jobs Initiative in 1995; and Casey's Making Connections initiative focuses on strengthening families and neighborhoods by increasing their earnings and income through workforce development strategies. Other foundations, such as the Charles Stewart Mott Foundation and the Ford Foundation, are working on similar projects.

(LaStar Matthews is Staff Associate, Research and Municipal Programs at National League of Cities.

William H Woodwell, Jr. is an independent writer, editor and author with 20 years of experience in public affairs and strategic communications.)

Notes

1. Source: "Non-metro Labor Markets Remain Soft," Amber Waves, February 2005.
2. Economic Research Service, 1999.
3. Rural America: Opportunities and Challenges (Amber Waves).
4. Rural Policy Research Institute, 1999.
5. Source: US Department of Transportation Federal Highway Administration URL: *www.fhwa.dot.gov/planning/rural.*
6. RUPRI, 2002.
7. ERS, 2002a.
8. Rural Policy Research Institute (RPRC).
9. Issues and Trends: Rural Housing in the US, Housing Assistance Council, Spring 2003.
10. *http://www.financeproject.org/Publications/workforcefunding.pdf*

Index

O

P

R

S

T

U

V

W